A VERY SHORT,
FAIRLY INTERESTING AND
REASONABLY CHEAP BOOK ABOUT
STUDYING LEADERSHIP

Also in this series:

Chris Grey, *A Very Short, Fairly Interesting and Reasonably Cheap Book About Studying Organizations*, 2nd edition

Robert Garvey, *A Very Short, Fairly Interesting and Reasonably Cheap Book About Coaching and Mentoring*

Chris Carter, Stewart Clegg and Martin Kornberger, *A Very Short, Fairly Interesting and Reasonably Cheap Book About Studying Strategy*

Ann L. Cunliffe, *A Very Short, Fairly Interesting and Reasonably Cheap Book About Management*

George Cairns and Martyna Sliwa, *A Very Short, Fairly Interesting and Reasonably Cheap Book About International Business*

Jim Blythe, *A Very Short, Fairly Interesting and Reasonably Cheap Book About Studying Marketing*

Irena Grugulis, *A Very Short, Fairly Interesting and Reasonably Cheap Book About Studying Human Resource Management*

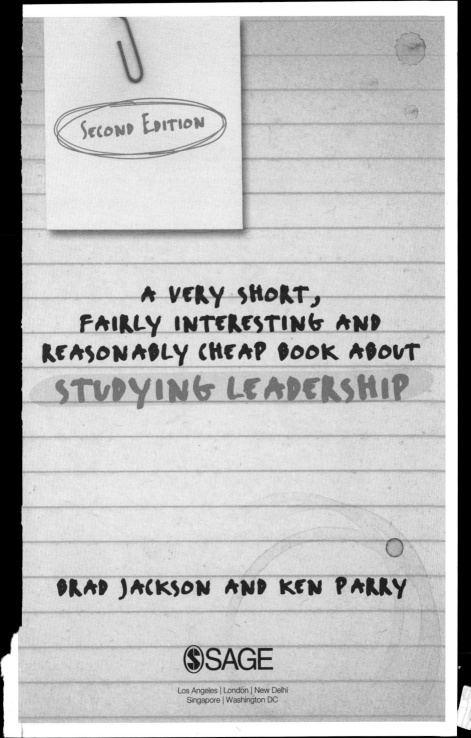

SECOND EDITION

A VERY SHORT,
FAIRLY INTERESTING AND
REASONABLY CHEAP BOOK ABOUT
STUDYING LEADERSHIP

BRAD JACKSON AND KEN PARRY

$SAGE

Los Angeles | London | New Delhi
Singapore | Washington DC

First edition published 2007
Reprinted 2008 (twice), 2009 and 2010 (twice)
This second edition published 2011
Reprinted 2012

The title for the 'Very Short, Fairly Interesting and Reasonably Cheap Book
about...Series' was devised by Chris Grey. His book,
*A Very Short, Fairly Interesting and Reasonably Cheap Book about Studying
Organizations*, was the founding title of this series.

Chris Grey asserts his rights to be recognized as founding editor of the **Very Short,
Fairly Interesting and Reasonably Cheap Book about...Series**

SAGE Publications Ltd
1 Oliver's Yard
55 City Road
London EC1Y 1SP

SAGE Publications Inc.
2455 Teller Road
Thousand Oaks, California 91320

SAGE Publications India Pvt Ltd
B 1/I 1 Mohan Cooperative Industrial Area
Mathura Road
New Delhi 110 044

SAGE Publications Asia-Pacific Pte Ltd
3 Church Street
#10-04 Samsung Hub
Singapore 049483

Library of Congress Control Number: 2010941808

British Library Cataloguing in Publication data

A catalogue record for this book is available from the British Library

ISBN 978-1-84920-738-6
ISBN 978-1-84920-739-3

Typeset by C&M Digitals (P) Ltd, Chennai, India
Printed and bound by CPI Group (UK) Ltd, Croydon, CR0 4YY
Printed on paper from sustainable resources

Contents

About the Authors   vi

Acknowledgements to the First Edition   viii

Acknowledgements to the Second Edition   x

Should You Buy This Book?   xii

1   Introduction: Why Studying Leadership Matters   1

2   Leader-centred Perspectives on Leadership   25

3   Follower-centred Perspectives on Leadership   45

4   Cultural Perspectives on Leadership   68

5   Critical and Distributed Perspectives on Leadership   95

6   Leadership with a Higher Purpose   112

7   Conclusion: Take Your Lead   134

Appendix: Resources for Studying Leadership   152

References   157

Index   186

About the Authors

Brad Jackson is the Fletcher Building Education Trust Chair in Leadership at the University of Auckland Business School and co-director of the New Zealand Leadership Institute. He was formerly Director of the Centre for the Study of Leadership and Head of School of the Management School at Victoria University of Wellington in New Zealand. Brad has been a Visiting Professor with the Copenhagen Business School, Doshisha University, Peking University, University of Pretoria and Worcester Polytechnic Institute and was an Associate Professor of Continuing Education at the University of Calgary.

Jackson's primary research foci centre on understanding the role of communication processes in the social construction of leadership with a special interest in the visual representation of leadership; examining the relationship between leadership and governance processes; and exploring how geographic perspectives might advance our understanding of leadership. He has taught courses in leadership, organizational behaviour, change management, corporate culture and ethics, qualitative research methodologies, intercultural management, organizational communication, and management learning.

Jackson has spoken to academic and business audiences throughout the world and has published five books – *Management Gurus and Management Fashions* (2001), *The Hero Manager* (with Ken Parry, 2001), *Organizational Behaviour in New Zealand, A Very Short, Fairly Interesting and Reasonably Cheap Book About Studying Leadership* (with Ken Parry, 2008) and *Demystifying Business Celebrity* (2009). He is a co-editor of *The Sage Handbook of Leadership* (2011) and *Sage Major Works in Leadership* (2011). Brad is a board member of the International Leadership Association and a Fellow of The Leadership Trust. He has a PhD in Management Learning from Lancaster University and has also obtained an MA from the University of British Columbia and a BSc from the University of Bristol, both of which are in Geography.

Ken Parry is Professor of Leadership at Bond University and Director of the Centre for Leadership Studies. Prior to this, he was the Foundation Director of the Centre for the Study of Leadership. The centre was a joint venture between Victoria University and the New Zealand College of Management, a private industry training provider. In the interim, he had a research and teaching position at Griffith University. Before taking up his first academic post at the University of

Southern Queensland, Ken spent nine years in the private sector as an inventory manager in the manufacturing industry.

Ken was the Founding Editor of the *Journal of Management & Organization* and is a Fellow of the Australian Institute of Management and the Australian Human Resources Institute. He is also a Fellow of The Leadership Trust Foundation in England. He regularly teaches and researches in England and Europe. He teaches courses in leadership, organizational change, organizational behaviour and human resource management.

His research interests include leadership, organizational change and chief executive-board leadership, as well as autoethnography, grounded theory and other qualitative methods. Ken has written and edited several books, including *Grounding Leadership Theory and Research* (2002), *The Hero Manager* (with Brad Jackson, 2001), *Leadership in the Antipodes* (2001), *Human Resource Management* (1998), *Transformational Leadership* (1996) and *Leadership Research and Practice* (1996).

Ken has a PhD from Monash University, a Master of Business from the University of Southern Queensland and a BA from the University of Queensland.

Acknowledgements to the First Edition

We'd like first and foremost to acknowledge Christopher Grey, who came up with the idea for this type of book with his own *A Very Short, Fairly Interesting and Reasonably Cheap Book About Studying Organizations* (Grey, 2005). We'd also like to thank Sage for believing in and supporting that book and for coming up with the distinctive Adrian Mole-like cover which this book cover echoes. When we first saw Chris's book we thought 'Now, why didn't we write that book?' It was clever, fresh, edgy and actually quite funny and it created a valuable new niche for organization and management studies books which have traditionally been quite staid and generally dull. Several months later we were delighted when Kiren Shoman from Sage invited us to write a sequel to this book which would focus its attention on studying leadership. Anne Summers and Katherine Haw have also assisted the publication of this book with admirable aplomb and professionalism.

The majority of the ideas and much of the material for this book have been road-tested with postgraduate and undergraduate, MBA and executive programme students in Australia, Canada, Denmark, New Zealand and the United Kingdom. The enthusiasm with which these students have participated in our courses and the feedback they provided have been very helpful in shaping the book's content and style – we have kept them first and foremost in our minds while writing it.

In researching this book we would especially like to acknowledge the efforts of Dale Pfeifer, Research Fellow for the Centre of the Study of Leadership (CSL) at Victoria University of Wellington, who helped us formulate the scope and intent of the book and dug out a lot of key sources for it, as well as providing thoughtful feedback. The commitment to leadership that she and her colleague, Pam Blakemore, evinces is an inspiration to us. Though now both former directors of the CSL, we are pleased to see the Centre endure and thrive.

We are also indebted to the institutions in which we have taken up chairs in leadership. Ken joined Griffith University in April 2003 and would like to acknowledge his colleagues Paul Rowland, Michael Powell, Ray Weekes, Ashley Goldsworthy, Brian Finn and Soheil Ebedian. Ken is also grateful for the generosity of spirit and visionary thinking of members of the New Zealand College of Management, including Mike Louden, George Hickton, Lyn Provost and David Moloney.

In the middle of writing this book Brad took up the post of Fletcher Building Education Trust Professor of Leadership at the University of Auckland Business School. He would like to thank all of his colleagues in the Department of Management and Employment Relations as well as Excelerator: The New Zealand Leadership Institute for making him so welcome, especially Mark Bentley, Judy Bonny, Giles Burch, Brigid Carroll, Liliana Erakovic, Annick Janson, Darl Kolb, Jolene Francouer, Lester Levy, Barry Spicer, Margaret Tibbles, Mattie Wall, Marie Wilson and Rachel Wolfgram.

We have been very fortunate to have either worked or interacted with some of the best minds in the leadership studies business. We would particularly like to acknowledge the influence of Nancy Adler, Bruce Avolio, Bernie Bass, Alan Bryman, John Burgoyne, Timothy Clark, David Collinson, Patrick Dawson, Deanne Den Hartog, Peter Dorfman, Graham Elkin, Michael Elmes, Keith Grint, David Grant, Eric Guthey, Kerr Inkson, Janet Holmes, Steve Kempster, Alan Lind, Ngatata Love, Meredith Marra, Pushkala Prasad, Arja Ropo, Majken Schulz, Amanda Sinclair, Dennis Tourish and Mary Uhl-Bien.

Finally, we'd like to thank our families for letting us write a second book together and for allowing us to slip away on weekends to get this book written. Brad has learned more about leadership from his wife Jacquie and two children, Devan and Colin, than he is generally willing to admit. Ken would like to say a heartfelt thanks to his wife Margie, and sons Hamish and Jonathan.

Acknowledgements to
the Second Edition

We'd like first and foremost to acknowledge Christopher Grey, who led the way again by writing a fine second edition of his pioneering book, *A Very Short, Fairly Interesting and Reasonably Cheap Book About Studying Organizations* (Grey, 2009) – we duly followed. Before we could do this, of course, we had to be invited. We would, therefore, like to thank Sage for continuing to believe in and support us and for coming up with an even better cover for the second edition! Kiren Shoman, our Editor at Sage, is a great believer in the field of leadership studies and has made an important contribution to its development. Her colleagues Alan Maloney, Natalie Aguilera and Rachel Eley have provided terrific rapport, combining consummate professionalism, infectious enthusiasm and admirable patience.

We are grateful to all those people who wrote to us with their comments on the first edition. We were pleasantly surprised by how many took us up on our invitation to write in with their comments, questions and suggestions for improving the book, some of which we have incorporated in this edition. A few of you are featured in the testimonials to this book. Our students in our MBA and Honours courses were instrumental in testing out our ideas and material in the first edition. They've played an even stronger role in the revisions we have made to this second edition.

Brad would especially like to acknowledge the efforts of Robert Strand, from the Centre for Corporate Social Responsibility of Copenhagen Business School, who undertook extensive bibliographic research into leadership research that had been published since the publication of the first edition. He would also like to acknowledge the many colleagues, students and practitioners whom he had the pleasure to meet and work with during his 'Geography of Leadership' world tour, conducted between July 2009 and June 2010. Most especially, he would like to warmly thank his generous hosts: Michael Elmes from Worcester Polytechnic Institute, Professor Yoshi-Fumi Nakata, Director-General of the Institute for Technology, Enterprise and Competitiveness at Doshisha University, Professor Hector Rene Diaz Saenz from EGADE at Tecnólogica de Monterrey, Professor Eric Guthey from the Copenhagen Business School, and Professor Liu Hongzhong from the New Zealand Center at Peking University.

Ken is indebted to Bond University, which he joined in 2008. Thanks also go to Julie Gabriel-Clarke, Sarah Gregory and other colleagues at Lancaster University where he is a regular Visiting Professor. He would especially like to acknowledge Audun Fiskerud from Bond University for his bibliographic work in preparation for this and other documents for Sage. To Ray Gordon, Steve Sargent and Pat Grier, thank you for your Chief Executive wisdom, advice and willingness to participate in the MBA learning experience. Thanks also to Werner Nienhüser at the University of Duisburg-Essen for your help and support.

Once again, we close our acknowledgements by thanking our families, who continue to go well beyond the call of duty in supporting our writing habits and encouraging us to get this second edition completed. Brad wants to offer his sincerest thanks and love to his wife, Jacquie, for being such a tremendous globe-trotting mate and to thank his two children, Devan and Colin, for loyally staying behind in New Zealand to hold the fort and look after Skippy, the dog. Ken would like to say a heartfelt thanks to his wife Margie, and sons Hamish and Jonathan.

Should You Buy This Book?

In common with the first and very original book in this series, Christopher Grey's *A Very Short, Fairly Interesting and Reasonably Cheap Book About Studying Organizations* (2005), this book is designed mainly for university students who are studying leadership, or who are perhaps contemplating studying leadership as part of a senior undergraduate or a postgraduate course. You may, in fact, be on the verge of starting a project, dissertation or thesis on leadership and want to get a handle on the various ways that you might go about doing this. We have been gratified to learn that this book has been taken up as required reading for a number of MBA programmes in Business Schools throughout the world.

It is not a textbook. As the title infers, it is much shorter, hopefully more interesting and considerably cheaper than a text – and it is a lot more portable. Indeed, we have written this book so that it can be comfortably read on a four-hour plane or train ride with time built in for dinner – think of it as middle-brow 'in-flight edutainment'. Feedback from the first edition suggests that we were perhaps a little too optimistic in how long the book would take to read but, of course, we were allowing for the inevitable delays and hold-ups! The downside of this condensed format is that it is a lot less colourful than a textbook and there are no pictures. We have tried to make up for this lack of visual content with our lucid prose, graphic imagery and biting wit, but we'll let you be the judge of that.

This book may also be of interest to those who are not currently engaged in a formal programme of study but have always had an interest in leadership. Understandably, you may be getting more than a little tired and somewhat disenchanted with the same old ghost-written 'I did it my way' biographies of business leaders or the 'Eleven leadership secrets' book-sized business cards written by faceless consultants. In fact, you may be looking for something with a little more intellectual grunt but aren't quite ready yet to dive into the academic abyss. We hope, of course, that after reading this book, you'll promptly march down to your nearest seat of learning and sign up for a formal programme to find others who have already decided to make that fateful leap. But we would say that, wouldn't we?

Finally, the book may also be of interest to our academic colleagues who have heard a lot about this thing called leadership recently and are curious to find out what all the fuss is about – and potentially about how they might add to this fuss. We spend a lot of time trying to convince our colleagues from other disciplines, such as anthropology, classics, history and political science, that leadership research is (a) a legitimate academic pursuit and (b) what they might already be doing themselves but are not explicitly aware of. To you we say: 'the more the merrier'.

If you do buy this book and would like to enquire further, take issue or even praise this book, you can email either Brad at b.jackson@auckland.ac.nz or Ken at kparry@bond.edu.au. We look forward to hearing from you.

Introduction: Why Studying Leadership Matters

I believe that we are more likely to secure responsible leadership in the future if we can demystify its constituent processes. In that sense, enhanced knowledge about leadership may go hand-in-hand with more morally desirable forms of leadership.

Howard Gardner (1995)

on studying leadership

The *Concise Oxford Dictionary* defines 'study' variously as 'a thing to be secured by pains or attention', 'devotion of time and thought to acquiring information, especially from books', 'be on the watch, try constantly to manage', 'a thing that deserves to be investigated' and the definition we particularly enjoy, 'a fit of musing, reverie' – something that we hope this book might invoke for you. There are broadly five ways that one can go about studying leadership. You can actually attempt to lead, you can observe leadership in action, you can talk about leadership, you can read about it and you can write about it.

Given that we are both professors, it won't surprise anyone to learn that we find it easiest to *talk* about leadership. After all, we do this every day in our lectures, seminars and workshops. We are greatly assisted in this regard by the fact that everyone has a fundamental interest in leaders and leadership. It's certainly true that everybody we have ever talked with has developed some kind of opinion on what constitutes good and bad leadership. Whether it's teenagers' views on the adequacy of their parents' or teachers' leadership skills or a colleague questioning the wisdom of promoting someone at work or the election of a new political leader, leadership tends to be something that is high on a lot of people's agendas – and invariably it's a powerful way of dividing people into those who support a particular leader and those who do not. The most authoritative sources regarding matters of global as well as local leadership are, of course, taxi drivers. They should be consulted at every opportunity.

As we will see, there is no shortage of opportunities to read about leadership. Leadership books continue to be a mainstay of publishers' catalogues. At the time of completing the second edition in January 2011, Amazon.com listed a staggering 57,666 titles using the search term, 'leadership books'. Where we hope we can help rather than hinder by adding one more title to this list, is by guiding you through the maze and encouraging you to go beyond the conventional, mainstream, popular fare which dominates the shelves of airport book stores. People read leadership books for a number of reasons: to be inspired by others who have faced and overcome even greater odds than they are facing; to be reassured that they are not doing so badly after all; or simply to be entertained. We want to encourage you to select leadership books because they challenge, unearth, expand and perhaps even subvert your assumptions about leadership, and what it is to lead and to follow.

Reading about leadership should not be confined to books; the newspaper is a prime source of leadership stories. The next time you pick one up try counting how many times the term 'leader' or 'leadership' appears in it. Most students will recognize that these terms will show up quite frequently in the business and politics sections but will be surprised to learn how often 'leader' and 'leadership' will crop up in the sports and entertainment sections. Of course, the section in which these terms are most frequently mentioned is career opportunities – yet another reason for becoming interested in studying leadership.

Another great source for leadership stories can be found at the movies. While we do not wish to undermine any welcome relief from the worries of the world that you may derive from going to the cinema, we do hope that, like us, you will never be able to watch a movie again without thinking that it is about leadership. From *Alien* to *Zorro*, all you will see are leadership lessons; the fun is well and truly over! To get you started, we've provided you with our list of all-time favourite leadership movies in the Appendix.

Every year students say, 'I will never be able to just watch a movie again. Now I look for the leadership everywhere'. Movies like *Remember the Titans*, or *Shackleton*, or *The Blind Side*, or *Apollo 13* are based on real events. The leadership stories and messages are thinly disguised, if not blatant. Movies like *When We Were Kings* are documentaries or show *actual* events. These are as close as we can come to being there. The value of movies is that we cannot actually create the boardroom environment or the courtroom as a means of studying or learning leadership. However, these are as close as we normally will come to such a recreation. A movie like *Groundhog Day* is an exaggeration of events. It is make-believe, but we can all place ourselves within the narrative and see how the leadership phenomenon maps out in this exaggerated context. A movie like *The Dish* is loosely based on real events, but the humour highlights the paradoxes and ambiguities that are the daily grist for the mill of leadership.

Writing about leadership is more challenging. We find that the 'publish or perish' stick used in concert with the 'fame and fortune' carrot can prove to be surprisingly strong motivators for academics. Perhaps the relief of getting assignments done and out of the way, coupled with the affirming allure of superior grades, may well do it for you. Whatever it takes, it is vital to find the time to write as there is something very special about the writing process. Its solitary, reflective and permanent nature requires a much stronger commitment to say what you really think, compared to everyday conversation or discourse. The off-the-cuff remark or observation that seemed so appropriate and pithy at the time reveals itself to be less so once vulnerably placed on the written page for all the world to see. However, when you do finally work an argument through to its logical conclusion, you can reach a level of contentment that is hard to match.

We tend to value our leaders primarily for their abilities as orators. However, many of them use the written word through the medium of their diaries and memoirs to make sense of and to work through the dilemmas, doubts and frustrations associated with their leadership positions. Nelson Mandela's magnificent autobiographical bestseller, *Long Walk to Freedom*, is an exemplar of this form of leadership communication. It's not surprising, then, that these documents attract so much interest when they are made public. People are naturally curious to see what lurks behind the front-stage of the theatre of leadership. Unfortunately, they can occasionally be disappointed, as demonstrated in Bill Clinton's verbose and generally unrevealing autobiography *My Life*, as well as Tony Blair's *A Journey*.

Seeing leadership, if done superficially, is not difficult at all. It's something we all do day in and day out. To quote a well-worn epithet, leadership is like beauty – it is difficult to describe, but we certainly know it when we experience it. Most of the time we rely on the media to guide us, and make it easy for us to understand and judge. Whether it's a beleaguered politician, the coach of a sports team on a losing streak, or a business tycoon embroiled in a business scandal, the media can be especially persuasive about what constitutes good and bad leadership and how it needs to be addressed. Usually they will recommend instant removal. However, we believe it is important to want to see leadership though our own eyes. Having the discipline to observe leadership properly requires time, patience, imagination and the willingness to question constantly what one is observing and to see for new and perhaps disconfirming evidence. Most importantly, one needs to see beyond the obvious, take a contrary view and, occasionally, be willing to become unpopular because of one's views. In this book we want to develop and foster a multidimensional, a broader, and even an empathetic view of leaders and leadership.

Anyone who has attempted to lead will understand that the act of leadership is considerably more challenging than talking, reading, writing or seeing leadership all put together. There's no doubt that one can learn the most about leadership from actually trying to lead. That has certainly been the case for us in our efforts to do so. It is an inconvenient irony that there is an inverse relationship between the ease and comfort we experience in doing something and the quantity and quality of learning that is generated by it. This irony is further highlighted by the fact that we can often learn the most from those situations in which we have failed to lead. Indeed, there is a leadership book entitled *Firing Back: How Great Leaders Rebound after Career Disasters* by Jeffrey Sonnenfeld and Andrew Ward (2007). Everybody loves to hear about a comeback story – just don't make a habit of it.

Of course, we can all think of some leaders with whom we have worked who, in common with the infamous David Brent character from TV's *The Office*, and his American counterpart Michael Scott, appear to be incapable of learning anything from their efforts at leading or from their followers. Thankfully, most leaders we work with are keen to learn and improve their abilities. The experience of leading seems to sharpen their desire to learn and to change.

In light of the power and importance of experience, the idea of merely studying leadership might seem somewhat passive, evasive, and even frivolous. In our roles as directors of a Centre for the Study of Leadership, we were often quizzed about the desirability of having such a passive and weak term as 'study' associated with the Centre. Wouldn't it be more marketable to rename it the 'Centre for Leadership' or more simply the 'Leadership Centre'? We however held firm to the word 'study' because we believe that there has perhaps been too much emphasis placed upon 'just doing' leadership and not enough, as Howard Gardner's opening quotation signals, on 'demystifying its constituent processes'. We also ardently believe that in order to create the morally responsible forms of leadership that many of us crave, it is vital not only for leaders to demystify these processes but also for followers to do so as we are the people who will guide and influence those leaders. We are not alone: John F. Kennedy famously noted that 'leadership and learning are indispensable'.

When we talk about 'studying' leadership we are thinking of all five of these activities: doing, seeing, talking, reading, and writing. We not only need to learn to become better at doing all of these but, most significantly, we also need to recognize it is vital for us to learn how to better link and integrate these activities into a cohesive philosophical whole – so that what we read influences what we see about leadership, what we talk about helps us to write about leadership, which, in turn, helps us to do better leadership. This is by no means a linear process. In fact, you could easily reverse the sequence described above or use various combinations and the process would be equally valid. Though the primary task of this book is to help you learn more about leadership by reading about it, it is our hope that the process of reading about leadership will duly impact on and shape what and how you choose to see, talk, write and do leadership.

where we are coming from

While biographies of pre-eminent leaders will often reveal a desire to lead early on in the life of the leader, which has invariably been engendered by a major setback or by an inspirational figure or a general expectation placed upon them, it's fair to admit that nobody consciously sets out to study leadership. For reasons that we have yet to grasp, society places a greater premium on actually being a leader (assuming one doesn't fail or, more significantly, appear to fail) rather than on its citizens who make their living out of studying leadership. We suggest a variation of George Bernard Shaw's well-worn maxim (about those who can't do teach) might be particularly instructive here. However, we hope that you – fellow student of leadership – wouldn't have it any other way.

Most leadership scholars we are familiar with have come to leadership research in a somewhat indirect and roundabout way. This has begun to change with the advent of postgraduate and, increasingly, undergraduate programmes that are explicitly devoted to studying leadership. But this is only a recent development. Most leadership researchers will tend to have backgrounds in psychology (originally from social psychology but more recently from organizational psychology), or roots in sociology, history or political science. Most will also come to leadership studies having done something else beyond academe – frequently consulting, teaching, training or project management – and will have been drawn into academia because of a profound curiosity they have developed about leadership processes and, almost invariably, a vague desire to help make the world a better place. Leadership scholars tend to be the token dreamers, the chronic optimists and the hopeless romantics that you will find huddled together in small clusters at most business schools or elsewhere on campuses, such as in departments of communications, educational administration, psychology or student affairs. We are no exception to this pattern.

Brad developed his original interest in leadership dynamics for sound practical reasons. As a son of a soldier having to change schools and neighbourhoods on a regular basis, he developed a chameleon-like ability to fit into groups quickly and with minimal fuss. The ability to score a goal during the initial playtime was a particularly effective means of establishing credibility. The other important means for fitting in was to quickly read the prevailing leadership dynamics within the various sub-groups, cliques or gangs, and ensure that one quickly got onside with the good leaders and offside with the bad leaders. This came into sharper focus when he attended military boarding school, where he contended with a dual civilian and military hierarchy as well as the critical informal network that was constantly being negotiated, challenged and reinforced by the boys. It was only later as he moved from a background in geography into the executive and management development field in Canada that he became exposed to some first-rate leadership teachers, as well as legions of middle and senior managers craving enlightenment about the mysterious secrets of leadership. Looking to management gurus for the answer led Brad to explore through his doctoral thesis the peculiarly evangelical brand of charismatic leadership that these gurus wielded to such impressive effect over millions of managers throughout the world, persuading them to take on the latest management fashion that they were promulgating. While he has failed to cash in on the lessons learned from studying the *modus operandi* of gurus, he has finally found his true cause in life as New Zealand's first professor of leadership. This is a role he relishes because he is paid to see, talk, read, write and do leadership every day of the year in a country that contains so many leadership lessons.

Ken was also the son of a soldier, and an officer at that – a very assertive officer. Being the youngest child, Ken learned from an early age that he was supposed to be a follower and not a leader. But, like many of us, he stumbled into random leadership roles – captain of a sport team on one occasion – accused of being charismatic on another. Ken eventually learned that leadership was something to be cherished and savoured. Most of the time we are followers, but occasionally we can use leadership with astonishing effect. We both hesitate to write mini-autoethnographies, but everyone in the leadership field, and that includes you as the reader, should attempt to be reflexive about the development of your own leadership identity and character. We should say at this point that autoethnography is a good methodology for Master's-level research and for professional doctorates but probably not for PhD research. A PhD needs a far greater coverage of methodology than an autoethnography provides. However, don't adopt our personal theories of leadership as your own. As you reflect back upon your experiences, and upon the role of notable people in your life, you will be able to see how your leadership has developed. Develop your own theories of leadership.

Leadership is a fundamentally important human experience that evolutionary theorists argue was initially created as a survival mechanism by Early Man (see Van Vugt, Hogan and Kaiser, 2008). As then, leadership has a very significant bearing on the conduct and quality of our everyday lives. We say this not because we have the scientific evidence to back this up. In fact hard evidence about the impact of leadership is surprisingly and tantalizingly hard to find. We say this because through our own direct experience working in a range of organizations, participating in a number of community and public groups and networks, we have been constantly impressed by the influence that a leader or groups of leaders can have when they engage with followers to create this special thing called leadership. In fact this can be mildly addictive. When it is good, it is very good; when it is bad, it is very bad indeed. Moreover, we find ourselves being constantly amazed at the variety and complexity of the forms that leadership can take wherever we have cared to look for these. In truth, it is this never-ending fascination that keeps us going in our pursuit of studying leadership.

We mention our backgrounds and experiences with leadership because we want to encourage you to think about where your interest in leadership has come from and to consider how your own background and experiences have served to shape your interests and beliefs about leadership. Bruce Avolio describes this as your 'life stream' which, simply defined, 'represents events you accumulate from birth to the present that shape how you choose to influence others and yourself' (2005: 11). You will have already developed a fairly sophisticated philosophy of leadership, which is dubbed your 'implicit leadership theory' (Schyns and Meindl, 2005), whether you are explicitly aware of it or not. You will also have some clear convictions about what you think constitutes the right and the wrong way lead someone or be led by someone.

What we hope is that, through the formal and informal study of leadership, you will not only be exposed to other philosophies of leadership by individuals who have devoted their intellectual lives to clarifying, challenging and deepening their philosophies of leadership but, as a result, you will also have cause to question and deepen your own philosophy of leadership. This will stand you in good stead not only as a leadership researcher, but also as a leader and as a follower.

▬▬▬ why it is a good time to be studying leadership

As we said at the outset, this book is aimed at those people who are either studying leadership or are considering the possibility of doing so. Being passionately committed to studying leadership, we would of course argue that any time is a good time to be doing this. However, we would not be stepping out of line by suggesting that there has never been such a good time to study leadership for the following reasons.

To begin with there has never been so much interest in the field. Leadership is widely seen as both the problem and solution to all manner of contemporary issues: from ending world poverty to addressing global warming; from turning around ailing corporations to regenerating local communities; from reviving schools to creating scientific breakthroughs. The hunger and quest for leadership knowledge appear to be insatiable. Typing into the Google search engine on January 6, 2011, we noted more than 258 million entries when we typed in the word 'leader' and more than 125 million for the word 'leadership'.

The distinctive feature of leadership is that it would appear that the more we learn about leadership, the more we realize we have to and want to learn. This might go some way toward explaining the dramatic growth of the leadership development field into a multibillion-dollar global industry; an estimated $36 to $60 billion is expended annually on management and leadership development throughout the world (Burgoyne, 2004). Surprisingly, little of the money that has been invested has been put towards evaluating the impact of this investment. There appears to be blind faith in the efficacy of leadership development. In accounting for this, John Storey (2004) has pointed to four different types of explanation which probably all have some salience. The conventional explanation points to the increased complexity and rapid pace of contemporary society which demands higher and more creative levels of leadership. A meta-analysis of all experimental and quasi-experimental leadership research interventions (Avolio et al., 2009a) found that 66 per cent of these generated a positive or desired outcome, and that there was considerable variation or heterogeneity across those outcomes. The good news is that leadership works, generally-speaking, most of the time. The other good news is that there is much research still to undertake in order to understand how and why leadership does not work at certain times.

The institutional explanation emphasizes the pressure that is exerted on individuals and organizations to emulate others in order to maintain one's credibility. If everyone is doing leadership development, we had better do it too. The sociological explanation highlights the role that leadership can play in legitimizing the authority, power and privilege of elites. It provides a socially acceptable means of justifying the status quo. Finally, the strategic advantage explanation argues that leadership is an intangible asset that must be cultivated in order to gain a rare and valuable source of competitive advantage.

Given the spectacular growth in interest in leadership, it is not surprising to learn that leadership is also appearing on the radar screens of government funders, most notably in Europe and Asia. Traditionally, in North America, private and philanthropic sources have provided the bulk of the funding for leadership research. Consequently, we have witnessed a mushrooming of leadership institutes and research centres throughout the world, many of which are university-affiliated. Perhaps the best known of these are the Centre for Creative Leadership based in Greensboro, North Carolina, Harvard University's Center for Public Leadership, and the Centre for Leadership Studies located at the University of Exeter. These and others are listed in the Appendix. Leadership centres and institutes tend to have a twofold focus. The stated purpose of The New Zealand Leadership Institute is typical in this regard: 'To enhance the understanding of leadership in New Zealand and take action to ensure the country has talented and skilled leaders who will develop, guide and advance our organisations and communities'.

In addition to these research institutes, universities, particularly those in North America, are beginning to invest heavily in the provision of leadership development opportunities for students in the form of extra-curricular activities, such as in-service programmes, while they are pursuing either undergraduate and postgraduate degrees. In some universities, for example the Jepson School of Leadership Studies based in Richmond, Virginia, an undergraduate degree in leadership is offered, while Antioch University offers a PhD in leadership and change. These types of programmes aim to respond directly to the demands of employees, parents and students who are looking for a competitive edge when they move into the job market.

On the subject of job markets, the more astute reader (we expect all our readers to be astute, of course; that's why they have bought this book) will have already recognized that this frenzy of activity will generate – and is already generating – a significant demand for enthusiastic individuals at all levels of seniority who have been well trained in leadership development and research. Perhaps this is where you come in.

the interdisciplinary and applied nature of leadership

Those who work in the leadership research field have always made a point of recognizing its applied and interdisciplinary nature. We research leadership primarily because we want to make a difference by promoting a better understanding of leadership, from which we can help to promote better leadership in practice. While this rationale hangs together in theory, in practice we have probably not been as applied in our effects as we would have liked to be or perhaps should have been. As John Storey has noted, 'the accumulation of weighty and extensive reports to date tends, in the main, to regurgitate a now familiar thesis – but it is a thesis which remains incomplete, insufficiently tested, inadequately debated and not properly scrutinised' (2004: 6). An exhaustive review of the extant leadership research corpus similarly concluded that 'if we admit that current leadership measures only capture a set of relevant leaders behaviours – we will be forced to develop new methods for exploring alternative leadership conceptualizations. If, on the other hand, we continue to conduct typical leadership studies we are likely to find supportive results – but results that lack true meaning, substance and practice utility' (2007: 443). The bottom line here is that there is still plenty of work yet to do – you are most definitely not too late.

Moreover, we have not been as interdisciplinary as we probably should have been in terms of the approaches that we draw upon to conduct leadership research and also in terms of the kinds of question that various disciplines might inspire if applied to the study of leadership. Psychology and, to a lesser extent, sociology still tend to dominate the field. There have been, however, some encouraging signs that the leadership field is increasingly branching out and becoming more receptive to a wider range of quantitative as well as qualitative methodologies. For example, political psychology is making an impact. This is the psychology of the lived experience of the individual politician, as derived from biography and historical interrogation, rather than the psychology of a population, as derived from questionnaires and experiments. Anthropology has a long history of research into cultures via the means of ethnography. Now with autoethnography, or hyper-reflexivity, researchers are standing back and looking at their own experiences, warts and all, and learning about leadership from them. The predominant journal in the field and its ultimate arbiter, *The Leadership Quarterly*, has noticeably expanded its agenda since its inception in 1989 to encompass articles with disciplinary and methodological perspectives that would have had only a slim chance of being published in earlier years.

Another bottom line for you, then, is that even if you feel your disciplinary training might not be directly relevant to studying leadership, it may prove to be a real asset in that it can help you see and conceptualize elements of the leadership process. A good example of this would be one of Brad's former doctoral students, Ralph Bathurst, who drew on his training and experience as a musician (a violist to be precise) to create in his thesis what he described as an 'aesthetic ethnography' aimed at comprehending the 'music of organizations', which he applied to an empirical study of a symphony orchestra to revealing effect.

Leadership is beginning to attract established researchers who may have traditionally eschewed leadership research, either because they were philosophically uneasy about the idea of privileging leaders over followers or because of the field's predominantly functional and positivistic orientation. The arrival in 2005 of a new European-based journal, *Leadership*, is providing an alternative outlet for research, with its stated aims of stimulating interest in new methods and theories of leadership; encouraging interdisciplinary, diverse and critical analyses of leadership processes; and providing an international forum for leadership research.

The father of modern leadership studies, James MacGregor Burns, has noted two striking recent developments in the field of leadership studies. The first is the internationalization of the study of leadership. Noting the blossoming of leadership as a discipline in the mid- and late twentieth century, he comments that 'theoretical work and practical application in non-American contexts will inevitably move leadership theory away from its overly American emphases and bias toward a more international perspective' (2005: 11). The second major development that Burns points to is the role of leadership research as an interdisciplinary endeavour that invigorates related disciplines. Obviously, leadership theory draws heavily from established disciplines, but it can also vitalize those disciplines. Burns notes, however,

> leadership, in common parlance, is a 'good'. When people call for leadership, or deplore the lack of leadership, they see it not as a needed spur to human progress but, as in itself, a moral and ethical entity and a necessary gauge of action. Leadership, in short, becomes an activity as well as an academic enterprise. (2005: 12)

Leadership scholars are not only growing in number, they are also starting to get better organized (something you would reasonably expect them to do well, given their subject matter). The International Leadership Association (ILA) was formed in 1999 as a means to strengthen ties and share ideas and resources among those who work in leadership studies, leadership developers, educators, practitioners and scholars. In January 2011 it had 2,200 members from 70 countries. Its 2010 conference in Boston attracted 1,048 attenders. In the past five years, the Academy of Management (AOM) has created a Network of Leadership Scholars which brings together several hundred leadership academics who are primarily based in universities. It is remarkable that 200 of the 2,000 papers presented at the 2010 annual meeting in Montreal had 'leadership' in their title. At the end of 2010, Lund University in Sweden played host to the ninth International Conference on Studying Leadership – a conference that regularly attracts critically-oriented leadership researchers from throughout the world.

the problem with leadership

You've had the good news. Now here's the not-so-good news. Leadership is a phenomenon that everyone has an opinion on but few of us seem to agree exactly on what it really is. Bernard Bass (1990) has famously observed that 'there are almost as many different definitions of leadership as there are persons who have attempted to define it'. From his exhaustive survey of leadership definitions through the twentieth century, Joseph Rost concludes, with more than a hint of lament, that a major problem with leadership studies as an academic discipline, and with the people who do leadership, is that 'neither the scholars nor the practitioners have been able to define leadership with precision, accuracy, and conciseness so that people are able to label it correctly when they see it happening or when they engage in it' (1993: 6). We will exemplify what he means with two definitions.

At one end of the continuum of leadership definitions we have the workmanlike but eminently robust definition offered by Stogdill (1974: 3) that conceives leadership as 'the process of influencing the activities of an organized group in its efforts toward goal setting and goal achievement'. There are three key components of this definition that are worth emphasizing: it is an interpersonal process between one person and a group; you cannot have 'leaders' without 'followers'; and the criterion for effective leadership is goal achievement. If there is no commonly agreed upon and generally understood goal, if it is basically a group of people doing various tasks in an independent fashion, then it is not leadership. At the other end of the continuum, we have the considerably more expansive and flamboyant view of leadership promulgated by Tom Peters and Nancy Austin in their book, *A Passion for Excellence* (1985):

> Leadership means vision, cheerleading, enthusiasm, love, trust, verve, passion, obsession, consistency, the use of symbols, paying attention as illustrated by the content of one's calendar, out-and-out drama (and the management thereof), creating heroes at all levels, coaching, effectively wandering around, and numerous other things. ... Leadership must be present at all levels in the organization. It depends on a million

little things done with obsession, consistency and care, but all of those million little things add up to nothing if the trust, vision and basic belief are not there.

You couldn't find two more totally different definitions. Yet from our experience they both point to and illuminate something significant with respect to the experience of leadership. One is more precise and functional, the other is more emotive and suggestive and, some would maintain, hopelessly romantic.

Keith Grint in his book *Leadership: Limits and Possibilities* (2005a) suggests that leadership has traditionally been understood in four quite different ways:

- Leadership as Person: is it WHO 'leaders' are that makes them leaders?
- Leadership as Results: is it WHAT 'leaders' achieve that makes them leaders?
- Leadership as Position: is it WHERE 'leaders' operate that makes them leaders?
- Leadership as Process: is it HOW 'leaders' get things done that makes them leaders?

We can illustrate these four ways of thinking about leadership with reference to the person who has done more to generate media attention on the leadership phenomenon than any other world figure in the past three years – Barack Obama. By virtue of the fact he ran and was successful in his bid to become President of the United States, both Americans and many in the rest of the world automatically associate him with leadership (i.e. Leadership as Position). Barack Obama will always be compared with his 43 predecessors, even long after he has left office, and his stock will rise and fall depending on the stance of the latest biography that reaches *The New York Times*' bestseller list. But, of course, it has been the 'Leadership as Person' lens that has been working overtime since his arrival on the political stage. Much attention has obviously been paid to the fact that he is the first black president ... even though he chose to run as a president who happened to be ... number of his other personal characteristics and ... have been and continue to be put under the micro- ... the most widely exposed political figure in history, ... uring fascination with who Barack Obama *really* is. ... narked during the lengthy and frequently poison- ... alth reform bill. The 'Leadership as Results' lens ... a lack of sufficient results during the first two years of his tenure – something that was inevitable given all of the hype that was generated during his spectacularly successful campaign, or to the wrong results – focusing on health when the economy should have been the key priority. With respect to 'Leadership as Process', Obama has been seen to have been far too cautious and conservative by many of his more left-wing supporters and far too radical and pandering to special interests by his vocal right-wing detractors.

The fact that we look at leadership in these four different ways goes some way towards explaining why we have so much trouble in explaining leadership, and in trying to understand it, teach it, and reward it. In Grint's view, each of these ways of thinking about leadership is valid and potentially useful. He therefore does not advocate that leadership scholars should attempt, as Joseph Rost has argued, to develop and agree upon one universal definition of leadership. Instead, he believes it should remain an 'essentially contested concept' that is constantly being discussed and debated.

The way in which we have organized this book follows this line of thinking by presenting five different perspectives on leadership, which we believe bring something quite valuable to the table in response to the challenge laid down by Howard Gardner in this chapter's opening quotation: to demystify 'the constituent processes of leadership'. It is when we find ways to share and pool our understanding of what constitutes good and effective leadership that we have the opportunity to foster and encourage exceptional leadership within a particular context.

While the importance of the role of individual leaders tends to be overestimated, the significance of leadership itself should never be underestimated. Grint (2005a) believes we have become overly preoccupied with individual leaders when, in fact, we should have been focusing more on leadership. As a result, he urges us to 'put the *ship* back into leader*ship*'.

Joseph Rost has attempted to systematically formulate the co-production of leadership by leaders and followers with his definition of leadership, which he believes is most appropriate to the 'post-industrial world' within which many of us are increasingly working. He defines leadership as 'an influence relationship among leaders and followers who intend real changes that reflect their mutual purposes' (Rost, 1993: 102).

Rost highlights three essential elements that must be present for genuine leadership to take place. First, the relationship should be based on influence that is multidirectional (i.e. it is exerted downwards, upwards, laterally, within and beyond a particular organization) and non-coercive that it is not achieved through force. Second, there is typically mor one leader and always more than one follower in the relation followers are active partners but, even in the most democr the relationship is inevitably, usefully, and even necessarily unequal. In responding to the 'Burns Paradox', which asks why we need to differentiate between followers and leaders when they are so intertwined, the eminent leadership scholar James MacGregor Burns observes:

> The key distinctive role of leadership at the outset is that leaders take the initiative. They address their creative insights to potential followers, seize their attention, spark further interaction. The first act is decisive because it breaks up a static situation and establishes a relationship. It is, in every sense, a *creative* act. (2003: 172)

Another key task for leaders to take on according to Ron Heifetz and Donald Laurie is to ensure that they and their followers are able to respond to 'adaptive change' – the sort of change that occurs when people and organizations are forced to adjust to a radically altered environment (Heifetz and Laurie, 1997). In order to do this, they provocatively argue that, 'leaders who truly care for their followers expose them to the painful reality of their condition and demand that they fashion a response. Instead of giving people false assurance that their best is good enough, leaders insist that people surpass themselves. And rather than smoothing over conflicts, leaders force disputes to the surface' (1997: 2).

The third element of Rost's definition is that both leaders and followers work together to bring about substantial rather than superficial changes. These changes are driven by a mutual purpose that is forged through a non-coercive influence relationship. This asymmetrical view of leadership, therefore, does not preclude followers from being active co-producers. In fact, it emphasizes the idea that leaders and followers should share responsibility for any consequences that might arise in the execution of the leadership relationship.

Think about the leadership relationships of which you have been part. How many of these do you think would pass the demanding standards set by Rost's definition? Looking back on our careers, we have rarely been part of a genuine leadership relationship within the workplace. The nearest we have come to this has been through our involvement in the wider community through volunteer work. This kind of leadership relationship is something that is quite special and memorable. The point here is that this definition is probably best thought of as an aspirational rather than a descriptive one. It's something that we should aim for if we wish to secure a sustainable future for everybody on the planet: the kind of leadership that is required if we are to confront complex and massive-scale issues such as global warming, poverty and the control of virulent diseases. Leaders will continue to play an important role in this relationship. We will still need leaders, but they will be different types of leader.

⬤⬤⬤ the three questions that are most asked about leadership

We are regularly asked by students, friends and journalists alike three questions about leadership that we think it would be wise to address early on in the proceedings. What we are keen to show in this book is that, while these questions are not unimportant to leadership scholars, there are many other questions that leadership researchers are actively engaged in answering.

⬤⬤ question 1: are leaders born or made?

We are frequently struck by the number of people we come across who believe that leaders are born and not made. Some will defend their position by observing that they have always known – and have been told by others – that they are 'natural' leaders. Certainly, a strong core self-concept is an important trait for leaders to possess, unless it verges on arrogance. Others may not believe that they themselves are natural leaders but they can point to a number of people whom they believe are. We are inclined to react critically to this view on two levels. First, on an intellectual level, because we want to know what 'natural' means, where it comes from and how it can be distinguished from 'unnatural'. Second, on a more practical level, we are concerned that this stance, by definition, is self-defeating because it rules out the possibility that leadership can and should be learned and, thereby, serves to deter people from developing their full potential.

Bruce Avolio has been tackling this question with admirable gusto. He has estimated, from extensive longitudinal research conducted on identical twins born in Sweden, that the 'born' side of the leadership development equation accounts for, on average, approximately 30 per cent of leadership effectiveness. The 'made' side of the equation (i.e. what happens to you after birth) accounts for 70 per cent. He concludes that 'leadership and wisdom are both made, even if both are built on the genetic abilities people are endowed with at birth like cognitive abilities, energy levels, and how attractive we are to others' (2005: 25). The latter quality, attractiveness, is probably more important than any of us would be willing to admit, particularly in persuading others that we should be given the opportunity to lead.

With respect to the making of leadership, Bruce has observed that a combination of authoritative parenting and a proclivity towards modest (but not serious) rule-breaking are strong predictors of leadership emergence. The next time you think that your parents may have been a little too strict with you, perhaps there were some benefits to this after all, especially if they allowed you to get away with occasionally bending the rules. Similarly, Manfred Kets de Vries argues that the experience we gain in our first five years plays a most profound role in shaping our desire to lead, as well the ways in which we choose to lead. He describes how the parental disharmony between King Philip and Queen Olympias sowed the seeds for the intense ambition of their son, Alexander the Great, to become an all-conquering leader. Alexander was desperate to take over from his father as the rightful king – an ambition that his all-loving mother did little to dissuade him from harbouring (Kets de Vries, 2004). We might not have accurate historical records from those days, but we do know that any child who saw its mother murdered and was raised in a world of criminal violence will grow to be a psychopath and have dif-ficulty in distinguishing between right and wrong. We have no doubt that many leaders throughout history were raised in an environment some-where between 'parental disharmony' and 'criminal violence'. In spite of their inherited personality, these experiences have determined the means by which they influence others and thereby demonstrate leadership. Amit et al. (2009) confirmed via empirical research that by comparing 'leaders' and 'non-leaders', the leaders had more leadership experiences in their youth. These experiences have an impact upon self-perception as a leader, a sense of self-efficacy, and an accumulation of psychological and behavioural knowledge related to the manifestation of leadership.

While this question has some value in stimulating debate and discussion, and occasionally earning a free drink, it doesn't really help us move forward on the real issue: namely, how do we go about developing the next generation of leaders? We have come across plenty of people who were apparently 'born' to be leaders (i.e. they had the 'right' genetic mix, background, etc.) but have not assumed leadership roles or failed miserably as leaders because they were either unable or unwilling to learn. We've also come across those who, on the surface, appear to have been born to follow but choose to learn and succeed in leading instead. It ultimately comes down to aspiration, to the desire to lead.

question 2: what makes an effective leader?

We need to distinguish between two different ways of answering this question: 'the common-sense way' and the 'scientific way'. The 'common-sense way' is an inductive approach which attempts to isolate fundamental truths about leadership that are based on direct and indirect experience with successful leaders. The 'scientific way' is a deductive approach that involves developing a theory of how leadership ought to work and then conducting rigorous analytical experiments to test that theory.

Our own common-sense response to this question is that if people follow another person, then that other person is demonstrating leadership. Leadership is probably easier to find than a leader. So, who is a leader? Usually, people will follow the lead of someone who possesses certain qualities or characteristics. If we are pressed, we will concede that five qualities are particularly vital in order to promote effective leadership: confidence, integrity, connection, resilience and aspiration. Confidence creates the essential sense of self-worth and self-efficacy that is needed to put oneself forward in order to lead and to sustain oneself in a leadership role. Integrity helps leaders to be consistent and allows them to be clear about what they stand for and believe in. Connection is the ability to translate those values through a genuine and authentic link with followers – this is much more than communication, which is often the first choice whenever we ask groups to name what they believe to be the most important quality for a leader to possess. To this we would add resilience, the ability to withstand emotional and physiological stress, setbacks and conflict. Leading can be both psychologically and physiologically draining. You shouldn't be surprised to learn, given our comments above, that we place aspiration at the top of the list of qualities which we believe an effective leader must possess. If you do not aspire to change something and you don't have a good reason for changing it, you cannot and should not lead.

The scientific response to this question adds five more traits to this list. In his review of major research programmes that have attempted to identify predictors of leadership effectiveness, Yukl (2002) points to the following prerequisites. First, a high internal locus of control, which means that leaders believe that events in their own lives are determined more by their own actions than by chance or uncontrollable forces. Second, effective leaders also require a high degree of emotional maturity and stability, which has been memorably labelled by Goleman (1995) as 'emotional intelligence'. This means that leaders are able to monitor their emotional state and be well aware of their strengths and weaknesses. Third, leaders should also have a high socialized power motivation. This means they should derive enjoyment and fulfilment from influencing people and events for the benefit of others and not themselves. Fourth, leaders should also have a moderate but not excessively high achievement orientation as they need to be willing to work with others who may be less capable. Finally, effective leaders should have a low need for affiliation, which means that being liked should not be a strong motivator. While leaders should not relish making tough and unpopular decisions, they should not shy away from doing so.

question 3: what's the difference between leadership and management?

There is considerable debate about the relationship between leadership and management. For many years, learned scholars have concluded that management and leadership are two different functions that require different skills and, usually, different types of people. Most influentially, Zaleznik (1977) has suggested that leaders develop visions and drive changes whereas managers monitor progress and solve problems. Along the same lines, Bennis and Nanus (1985) argued that 'managers do things right, while leaders do the right thing'. Kotter (1990) makes the point that not all managers are leaders and, equally, not all leaders are managers.

Arguing against this view, Peter Drucker, the management guru's guru, believes that effective managers should strive to be both formal and informal leaders within their organizations (Drucker, 1955). Leadership is one of the key tasks of management alongside planning, controlling and organizing. We can personally attest to the wisdom of this argument having worked for individuals who considered themselves to be leaders and would not denigrate themselves by engaging in any form of management activity. They preferred instead to leave the operational details to others, so that these would not cloud their 'big picture' thinking and get in the way of their vital vision-building activities. We, and the organizations they aspired to lead, ultimately found to their cost that the devil was in the detail.

Drawing on data they collected from their intensive leadership development work with senior and middle managers, Carroll and Levy (2008) have noted that, while they tended to revere and strive for the leadership identity, the management role was what they tended to hold as a 'default identity'. When push comes to shove, many managers will drop the leadership identity that they and their companies invest so much time and effort in developing and revert back to a default identity that is considerably more familiar, simpler to comprehend, and safer to hold. It is important to recognize the different emphases that leadership and management and values each brings, but equally these need to be blended and intertwined to work effectively together. We should resist the trap of ghettoizing leaders and managers, demarcating those who should lead and those who should manage. We agree with Lester Levy when he remarks, 'in each individual you need to have the mind of a manager and the soul of a leader' (2004: 3).

Keith Grint has further served to elevate our thinking when making the distinction between leadership and management with his typology of authority, which is rooted in a social constructionist perspective of leadership. He begins by distinguishing between three general types of problem that need to be addressed by organizations: 'tame' problems (i.e. complicated problems which can be solved through unilinear acts and are likely to have been faced before); 'wicked' problems (i.e. complex problems with no apparent solution and where there is no 'right' or 'wrong' answer); and 'critical' problems (i.e. a crisis in which there is scant time for action and little uncertainty about what needs to be done). 'Tame' problems, he argues, are best suited to management in that they can be solved by the deployment of tried-and-tested processes. Leadership, by contrast, is the authority best suited to the collective addressing of 'wicked' problems. 'Critical problems' generate a compelling case for using forms of coercion or 'command' form of authority. Of course, the categorization of the problem is rarely pre-assigned. In fact, one of the key tasks of the leader is to persuade followers that the leader has defined the nature of the problem correctly. This is not as straightforward as we might imagine. Referring to the Brent Spar controversy, Grint notes that what seemed to Shell to be a tame problem requiring management action was turned into a critical problem by and through the coercive acts of Greenpeace activists who had tried to keep it as a wicked problem. He concludes by noting a 'irony of leadership': because it is the most difficult of the three approaches, decision-makers will understandably try to avoid it at all costs because the leader does not have the answer when their followers still fully expect them to have it. Indeed, the leader's primary task is to make the followers face up to the problem and help to formulate the answer, something which will take considerable time and may never be universally seen as being the 'best' solution (Grint, 2005b).

One final processual strand to add to this discussion is the place of governance with respect to leadership and management. This question has gained considerable practical as well as academic poignancy in the aftermath of the collapse of so many financial institutions during the 'global financial meltdown'. Jackson and Erakovic (2009) have pointed out that a major contributing factor to the spectacular failure of these organizations is that governance and leadership processes have been disconnected in many organizations, frequently by design. Conventional wisdom suggests that governance functions are the responsibility of the board whereas leadership is the prerogative of senior management. This belief has unfortunately led to a critical disconnection between the two functions when, in fact, these need to be carefully integrated in a dialectical fashion. One should influence and challenge the other as:

> Corporate governance provides the organizational framework within which leadership is enacted – it sets the stage for leadership at the top of the organization and has an indirect but significant impact upon

leadership processes at other levels within the organization. While corporate governance provides a structure for the relationships among organizational core stakeholders (e.g. shareholders, boards and managers), leadership provides the motivation and impetus to make corporate governance effective towards achieving the organization's purpose and goals. In this respect, good leadership can 'energize' governance, while good governance can serve to sustain leadership. (Erakovic and Jackson, 2009: 3)

At the end of the day, it is important to recognize that all four of these processes – management, leadership, command and governance – are properly developed and are allowed to make an important contribution to the vitality and sustainability of all organizations, whether private, public or not-for-profit. It is very important to ensure that none of these processes dominates, that they are mustered to address the appropriate problem and they are properly interconnected, not detached. Perhaps the Danes have it right when they use just one word, '*ledelse*', to cover leadership, management and governance.

how the book is organized

Given the vast scale of the leadership literature, it would be impossible to distil every word that has been written about leadership to fit in a book of even conventional length. In the Appendix we have included some excellent reference sources which can provide such a comprehensive review of leadership research. However, given the space constraints implied by the 'very short' promise in the title of this book, we've decided not to rehearse the history of the theoretical development of leadership studies.

This departs from the strong historic focus of Chris Grey's original (2005) book on studying organizations. Our reasoning is that any standard organizational behaviour (OB) textbook will do a sound job of providing a historical overview of the development of leadership theories. These accounts invariably begin with what Huczynski and Buchanan (2006), in their own OB text, describe as the 'trait spotting' theories of leadership, which attempt to identify personality traits with a view to selecting leaders – much as we did in the section above on what makes an effective leader. They then move on to the 'style counselling' theories which characterize and develop appropriate leadership behaviour patterns, invariably divided into task and relationship orientations. Following this, they examine 'context fitting' or contingency theories, which emphasize the need to change leadership styles in order to adapt to a particular situation. The situation here invariably incorporates factors such as the state of employee morale, the complexity of the task, and the level of senior management support. Conventional accounts of leadership theories inevitably conclude with a discussion of 'new' leadership theories, which emphasize visionary and inspirational leadership in order to transform organizations (i.e. transformational versus transactional leadership theories). Irrespective of the impact of leadership within organizations, the current directions of research revolve around the question of 'what is going on?' rather than the old questions of 'who is the leader?' or 'what does the leader do?' or 'how does the leader get the most out of other people?' These 'new leadership' theories will primarily be the focus of the next chapter, although, technically speaking, they are no longer very new.

What we've chosen to do instead is look at some of the more interesting questions that are currently being asked by those who are studying leadership. While we are not suggesting that one should consider studying only what is currently being studied by other leadership researchers, when one pursues postgraduate studies it is generally wiser to at least begin where other scholars are currently theorizing and proceed from there.

In common with Chris Grey, we have taken a very personal view on this subject, which is so near and dear to our hearts. We have attempted to write this book in a direct, concise and opinionated way using relatively simple language. You will see that we have attempted to keep the academic terminology to a minimum. We are well aware that many students can be initially put off by the dense conceptual language that is used by academics to communicate with each other and conclude that perhaps leadership research or academic research in general is not for them. In this book we want to provide a bridge into this literature and, in the process, show you that there may very well be a place for you. In fact, you may well be able to make a contribution to the literature sooner than you imagine.

We also want to help you develop your critical appreciation of some of the very fine work that is being done in this area but rarely receives any exposure beyond academe. By endeavouring to make this book 'short, interesting and cheap', we realize that we have made a trade-off with the precision, sophistication and depth that you will find in more conventional academic treatises on leadership. Again, for those who wish to consult with more authoritative academic sources, we strongly encourage you to begin with the ones we have listed in the Appendix.

In Chapter 2 we will focus on leader-centred perspectives on leadership. The chapter begins with a discussion about the relationship between the identity of a leader and his or her behaviour, and includes a consideration of the influence of gender on leadership. It then contrasts transactional, transformational and charismatic leadership and explores both the 'light' and 'dark' sides of these forms of leadership. These three conceptions of leadership have been a central preoccupation for most leadership researchers in the past two decades. It is this work that most people outside the field would identify as being leadership research; indeed the bulk of research papers and postgraduate theses still fall within this particular bailiwick.

Subsequent chapters focus on research that has been done in response to the perceived shortcomings and limitations of this work. In Chapter 3 we survey work done by those who have been curious about that other generally unheralded group of people when it comes to leadership, namely the followers. We specifically look at various theories that have conceptualized followers as moderators or constructors, or substitutes or co-producers of leadership. This work has sought to provide a much needed rebalancing of a lopsided focus on leaders. This is somewhat surprising as most of us are, and always will be, followers and yet Western society tends to take a 'second best' view of followership despite the fact that we all know it – and we all play a vital role in the leadership equation.

In Chapter 4 we bring culture into our analysis. Most of the extant leadership research has been conducted within the United States. It is research that has been undertaken by American researchers predominantly on American subjects while working in American organizations. The growing interest in leadership research throughout the rest of the world has revealed contributions as well as limitations in the applicability and relevance of this research to other national and local contexts. In response, a subfield of leadership research, generally described as cross-cultural leadership, has emerged which has endeavoured to address this issue by seeking explanations for cultural variations in leadership behaviour. However, others have argued that it is not just the specificity of the cultures being explored but the culturally specific way in which they have been explored that has limited our ability to understand the full range and depth of leadership practices throughout the world.

In Chapter 5 we describe some of the growing body of work that takes an explicitly critical stance against mainstream leadership research of the kind we review in the first four chapters. In common with their more established peers in the field of Critical Management Studies, these writers argue that conventional leadership studies tend to reinforce and preserve the status quo rather than challenge it by focusing on how to improve current leadership practices and by relying primarily on quantitative analyses to conduct their research. We also look at attempts by various theorists to develop 'leaderful' leadership models which will enable followers to take on leadership responsibilities either at the top of the organization, through co- or shared leadership models, or throughout the organization via the creation of dispersed leadership models. We take this argument one stage further by considering the possibility of doing away with the idea of leadership altogether and giving it a well-deserved retirement.

In Chapter 6 we look at a series of related efforts to rehabilitate and invigorate leadership in response to widespread concerns brought into dramatic relief by a number of corporate scandals and financial crises that erupted in the first part of the century, the most infamous of which was the spectacular and very public collapse of Enron. Such concerns came into sharp relief again with the collapse of an alarming number of banks and other financial institutions throughout 2008 and 2009. We may have done a good job at improving leaders' abilities to influence their followers, but what kind of job have we been doing in leading them to do the right thing? Three rapidly growing areas of leadership scholarship are examined which have sought to respond to the shortcomings of mainstream leadership: ethical leadership, authentic leadership, and spiritual leadership. The chapter closes with a consideration of how a more aesthetically informed approach to leadership might improve our understanding and the practice of leadership, particularly when we look at it through the lens of the arts.

Finally, in Chapter 7, we look at what is being done – in light of all the research that has been presented in the preceding chapters – to develop more and better leaders throughout the world. We examine the still nascent field of leadership development, identifying the conventional means by which leaders are developed as well as the limitations of these methods. We also consider how you might best prepare and position yourself to become an active contributor in advancing this still young, but rapidly expanding field. To this end, we provide some guidance and advice about what you can do to develop your abilities as a student of leadership, most particularly how you might begin to construct your own leadership research – be it a project, a thesis, or a dissertation.

For now, content yourself with the knowledge that you are making a good start in this endeavour by reading the rest of this 'very short, fairly interesting and reasonably cheap book about studying leadership'.

2

Leader-centred Perspectives on Leadership

It is important to realise that the quality of all of our lives is dependent on the quality of our leadership. The context in which we study leadership is very different from the context in which we study, say, astronomy. By definition, leaders wield power, and so we study them with the same self-interested intensity with which we study diabetes and other life-threatening diseases. Only when we understand leaders will we be able to control them.

(Warren Bennis, 2007, p. 4)

leader identity and leader behaviour

It seems sensible to start a discussion about leadership with a discussion about leaders. In fact, leadership research has been dominated by an interest in leaders. To be specific, research has looked at who the leader is (leader identity) and what the leader does (leader behaviour). Indeed, these two issues are still very important in leadership research. We shall first say a few words about leader identity and then move on to leader behaviour.

All textbooks on leadership seem to commence with a treatise on the trait approach. As a courtesy to thirty years of good-quality publishing, we should do so as well. The trait approach seeks to determine the personal qualities and characteristics of leaders. This orientation implies a belief that leaders are born rather than made – in other words, nature is more important than nurture. As we saw in the introductory chapter, Bruce Avolio has been active in researching the nature–nurture debate with regard to the development of leaders. Refreshingly, the conclusion seems to be that it is a 50–50 bet. Yes, heredity and pedigree determine some elements of leadership, but the experiences that we have at home and in life determine our leadership capabilities just as much.

Early research tended to be concerned with the qualities that distinguished leaders from non-leaders or from followers. For many writers concerned with leadership, the findings of such research had implications for their area of interest because of a belief that the traits of leaders would distinguish effective from less effective leaders. In general, the simplicity of the trait theory has reduced its attractiveness for scholars and, since the 1940s, a more persuasive trend has shifted to the examination of leadership behaviour. In summary, the trait approach to leadership has had problems, has been discredited, and is really not valid now.

What does happen in the modern era is a continued assumption that the person in charge is the leader, and therefore is the subject of leadership research and scholarship. We have found that this potential problem of confusing the manager-in-charge with the 'leader' is more prevalent in North America, but is nonetheless an issue all round the world. We have had confusing and at times frustrating conversations with colleagues, usually in the USA, who will claim to be researching 'leadership', and will keep talking about the 'leader'. When pressed further, they have actually been talking about the manager of the work unit. It all gets confusing when we are not sure whether we are studying leadership, or a leader, or the manager. It might be splitting hairs, but the basis of the research needs to be clear from the start. The value is that if you say that the person in charge is the leader, then at least you will know who you are talking about. What you are probably saying is that the person in charge has the greatest leadership role to play in their management responsibility. That is a perfectly sound premise upon which to base your investigation, and an important basis for your research.

One problem with this research direction is the implication that either you are a leader or you are not. If you don't have the right demographic characteristics or even the right rank in the hierarchy, then you cannot be the leader. Another challenge can be that if you are the manager in charge you must be the leader, and if you are not the manager then you have no leadership role to play. This dichotomy can be a huge burden to bear for the (unfortunate) person who happens to be the manager in charge of a work unit. Perhaps we should remove the word 'leader' from our lexicon. It carries far too much baggage. We should just stick with 'manager' as the person and 'leadership' as the phenomenon under investigation. Try it for yourself. See if you can get through a whole leadership seminar without mentioning the word 'leader'. We bet you will have clear discussion and a successful seminar.

Another problem is that people other than the manager-in-charge will demonstrate leadership from time to time, and from time to time the manager-in-charge will be a follower rather than a leader. Therefore, research questions can be confused as a result of this potential dislocation between research subject (manager) and research phenomenon (leadership).

It is partly because of this dislocation that we must move now from leader identity to leader behaviour.

The implication of concentrating on leader behaviour rather than leader identity is that the leader can get better at his or her leadership role by behaving in the most appropriate way. If you strike the right balance between a concern for people and a concern for production, you will be the most effective leader. There are other ways in which this balance has been articulated: employee-centred versus production-centred; supportive versus directive; consideration versus initiating structure; relationship-oriented versus task-oriented. These labels pepper the organizational behaviour textbooks and are all essentially talking about the same dichotomy. Some taxonomies of leader behaviours can be quite complex, but the point has been well and truly established that the most effective leaders will achieve a balance between the twin challenges of getting the job done and looking after the welfare of the workers.

The behavioural approach to leadership has also gone out of favour in recent years, with the exception that transformational leadership has been criticized as another behavioural theory under a different guise. We will say more about that later.

gender and leadership

In the previous chapter, we referred to the three most commonly asked questions about leadership. If we had included a fourth it would most definitely have been the one that asks: 'What differences are there between male and female leaders?' The trait approach to leadership seemed to say that men were better leaders than women. The behavioural approach now seems to suggest that women demonstrate better leadership than men do, on average.

Actually, there is no consensus in the literature about gender differences in leadership styles. For example, only weak evidence exists suggesting that women display more transformational leadership than men. Examples include Eagly and Johnson's (1990) meta-analysis and Bass and Avolio's (1994) research. Another meta-analysis is Eagly et al.'s (2003) work on transformational leadership research, which revealed a slight but significantly more frequent display of transformational leadership by women over men, across a large number of studies. Some of our research in New Zealand also found this.

Some studies point to gender differences in particular behaviours. For example, Astin and Leland (1992) found that women believe more strongly than men that listening to and empowering followers is important, and women are more likely to use conferences and networks to achieve results. Burke and McKeen (1996) suggest that such differences occur because men and women view the world differently, and consequently male leaders seek autonomy and control over their followers while women favour connection and relatedness. It is a complex area and a clear resolution of the issues does not appear to be forthcoming. The differences are modest and certainly not universal.

Eagly's (1987) social role theory suggests that to avoid criticism and to achieve praise, people will behave consistently with society's expectations of their gender. Therefore as leaders women will strive to be nurturing and caring, while men will be more task-focused, ambitious and competitive. In a large-scale meta-analysis of organizational, laboratory and assessment centre studies, Eagly and Johnson (1990) reported small but reliable gender differences in leadership style. Female leaders were found to emphasize both interpersonal relations and task accomplishment more than men. Behavioural theory would therefore conclude that women are better leaders. However, these differences reduced considerably among organizational leaders *vis-à-vis* leaders at lower levels. The problem with such small statistical differences is that the significant minority of people who do not conform to the stereotype are unfairly labelled with the characteristics of the majority. After all, the 'feminization' of leadership is equally applicable to men as it is to women.

As far back as the early 1990s, many commentators have called for the feminization of leadership as a way to improving long-term organizational effectiveness and well-being. The 'feminization' of leadership does not mean that women are better leaders than men. It means that leaders who conform to the feminized stereotype, that of a balance between relationship-orientation and task-orientation, will be the better leaders, irrespective of whether they are women or men.

Eagly and Johnson's findings suggest that leadership processes might vary according to the gender composition of the workplace as much as by the gender dominance of the industry. For example, Chatman and O'Reilly (2004) found that women expressed greater commitment, positive affect and perceptions of cooperation when they worked in all-female groups. Walker et al. (1996) found that in mixed sex groups, men were much more likely to exercise opinion leadership than women. Gardiner and Tiggemann (1999) found that women and men in male-dominated industries did not differ in their interpersonal leadership orientation, however women in female-dominated industries were more interpersonally oriented than men. Furthermore, women exhibiting an interpersonal-oriented leadership style in male-dominated industries reported worse levels of mental health. This finding suggests that both the gender of the leader as well as the gender ratio of the industry in general will affect leadership styles, although the findings are inconclusive overall.

Clearly, one future direction for research is to assess the impact on leadership of gender domination in the workplace and within the industry generally. On the one hand, the matter of gender and leadership seems to provide a fertile area for research and scholarship (Adler, 1996; Holmes and Marra, 2004; Sinclair, 2005). On the other hand, we would suggest that if all these esteemed researchers can come to no consensus about the thorny question of gender and leadership, then perhaps we are asking the wrong question. Ken has a mantra that if you can't find an answer to a question, then you are probably asking the wrong question. This claim relates to the study of leadership as much as to life in general.

Women appear to have a particular challenge when attempting to further their leadership careers. This challenge is known as the 'glass cliff'. Women are more likely than men to be appointed to leadership positions associated with an increased risk of failure and criticism because these positions are more likely to involve the management of organizational units that are in crisis. Haslam and Ryan (2008) posited this challenge a few years ago, and now have empirical evidence to support the presence of the glass cliff. Not only that, but they also found that glass-cliff appointments are associated with beliefs that these appointments suit the distinctive leadership abilities of women and that they provide women with good leadership opportunities.

They suggest that rather than the appointment of female leaders precipitating a drop in company performance, a company's poor performance is a trigger for the appointment of women to the board. Women then become lightening rods – blamed for negative outcomes that were set in train well before they assumed their new roles. Ryan and Haslam note that there is some anecdotal evidence for the glass cliff. Most famously, Carly Fiorina (Hewlett Packard), Kate Swan (W.H. Smith) and Patricia Russo of Alcatel-Lucent were all appointed to top positions at a time of tumbling share prices. Their empirical experimental research supports the presence of the glass cliff. Not only do you women out there have another challenge when deciding to take your lead, but we all have another great opportunity to research this phenomenon.

What does seem clear is that research in this area appears to be the domain of ageing male and female baby boomers trying to remedy the ills of the past. Experience suggests that Generation X and Y researchers have a different interest in studying gender issues within the phenomenon of leadership, if any interest at all. They would look at powerful women such as Margaret Thatcher, Anita Roddick and

Hillary Clinton and agree that issues such as power and communication are more influential than gender for the success of their leadership.

Ken often cites some fascinating work undertaken by Jenny Neale in the late 1990s. Jenny was part of a multinational study, which investigated the life stories of men and women who had made it to 'the top' as leaders in their industries (Neale, 2001). She looked specifically at Australia and New Zealand. She found that people who made it to the top had in common the privilege of having someone else to look after their domestic situation, such that they could concentrate on their careers. Men invariably had a wife to look after their domestic situation. Unless they were independently wealthy, women did not have a husband to look after their domestic situation. Therefore, those women had foregone a domestic situation by not having children and/ or not having a husband. One interpretation of this phenomenon is that leadership success was a function of power rather than gender. To be sure, there has always been a correlation between gender and access to power, but that correlation is becoming weaker all the time.

We have noticed that contemporary research appears to look at gender as a moderator rather than as a dependent or independent variable. As the twenty-first century unfolds, it appears that the characteristics of the individual workplace and the expectations of workforces will have more impact on leadership than does the gender of leaders. The future for gender research seems to be focused on context, power, leadership style, social construction and identity rather than biological gender. The bottom line is that gender differences with regard to leadership, even if significant, are slight. There seems to be little mileage in pursuing this as a specific research direction, unless gender is couched as a social identity rather than as a biological binary relationship.

transformational leadership

One approach to leadership research that has dominated the literature since the 1980s is transformational leadership. Research in this area continues unabated. In the three years since the first edition of this book, 380 articles have appeared in journals with the phrase 'transformational leadership' in the title. It has been hailed, somewhat unfairly, by some people as another behavioural theory of leadership. Transformational leadership is part of what Alan Bryman (1992) has called the 'new leadership'. Apart from the fact that new leadership is no longer strictly new, it has generated a great deal of excellent as well as mediocre research and acts as a powerful touchstone for many contemporary leadership researchers. For this reason, the term 'new' still holds some currency.

'New leadership' describes and categorizes a number of approaches to leadership which emerged in the 1980s and exhibited common, or at least similar, themes. Together these different approaches seemed to signal a new way of conceptualizing and researching leadership and they are still going strong. Writers employed a variety of terms to describe the new kinds of leadership that they were concerned with promoting. Among many others, Bass, Avolio, Alimo-Metcalfe, and Tichy and Devanna (1986) wrote about 'transformational leadership'. House and Howell (1992), and Conger (1990), wrote persuasively about 'charismatic leadership'. Sashkin (1988), and Westley and Mintzberg (1989), wrote about 'visionary leadership'. Finally, others such as Bennis and Nanus (1985), Kotter (1990), and Kouzes and Posner (1998) simply wrote about 'leadership', usually *vis-à-vis* 'management'. We will say more about charismatic leadership in the next section.

Together, these labels revealed a conception of the leader as someone who defines organizational reality through the articulation of a vision, and the generation of strategies to realize that vision. Thus, the new leadership approach is underpinned by a depiction of leaders as what Smircich and Morgan (1982) described as 'managers of meaning'.

Another persuasive distillation of the essence of leadership is that of 'sense-making', made famous by Karl Weick in 1995 and articulated further by Annie Pye in 2005. A third distillation of the essence of leadership is that of 'enhancing adaptability' (Parry, 1999). This third essence of leadership is not as famous as the first two, but the point is that the underlying nature of leadership has been explained as more than just an influence process that one imposes upon followers. Of course, arguably, the most popular essence of leadership is that of the transformation – a transformation in the attitudes and motivations, and consequently behaviours, of followers – which is generally termed 'transformational leadership'.

The all-important foil for transformational leadership is transactional leadership. Transactional leadership involves an exchange between the leader and follower wherein the leader offers rewards in return for compliance and performance. The transaction is usually represented in formal contracts, employment agreements, performance management systems and service-level agreements. As with behavioural theories of leadership, the most effective leaders are successful at enacting the transformation *and* the transaction. Transformational leadership theory owes a great deal to the ground-breaking work of Bernard Bass, often in partnership with his colleague of many years Bruce Avolio.

research on transactional and transformational leadership

For Bass, the ideal approach to leadership exhibits both forms of leadership – transformational and transactional. Bass developed quantitative indicators for each component. His specification of these components has varied somewhat as his model has undergone development. The seemingly simple dichotomy of transformation and transaction has been modified through richer and more detailed research to now reflect three higher-order factors that give greater richness to the transformation and transaction. According to Avolio, Howell and Sosik (1999b), the three main leadership factors are *transformational* leadership, which includes inspirational leadership and intellectual stimulation, *developmental exchange*, which includes individualized consideration and contingent reward, and *corrective avoidant leadership*, which includes active management-by-exception and *laissez-faire* behaviours. Each of these components is measured with the Multifactor Leadership Questionnaire (MLQ). Empirically, as well as conceptually and theoretically, this is a powerful way to explain transformational leadership.

The MLQ has a self-rating version, a team version and a conventional leader-rating version. The research, which has been conducted on a host of different levels of leader in a variety of settings, typically shows transformational leadership and developmental exchange to be the components of leader behaviour that are most strongly associated with desirable outcomes such as the performance of subordinates, followers and colleagues. Too much corrective avoidant leadership will result in reduced performance and reduced goal attainment.

Phil Podsakoff also developed a questionnaire to test for six factors of transformational leadership and four factors representing contingent and non-contingent reward, and contingent and non-contingent punishment (Podsakoff et al., 1990). Podsakoff's six transformational leadership factors are: articulates vision, provides appropriate role model, fosters the acceptance of goals, communicates high performance expectations, provides individualized support, and supplies intellectual stimulation. Like Bass's original operationalization of transformational and transactional leadership, these are pitched mainly at the individual level of analysis.

Alimo-Metcalfe and Alban-Metcalfe (2001) also developed a Transformational Leadership Questionnaire (TLQ). This measures nine factors, once again at the individual level of analysis and measuring 'close' or 'nearby' leadership as opposed to 'distant' leadership. Those nine transformational leadership factors are: possesses a genuine concern for others; empowers and develops potential; has integrity, trustworthiness, honesty and openness; displays accessibility and approachability; clarifies boundaries, involves others in decisions; encourages critical and strategic thinking; is an inspirational networker and promoter; shows decisiveness, determination and self-confidence; and possesses political sensitivity and skills. Once again, these have been adapted for the selection and training of leaders.

Importantly, Bass's and Podsakoff's measures of leadership contain a transactional component as well as a transformational one. Kouzes and Posner's (1998) and Alimo-Metcalfe and Alban-Metcalfe's (2001) measures do not. Waldman et al. (1990) drew attention to the importance of the augmentation effect of transformational leadership over and above the effect of transactional leadership. In other words, as the old mantra says, 'transactional leadership is necessary, but not sufficient'. The transaction seems to be the basis of human interactions. However, it is the transformation, in addition to the transaction, that enables followers to perform beyond expectations. This finding has been supported by Deanne den Hartog and colleagues in 1997, with questionnaire analysis. These theoretical findings, that transactional leadership by itself is necessary but not sufficient for optimal organizational performance, support the conceptual conclusions of Kotter (1990) and others that 'leadership' without 'management' is insufficient for optimal organizational performance.

The idea of transformational leadership has generated an impressive set of findings and has made a great impact on the study of leadership. We keep waiting for transformational leadership to reach its use-by date, and to turn from the fashion into an erstwhile fad. However, it remains a hugely powerful diagnostic. Given the volume and impact of transformational and 'new' leadership, it is clear that it won't go away in a hurry. Indeed, we believe that it will remain a key component of the study of leadership for many years yet. Some reflections about the new leadership approach can be found in the following overview.

the limitations of transformational and new leadership

With the exception of the research stemming directly or indirectly from Bass's work, the new leadership approach can be accused of concentrating excessively on top leaders. While a switch towards examining the leadership *of*, rather than *within*, organizations is in contrast to the small-scale, group-level studies of earlier eras, it could be argued that the change in focus has gone too far and risks having little to say to the majority of leaders. Also, as with earlier phases of research, the new leadership has little to say about informal leadership processes, although the qualitative case studies that have grown in popularity show great potential in this regard. On the other hand, quantitative approaches exhibited by the work of Bass, Podsakoff, Alimo-Metcalfe and Alban-Metcalfe, and Kouzes and Posner, are likely to replicate the tendency to focus on formally designated leaders.

Finally, there has been little situational analysis until recently. Much effort was exerted in the late 1990s towards testing the situational validity of the new leadership, and transformational leadership in particular. Attention has been drawn to a wide range of contextual factors that can limit the room for manoeuvre of prospective transformational leaders. These contextual factors might include technology, industry structure, the international trading environment, national public policy, and social and cultural transformation. We have no doubt that many moderating and mediating variables can be tested upon the relationship between transformational leadership and outcome variables.

However, further research along these lines will just be toying with what we already understand, and will probably add little to the body of knowledge. Therefore, there is growing evidence that situational constraints may be much more important in restricting the transformational leader's room for manoeuvre than is generally appreciated. On the other hand, Bass (1997) is insistent that transformational leadership works in almost any situation, except that the way in which it works is, very definitely, situationally contingent. There is a tendency for new leadership writers to emphasize the exploits of successful leaders, and to engage in insufficient examinations of the reasons for the loss of transformational attribution. This can generate a distorted impression since there may be important lessons to be learned from failed transformational leaders.

Apart from these concerns, Gary Yukl (1999) has typically provided the most cogent critique of transformational leadership theories. One weakness he identifies is the omission of the specification of important behaviours and ambiguity about other transformational behaviours. In part, this criticism has led to the development of Alimo-Metcalfe and Alban-Metcalfe's Transformational Leadership Questionnaire, with a broader range of leadership behaviours and interactions with followers.

Another weakness was an insufficient identification of the negative effects of transformational leadership. This shortfall has in part been rectified by Bass and Steidlmeier's (1999) examination of authentic and inauthentic transformational leadership, and also by a discussion by Maccoby (2000) and Kets de Vries and Miller (1985) and others on the problems of narcissism with people in senior leadership positions. A third weakness was ambiguity about the underlying influence processes associated with transformational leadership.

We expect that the greater use of qualitative methods to research leadership will remedy these perceived weaknesses over time (Bryman,

Stephens and à Campo, 1996). A final weakness identified by Yukl (1999) was an overemphasis on the dyadic processes of transformational leadership. Once again, the greater use of qualitative methods to research leadership, as a social process found generally within organizations, should move researchers towards a resolution of this problem. Either way, there are still many opportunities for broadening out research into leadership as transformation. We invite you to play your part.

We keep waiting for the transformational leadership 'bubble' to burst and for it to be relegated to the historical scrapheap as another management fad. However, Ken in particular continues to find that an appreciation of the notion of transformation and transaction is a powerful diagnostic and learning tool for managers and executives in executive development forums. Once people get the point, and it is an easy point to get, the leadership learning really takes off.

There are good reasons to continue studying the new leadership, and transformational leadership in particular. First, it is a well-worked area of research so there is a large body of theory upon which to build. Second, it has been dominated by questionnaire-based research, so there is a good opportunity to broaden the methodological base upon which this research is conducted. Certainly, a continued use of questionnaire research will be expected but, as we have suggested, people have an opportunity to research the contexts within which they live and work in order to gain an understanding about the processes that are at play in the leadership they are experiencing. Questions about 'what is going on?' will probably dominate the research agenda. For a good example of the benefits of applying a fresh perspective on transformational leadership one could do no better than looking at David Boje and Carl Rhodes' fascinating article which explores the process by which leaders are virtualised through the mass media to become what they describe as a 'Virtual Leader Construct' (VLC) which is a non-human image of a leader that is purposefully created by an organization. Referring to three examples from the fast food industry – Ronald McDonald, Dave Thomas, and Colonel Sanders – they argue that VLCs can and do perform potent transformational leadership functions for organizations, functions that are enabled the more they are virtualized. Indeed they are more reliable and dependable than many real leaders who will occasionally lapse into less than virtuous behaviour!

Having staked a claim for more qualitative research into leadership, we must add a rider here we see a need for more triangulation of data. In other words, both qualitative and quantitative data, used concurrently and within a broader framework of qualitative analysis, might well provide the greatest insights over time.

▬▬▬ charismatic leadership

As we suggested earlier, charismatic leadership is often thought of as a sibling of transformational leadership. It is also thought by other commentators to be a component of transformational leadership. Either way, it is another important aspect of the new leadership that needs to be considered. Much of the research into charismatic leadership has centred on community or political leadership (i.e. the sociological, psychoanalytic and political approaches), rather than leadership in organizations. The transitory nature of charismatic leadership makes it difficult to isolate and therefore to research. For example, Tony Blair was hugely charismatic in the early years of his prime ministership. By the end of it, his charismatic aura had lost much of its glow. For many 'charismatic' leaders, the gain and loss of charisma happens much faster than the ten years it took for Blair to lose his. Even so, striving to understand the process of gaining and losing charisma continues to be a fruitful and underutilized research avenue.

The main approaches that normally attract scholars are the behavioural approach, lionized by Bob House (1977), Bernie Bass (1998) and Jay Conger (1989), the attribution approach, articulated by Jay Conger (as well), Jane Howell, and the great conceptual thinker Boas Shamir (Shamir and Howell, 1999), and the follower self-concept approach (Shamir et al., 1993). Along the same lines, Zaleznik's (1977), Hummel's (1975) and Lindholm's (2002) psychoanalytic approaches to charisma emphasize the impact that leaders have on followers. These two follower-centred approaches to understanding leadership will be explored further in Chapter 3.

The key variable is the motivation and response of followers that charismatic leaders can tap into. This approach to leadership is best suited to political leadership; case studies such as Hitler, Gandhi, Mandela and various US presidential candidates are often analyzed. Whereas most work on charismatic leadership has focused on leader behaviours and follower effects as independent and dependent variables, Boas Shamir (1992) has added to the debate by positing an explanation for the intervening variable which links leadership and effect. He suggests that charismatic leadership has its effect by heightening the self-concept of followers. In particular, charismatic leadership generates heightened self-esteem and self-worth, increased self-efficacy and collective efficacy, a personal identification with the leader, an identification with a prestigious and distinctive social group, and an internalization of the values of the leader. Clearly, charisma is a complex psychosocial phenomenon.

Arguably the most striking case of charismatic leadership gone horribly wrong in the business world – the spectacular implosion of the Enron corporation – has been the subject of seemingly endless analysis and dissection. One of the most thoughtful of these has been provided by Dennis Tourish and Naheed Vatcha (2005) who draw out three distinctive and disturbing charismatic leadership practices that were perfected by Kenneth Lay and Jeffrey Skilling, Enron's celebrated and then vilified leaders. These were the promotion of a compelling vision by these leaders of a totalistic nature; individual consideration, expressed in a recruitment system designed to activate a process analogous to conversion; and the promotion of a culture characterized by conformity and the penalizing of dissent. Based on these observations, the authors conclude that Enron might be most usefully regarded as an example of a corporate cult that, while an extreme variant, has showcased some general and undesirable tendencies within many contemporary corporations.

Charismatic leadership really is a function of the whole situation. It is leader identity, leader behaviour, follower identity, sociocultural context and organizational setting all working together concurrently. Therefore, one should be researching that whole situation in its entirety to understand what is going on. The topic is perennially sexy. One metaphor for the charismatic leadership narrative is that of a 'love story'. Viewed through the frame of the aesthetic category of the sublime derived by Immanuel Kant combined with Max Weber's theory of charismatic authority, Ladkin (2006) suggests that the experience of charisma can be seen as a relational encounter between leaders and followers rather than one situated solely within the leader him- or herself. She helpfully distinguishes between 'generative' and 'degenerative' forms of charisma based on the relational quality rather than on the outcomes associated with it. She concludes that, 'as an expression of the sublime, charismatic leadership functions as a means by which followers are empowered to wake up to their own sense of urgency to respond in radical ways during times of crisis' (2006: 165). This narrative could be dangerous because it opens the door to the dark side of charismatic leadership and allows in a Jim Jones or a Charles Manson. Perhaps the metaphor for charismatic leadership could be that of the older sibling or the doting aunt or uncle – admired and respected from afar. The point is that these narrative perspectives on the phenomenon of charismatic leadership hold much potential for ongoing research.

leadership and personality

This is an issue that has always been best researched psychometrically with questionnaire instruments. Leadership has been linked to certain personality factors in leaders (Judge et al., 2002). Those personality factors are conscientiousness, agreeableness, extraversion and emotional stability. The works of Cable and Judge (2003) and Smith and Canger (2004) are probably good places to start.

It is important to recognize that the links between the demonstration of leadership and personality factors have always been modest, even though they are statistically significant. Bartone et al. (2009) found that personality explained only 3 per cent more variance in measures of leadership, over predictors like gender, course entry scores and social judgement. Strang and Kuhnert (2009) even found that the ability of leaders to make sense of their experiences and construct their own reality socially was a better predictor of leadership performance than personality. Certain personalities lend themselves more to demonstrating leadership than others. For example, a person who is organized, reliable and ambitious (high in conscientiousness) is more likely to be seen as a leader than someone who is unreliable and careless (low in conscientiousness). This finding makes sense, but ironically it is not strong and it is not universal. In other words, contrary to what we might think intuitively, some less reliable and careless people can and do have leadership attributed to them.

The point here is that, irrespective of your personality, you can engage in the behaviours of effective leadership. We would hate to have to say to someone, 'Sorry, but because of your personality, you cannot be a leader', or worse, 'Sorry, but because of your personality, you cannot be in a leadership position', or even worse, 'Sorry, but you cannot even be better at leadership because you have the wrong personality!' However, that being said, we believe it is important to be aware of the links between personality and leadership – to know how and why certain leader–follower relationships work. Perhaps a future direction for research should be an examination of the relationship between the personality of followers (or workers) and leadership by the manager. Either way, we need to understand where people are 'coming from', both figuratively and literally. By the same token, let's not lose sight of the idea that, in spite of our personality profile, we can *all* learn to become better leaders.

Craig and Gustafson (1998) developed an instrument to assess the perceived integrity of leaders. Not surprisingly, it is called the Perceived Leader Integrity Scale (PLIS). Ken utilized a modified version of that scale to test the relationship between transformational leadership and perceived integrity in one of his national surveys in New Zealand (Parry and Proctor-Thomson, 2002). As expected, he found a generally positive relationship between perceptions of integrity and attributions of leadership. However, an intriguing side issue that he also discovered was that 6 per cent of leaders in New Zealand organizations were found to be above average in their display of leadership yet below average in perceived integrity. In other words, some people in leadership positions can give all the inspirational speeches they want and get to know the needs of individuals and display a sense of power, yet followers will still believe that those same leaders lack integrity.

These figures resonate with Gustafson and Ritzer's (1995) and Babiak's (1996) finding that approximately one in twenty managers are aberrant self-promoters, a mild form of organizational psychopathy. The implication is that some people are enacting all the right transformational behaviours, yet what is in their heart is not as honourable as they would like their followers to believe. These and related findings have heralded an exciting new direction for research which examines why and how leaders do bad things.

when leaders go bad

In her (2004) book, *Bad Leadership,* Barbara Kellerman notes a marked and regrettable reluctance on the part of leadership scholars as well as those who study leadership to consider leadership that it is neither positive, ethical or uplifting. This is unfortunate and ironic because a large proportion of the world is led by bad leaders who employ coercion and terror. Furthermore, we have more to learn from bad rather than good leadership. By refusing to teach about bad leadership, she argues, academics are confusing, misleading and ultimately doing a disservice to their students.

She will no doubt be warmed by the growing and highly profitable line of research that has emerged in the past five years which investigates destructive leadership. For example, in a recently published collection of essays entitled *When Leadership Goes Wrong: Destructive Leadership, Mistakes and Ethical Failures* the editors claim that 'allowing for the possibility that leaders can also do harm, either intentionally or unintentionally, broadens the scope of leadership studies and serves to increase the practical implications of leadership research' (Schyns and Hansbrough, 2010). Researchers in this field most commonly concern themselves with the 'dark' or 'shadow' side of leadership (Kets de Vries and Balazs, 2011). The dark side includes among other facets of personality: narcissism, a passive-aggressive personality, an obsessive-compulsive personality, anti-social behaviour, and paranoid, schizotypal and histrionic personalities (Khoo and Burch, 2008).

It is not a simple case, however, of separating out the 'good' or 'bad' as many of the qualities that enable individuals to lead well can also serve to subvert and ultimately destroy. As Jay Conger observes, 'the very behaviours that distinguish leaders from managers also have the potential to produce problematic or even disastrous outcomes for their organizations. For example, when a leader's behaviours become exaggerated, lose touch with reality or become vehicles for purely personal gain, they may harm the leader or the organization' (1990: 44). In light of this Judge, Piccolo and Kosalka (2009) argue that it is important to consider both the positive and negative effects of specific 'bright side' personality traits of leaders: the Big Five Traits (discussed at the end of Chapter I), core-self evaluations, intelligence and charisma as well as the positive and negative effects of the 'dark side' traits: narcissm, hubris, dominance and Machiavellianism.

The 'bright' or 'dark' leadership behaviour that has received the most attention in this regard is narcissistic leadership. In their comprehensive review on this topic, Rosenthal and Pittinsky describe narcissistic leaders as having 'grandiose beliefs systems and leadership styles, and are generally motivated by their needs for power and admiration rather than empathetic concern for the constituents and institutions they lead' (2006: 617).

In one particularly well-cited issue of the *Harvard Business Review*, Michael Maccoby (2000) discussed the 'incredible pros' and the 'inevitable cons' of narcissistic leaders. There are any number of psychology textbooks that explain the narcissistic personality but, for our purposes here, the narcissistic leader is usually represented by the larger-than-life personalities whom we see running organizations and figuring prominently in our society – best personified by the likes of Richard Branson, Donald Trump and Jack Welch.

One strength of the narcissistic leader is an ability to energize followers with a grand and compelling vision. Another strength is to generate large numbers of followers who can enact the vision. In fact, the narcissistic leader is very dependent upon followers. There are also weaknesses to narcissistic leaders. They are sensitive to criticism. They are poor listeners. They lack empathy and have a distaste for mentoring, although they have an intense desire to compete.

The focus of research into the narcissistic leader could equally be the leader or the followers. A good example of the latter is the study by Elmes and Barry (1999) of narcissistic behaviour exhibited by mountaineering groups on the rock face which ultimately led to the tragic climbing deaths described in the bestseller, *Into Thin Air* (Krakauer, 1997). By the very nature of its subject, this research usually takes the form of a case study. The books and popular press articles on narcissistic leaders are effectively case studies, albeit lacking in empirical rigour. There is room for improvement in the quality of the research that goes into such case studies. Equally, by virtue of the impact of personality on leadership, there is also still great scope for more traditional questionnaire research into the narcissistic leader. In terms of some of the research that has been undertaken, Post (1986), Kets de Vries and Miller (1985), and Maccoby (2000) have discussed the impact of personality aberrations such as narcissism upon the performance of people in senior leadership roles.

While narcissism has attracted the lion's share of attention, there have been a number of notable efforts to conceptualise the causes, behaviours and effects of destructive leadership at a broader level. One focus has been to concentrate on the goal of leadership. In a seminal study, House and Howell (1992) make a classic distinction between 'socialized leadership' (i.e. leadership for the wider good) and 'personalised leadership' (i.e. leadership for the good of the leaders and his or her immediate followers). Building on this, Mike Mumford and his research team have drawn on an historiographic study of 80 historically notable leaders and classified these leaders according to four categories: 'violent/ideological leaders' (e.g. Vladimir Lenin, Pol Pot, Osama bin Laden); 'violent/non-ideological' leaders' (e.g. Adolf Hitler, George Patton, Idi Amin); 'non-violent/ideological' leaders (e.g. Mother Theresa, the Dalai Lama and Eamon de Valera); and 'non-violent/non-ideological' leaders (e.g. George Soros, Nelson Mandela, Margaret Thatcher) (Mumford et al., 2007). The extent to which leaders are truly capable of being totally 'non-ideological' and 'non-violent' is a moot question but this is an intriguing list nonetheless.

when leaders stay good

Perhaps the most influential leadership idea to emerge in the popular realm in the first part of the twenty-first century has been the notion of 'level 5' leadership, a term coined by Jim Collins in his best-selling business book, *Good to Great* (2001a). Continuing the theme of sustainable corporate success that was so profitably mined in his earlier bestseller, *Built to Last* (Collins and Porras, 1995), both he and his research team set out to discover what lay beneath the continued superior performance of a handful of American corporations over several decades rather than in the short term.

Despite their best efforts not to pin success on the quality of the leadership at the top of the organization, that is in fact what they found. In particular, they discovered a CEO at each one who had well and truly paid his dues (they were all males) in the company and the industry, and had steadily and patiently worked his way to the top of the organization, sticking around through thick and thin. By no means overnight sensations, these CEOs represented the antithesis of the charismatic and narcissistic turnaround kings who were held up as archetypal CEOs during the financial booms of the 1980s and 1990s. Collins suggests that the latter 'magic leaders' exemplified what he terms 'level 4 leadership' – highly effective in the short term but, due to their character flaws, doomed to fail in the longer term. They fall short of 'level 5 leaders' who, by contrast:

> are a study in duality: they are modest and willful, shy and fearless. They act with quiet, calm determination and they rely principally on inspired standards, not inspiring charisma, to motivate. They channel their ambition into the company, not the self. They also 'look in the mirror, not the window, to apportion responsibility for poor results, never blaming other people, external factors or bad luck. Similarly, they look out of the window to apportion credit for the company's success to employees, external factors or good luck. (Collins, 2001b: 73)

The level 5 leader was personified by Wade Thompson, the co-founder with Peter Orthwein of Thor Industries, the world's largest recreational vehicle company. Since purchasing the iconic but financially ailing Airstream company in 1980, Thompson and Orthwein slowly but surely built up a highly successful company that has become one of America's 15 most admired companies. They did this by consistently adhering to a few basic principles rooted in integrity, responsibility and accountability, many of which they share with the legendarily low-key yet spectacularly successful investment guru, Warren Buffet. They achieved all of this in a studiously understated manner, miles away from the media spotlight. Brad was fortunate to have the opportunity to make a documentary called *The Open Road*, which describes the historic growth of this multibillion dollar company, as a means to teach the next generation of strategic leaders.

This discernible weather change that moved away from celebrating the 'loud and proud' charismatic leader archetype to embracing a more humble, ethical anti-charismatic leader has also found its way into popular accounts of leadership at other levels within the organization and the community at large. Most notably, Joseph Badaracco (2002: 3) in his book, *Leading Quietly*, compellingly observes:

> They're not making high stakes decisions. They're often not at the top of organizations. They often don't have the spotlight and publicity on them. They think of themselves modestly; they often don't even think of themselves as leaders. But they are acting *quietly*, effectively, with political astuteness, to basically make things better, sometimes much better than they would otherwise.

Early in 2008 Jeff Immelt, CEO of GE, told his worldwide senior management group to 'prepare for a global financial meltdown like we have never seen before'. The managers thought he was crazy. Both their business and the world economy were stronger than ever. Nonetheless, he had the credibility and plausibility to ensure that his managers did indeed prepare for such an eventuality, which was lucky for all of them. He did not *know* what was going to happen. He was probably not being pessimistic or crisis-mongering. He was simply attempting to avoid complacency. He was calmly showing sufficient wisdom and intellectual stimulation to ensure that his managers were ready for one of several scenarios.

Brad and his colleague Eric Guthey, from the Copenhagen Business School, have investigated what they describe as the 'hero manager backlash' that gathered momentum at the beginning of 2002 with the advent of the widely vilified corporate scandals and the bursting of the dot.com bubble (Guthey and Jackson, 2005; Guthey, Clark and Jackson, 2009). They traced the media backlash through an analysis of the changing portrayals of CEOs featured on the covers and within the pages of high-profile business periodicals such as *Business Week*, *Fortune* and *Forbes*. They noted the tendency of the media not only to seek to demonize heroic leaders, pillorying them in a quite shocking, visual fashion (after celebrating them only a year prior), but also to find new heroes to replace them. In this regard, they note that the media have replaced the 'Men in Black' level 4 leaders with the 'Men in Beige' level 5 leaders. At what point and in what form these leaders will be subsequently knocked down and replaced by the 'level 6' leaders (whomsoever they may be) is anyone's guess.

As we shall see in Chapter 6, leadership scholars have not been impervious to this tectonic shift in popular attitudes towards business leadership. In Chapter 6 we describe the three-pronged quest for leaders who have a higher purpose (i.e. one that is above the grubby preoccupation with hard cash and absolute power) by exploring authentic, ethical and spiritual leadership. Much of this work has sought to invigorate the theory and practice of transformational leadership yet also drive charismatic leadership to the sidelines. Typical of this search is the observation made by Gardner and his colleagues about 'the authentic leader':

> We are struck by the uplifting effects of lower profile but genuine leaders who lead by example in fostering healthy ethical climates characterized by transparency, trust, integrity, and high moral standards. We call such leaders authentic leaders who are not only true to themselves, but lead others by helping them to likewise achieve authenticity. (Gardner et al., 2005: 344)

Essentially, what we are witnessing here is the continued desire by leadership scholars to solve what are perceived to be problems created by poor leadership by selecting and developing the 'right' type of leader. New leadership theory emphasized the dramatic performance improvements that could be realized by visionary leaders who were able to inspire their followers through their charismatic rather than their formal authority. While results have often been dramatic, they have sometimes been achieved with unacceptable ethical, moral and psychological costs. This has caused leadership scholars to shift their focus away from the 'means to the ends' of leadership, specifically to inspect the moral and ethical bases of leadership goals. Their quest for genuinely authentic, ethically sound and spiritually enlightened leaders maintains the leader-centric perspective which endeavours to solve leadership problems by focusing on the leader. Their followers, therefore, continue to play a marginal and incidental role. In Chapter 3 we will look at a number of bold but isolated efforts to redress this situation by finally bringing these followers into the analysis.

conclusion

This chapter began with a discussion regarding the relationship between the identity of a leader and his or her behaviour. Related to this, we considered the influence of gender on leadership and concluded that, while biologically-oriented research had revealed surprisingly little difference, those who had looked at gender from a social identity perspective had provided comparatively more fertile terrain for leadership researchers. We reviewed the substantial contribution that new leadership theory (encompassing transformational, transactional and charismatic leadership) has made to our understanding of what constitutes effective leadership and how to promote it. We also noted a number of criticisms that have been levelled at this impressive and still highly influential body of work.

In exploring the relationship between personality and leadership, we noted that most of the research has focused on the positive and rational aspects of personality that were seen to be conducive to fostering good leadership. We also noted and welcomed a growing interest in understanding the 'dark' as well as the 'light' side of leadership personality, pointing specifically to the role of narcissism in promoting good and bad leadership. We closed the chapter by discussing the shift that has taken place in the popular archetypes of sound strategic leadership from the larger-than-life visionary charismatic business leaders of the 1980s and 1990s to the more humble, ethical and understated business leaders of the 2000s, in the aftermath of corporate scandals and the global financial crisis.

3

Follower-centred Perspectives on Leadership

New insights into the processes of leadership can be gained by focusing attention squarely on processes connected to followers and their contexts, independently of what leaders are actually doing.

Meindl, Pastor and Mayo (2004: 1347)

introducing the follower

In Chapter 1, we introduced Joseph Rost's definition of leadership as an influence relationship among leaders and followers who intend real changes that reflect their mutual purposes. In Chapter 2 we focused our attention on the leader's role in this relationship. In this chapter we turn to the role of the follower.

At the beginning of the presentation on leadership that Brad gives to undergraduate students he conducts a quick poll. He asks how many of them aspire to be a 'good leader'. Invariably, between 10 and 15 of the class of 200 will put up their hands. When he asks how many of them aspire to be good followers, either none or one lone maverick student will put up a hand. This does not change even when Brad puts up his hand – such is the level of influence that he exerts on the class.

Setting aside the concern that the vast majority of undergraduates aspire to be neither a good leader nor a good follower – or at least are not willing to publicly declare their intentions, good or bad – the almost non-existent desire to be a good follower is striking and potentially unsettling. We all know instinctively that we will spend most of our life as a follower and only a small proportion of it as a leader, but it is not something that we are generally proud to admit, let alone celebrate. Even the most powerful world leaders, whether it's the President of the United States, the Pope, or even Bono, will spend most of their lives as followers too. In fact, the public are quite amused when they catch prominent leaders acting as followers, whether it's being cajoled by an adviser or a protester or being gently reprimanded by their spouse or children. We all have to follow: as Bob Dylan wryly observes, 'You Gotta Serve Somebody'.

Being reticent or reluctant to follow is not something that is peculiar to undergraduate students but, as we will see in Chapter 4 on culture and leadership, it is a strong feature of individualistically oriented Western societies, especially those that are characterized by low power distance values. Part of the problem is the word 'follower' itself. Being a follower implies that you are second best, that you are not good enough to lead. Clearly, there is a pejorative tone to it. For some, the notion of following has strong religious overtones, suggesting blind devotion, which further serves to undermine the currency of the term.

The uneasiness or lack of interest in either talking about or understanding followership is reflected in how much less the term crops up on the Internet. Karl Weick notes from a Google search that he found 57 items relating to the word 'leader' for every one regarding a 'follower' (Weick, 2007). Three years later, Bligh (2011: 431) discovered that this ratio had plummeted to 22:1. This fundamental imbalance and the recent readjustment in favour of followers are reflected in the number of books that are published on the subject. While just over 5,000 non-fiction books can be ordered through Amazon.com with the word 'leadership' in their title, only 37 books can be ordered with the word 'followership' in their title. The figure for leadership has changed little, but the figure for 'followership' titles is up from the six we found three years ago when we wrote the first edition of this book. Most notable among these is the edited volume entitled *The Art of Followership: How Great Followers Create Great Leaders and Organizations* (Riggio, Chaleff and Lipman-Blumen, 2008).

Clearly, the interest in followership is increasing to such a point that it has prompted Michelle Bligh, in her recent review of follower-centred research, to conclude that 'there is evidence that followership is entering the second stage of conceptual development, one of evaluation and conceptual development' (2011: 431). Baker (2007) has further aided us in this regard by pointing to the rich theoretical foundation of work on followership that has been conducted by non-leadership scholars since the 1950s but has been largely ignored by contemporary leadership researchers. One of the pioneers of followership, Edwin Hollander, soberly suggests that we might profitably look back much further, observing that 'followership is periodically rediscovered as important to leadership, despite a long tradition of usage' that has emerged and re-emerged since at least the sixth century BC (Hollander, 1995: 56).

One response to the reluctance to acknowledge the term 'follower' has been to look for alternative terms. Various replacements have been proposed from 'team member' to 'collaborator', 'associate', 'colleague', 'partner', or even 'peer', but none of them has caught on in either popular or academic discourse. The word 'follower' persists, albeit with grudging and somewhat embarrassed acceptance, in our leadership lexicon. We will, however, be using the term in this chapter with unbridled enthusiasm as we strive to show that it is not the act of following that is necessarily problematic – indeed it is vital to leadership – but, as with leading, there are more and less effective ways in which we may follow.

The undue primacy that is placed on leaders over followers has been reinforced by leadership scholars. A major exception to this was Jim Meindl, the Director of the Center for Leadership Studies at the State University of New York, at Buffalo, who sadly passed away at the peak of his career in 2004. Meindl's major contribution to leadership studies was to head up a 'follower-centric' approach to leadership studies offered by way of a much-needed counterweight to an almost exclusive preoccupation with leader-centric approaches. Consolidating earlier arguments made by Pfeffer (1977), Pfeffer and Salancik (1978) and Calder (1977), he observed that while most leadership scholars would have little difficulty in recognizing that leadership is fundamentally predicated on the relationship between leaders and followers, the follower almost invariably took a minor supporting role in the analysis of leadership.

Reading Meindl's work, one is struck by his deep-seated discomfort with the tendency for his peers and his fellow citizens to place such great stock in the role of leaders, especially those at the apex of the organization. This misplaced faith was held despite the overwhelming weight of evidence showing that external forces and a myriad of alternative internal factors could be considerably more influential in determining organizational performance. He concluded with more than a hint of resignation that, 'the concept of leadership is a permanently entrenched part of the socially constructed reality that we bring to bear in our analysis of organizations. And there is every sign that the obsessions and celebrations of it will persist' (Meindl, Ehrlich and Dukerich, 1985: 78). The twenty or so years since he made this observation have only served to further reinforce his conviction.

Another notable addition to the growing followership canon, *Follower-Centered Perspectives on Leadership* (Shamir et al., 2007), collected together in a tribute to the memory of James Meindl a number of researchers who actively work towards the development of new follower-centric approaches to leadership. In the book's introduction, Boas Shamir provides a helpful overview of this work and identifies five roles that followers have traditionally played in leadership theories: 'followers as recipients of leader influence', 'followers as moderators of leader impact', 'followers as substitutes for leadership', 'followers as constructors of leadership' and 'followers as leaders'

(2007). We have used these categories to organize our discussion. We will close the chapter by considering a sixth role that Boas and his colleagues have advocated for followers: 'followers as co-producers of leadership'. This perspective has been developed as a critical alternative to the five ways in which followers have been traditionally conceptualized. This is a conceptualization which is very much in tune with our own thinking and also ripe for further study and investigation.

followers as recipients of leadership

The passive conception of the follower's role in leadership has been the traditionally dominant view. As such it has done little to challenge the popular stereotypes about followers and followership. As we saw in Chapter 1, traditional leadership theories posit the leader's traits and behaviour as the independent variables and the followers' perceptions, attitudes and behaviours to be explained as the dependent variables in the leadership equation.

Even with the more recent theories of transformational, transactional and charismatic leadership discussed in Chapter 2, the onus is still firmly placed on the leader to create one or various of these forms of leadership for followers to respond to. If the leader follows the correct procedures, he or she will succeed in creating transactional or charismatic or transformational leadership, irrespective of these followers. Because of the way these theories perceive the leadership process, it does not really matter who you are trying to lead. Followers do not play an active role in the leadership process. It is an essentially linear, one-way relationship between leaders and followers. Each follower is, in effect, a blank slate upon which the leader writes the script.

followers as moderators of leadership

As we saw in the first chapter, contingency theories of leadership acknowledge that the leader's influence on followers' attitudes and performance depends on the individual follower's characteristics. This view of followers still thinks of them as primarily passive recipients of influence, but also acknowledges that the leader's influence may have to be moderated by the characteristics of the follower.

Brad recalls from the first leadership training course he took, which was on 'situational leadership' (Hersey and Blanchard, 1977), that he had to learn to change his leadership style depending on the level of 'maturity' of the follower. This was determined by the ability and motivation of the follower. With an immature follower he should take on a 'telling style' of leadership, in which he would tell the employees what needed to be done but not be too interested in them as people. 'Relationship behaviour' would come later. As the follower became more capable and motivated, Brad could then move on to a 'selling style', in which he would keep up the task pressure but also begin to cultivate a good relationship with the employee.

Moving around the compass he could then progress to a 'participatory style', in which he could cease to give direction and allow the follower to direct themself and devote his attention to relationship-building activities. In the final stage, presumably some form of leadership nirvana, Brad could take on a 'delegating leadership style' (sometimes derogatively referred to as '*laissez-faire*' leadership), by which he could leave the employee to their own devices and let them lead themself. This all sounded so enticing in theory, but in practice followers would rarely stuck to the same script. They had obviously been on a different course! They kept throwing up all kinds of complications, such as having different opinions, not sharing the same motives, and plunging various spanners into the works.

Perhaps they had attended a course inspired by Kelley (1988, 1992), whose provocative explanation of follower communication styles did much to popularize the notion of 'followership'. Based on his own 2 × 2 matrix, which used the twin axes of independent thinking and active engagement, followers could be classified as being either 'the sheep', 'the yes-people', 'the alienated', 'the pragmatic' or 'the star followers'. Now which one of these are you?

Contingency theorists have pointed to a number of other aspects of followers that leaders need to take into account when leading. These include: the follower's initial attitude towards the leader and their acceptance of the leader (Fiedler, 1967); the follower's need for either technical or emotional support (House, 1971); and the follower's knowledge together with the congruence of their values with their leader's (Vroom and Yetton, 1973). While each of the theories tries to point to another aspect of the follower that the leader must take into account when determining how to behave, the overriding expectation is for the leader to be the active partner in the leadership process.

followers as substitutes for leadership

From time to time the careers section in the newspaper runs articles publicizing the latest HR consultancy survey, highlighting the finding that the number one reason why most people leave their jobs is because of a bad boss. Money, conditions, benefits and prospects pale into insignificance compared to an abusive or inconsiderate boss, it would seem. Leaving is, of course, one way to deal with a bad boss. Another way is to find ways to avoid him or her and minimize the damage.

The 'substitutes for leadership' theory originated by Steven Kerr and John Jermier provides some encouragement in this regard (Kerr and Jermier, 1978). It argues that, under certain conditions, the influence of a leader over a follower may actually be neutralized or even substituted. If it is neutralized, this means that it is impossible for either the task-oriented or the relationship-oriented activities of a leader to make a difference to a follower's attitudes or behaviour. If leadership is substituted this means that the leader's activities are not only impossible, but they are also largely unnecessary.

Returning to the problem of avoiding a bad boss, those followers who have high levels of ability, experience, training and knowledge – as well as a high need for independence and a strongly 'professional' orientation – are usually quite self-aware and possess self-efficacy and therefore have little need for a boss's feedback. Moreover, when the task at hand is relatively straightforward and routine, you have little need for a boss. Alternatively, if you can get into a job that is intrinsically satisfying or like a tradesperson, you can see directly what you have achieved. You do not need a boss to explain to you how important your work is or how you are doing. Finally, you might consider joining an organization which is highly bureaucratic in that the work and the rewards are highly formalized and little is left to the boss's discretion. Best of all, try taking a job in which there is considerable spatial distance between you and your boss, but beware of the remarkable reach of the BlackBerry or iPhone.

Perhaps not surprisingly, the substitutes for leadership theory have strong intuitive appeal for those who do not subscribe to the importance of leadership in organizational processes. It serves quite effectively to take the wind out of the sails of leadership scholars who trumpet the central importance of leadership in organizational success and failure. It has, however, failed to lead to much in the way of subsequent research, serving primarily as an act of protest. A series of exchanges published in *Leadership Quarterly* did, however, try to generate further theoretical and methodological refinements to the substitutes for leadership, particularly as it applies to strategic leadership at senior levels within organizations (Dionne et al., 2005).

Boas Shamir (2007) characterizes the way in which the substitutes for leadership theory perceive the followers' role as an extreme version of seeing followers as moderators of leadership. In common with this perspective, the specific activities of followers in substituting for leadership are not actively theorized. The theory has been developed primarily to de-emphasize the significance of the leader, but it does not do a lot to explicate the role of followers in creating leadership. As we shall see in the following section, the next group of theories have made this task their central concern.

followers as constructors of leadership

In this section we will talk about research that has examined the way in which followers make or construct leadership. Researchers here are preoccupied with the thoughts of followers, most especially how they construct and represent leaders in their thought systems. They make the fundamental point that leadership is essentially in the eye of the follower. Unless followers recognize it as leadership, it isn't leadership. We will distinguish between three groups of theories that have identified a different aspect of this construction process: the romance of leadership theory, the psychoanalytic theory of leadership, and the social identity theory of leadership.

the romance of leadership

At the beginning of this chapter we noted that the follower-centric view of leadership emanated from a concern that most leadership scholars had become overly preoccupied with the role of the leader in creating leadership, while virtually ignoring the role of the follower. Essentially, leadership scholars were mirroring, and indeed perpetuating, the hype and unrealistic expectations that are routinely placed on leaders in all spheres of human endeavour, but most especially in the world of business and politics. Rather than turn their back on leadership studies, Jim Meindl and his colleagues decided to make this tendency to overestimate the significance of leadership their central concern.

At the heart of their analysis lies the notion of the 'romance of leadership', which they suggest 'denotes a strong belief – a faith – in the importance of leadership factors to the functioning and dysfunctioning of organized systems' (Meindl and Ehrlich, 1987: 91). A series of empirical studies conducted in laboratory settings – through the development of a survey instrument, the Romance of Leadership Scale (RLS) – and the analyses of media reports revealed a consistent pattern of follower behaviour (Meindl and Ehrlich, 1988). In the absence of direct, unambiguous information about an organization, respondents would tend to ascribe control and responsibility to leaders, with events and outcomes to which they could be plausibly linked (Meindl, Ehrlich and Dukerich, 1985). In effect, leadership acted as a simplified, biased and attractive way to make sense of organizational performance. Moreover, this romantic tendency seemed to have the greatest sway in extreme cases – when things were going either extremely well or extremely badly observers tended to lay the credit or blame at the leader's door.

Meindl did not advance the follower-centric approach in an effort either to compete or to replace the dominant leader-centric approach. As he noted: 'Rather than being anti-leadership, the romance of leadership, and the perspective it provides, is more accurately portrayed as an alternative to theories and perspectives that place great weight on "leaders" and on the substantive significance to their actions and activities' (1995: 330). Looked at through the romance of leadership lens, you could see that a superior performance was perhaps, in fact, the cause and not the consequence of charismatic leadership (Awamleh and Gardner, 1999: 346). Put succinctly, leaders keep on winning largely because their followers perceive them to be winners. They therefore do everything they can to ensure this continues to be the case. For example, Manchester United players would do everything they could to keep Sir Alex Ferguson and his winning ways.

Meindl described the romance of leadership as a social construction. Followers construct their opinion about the leader by interacting with other followers. Central to this process is something he called social contagion, which he described as 'a phenomenon of the spontaneous spread of affective and/or behavioral reactions among the members of a group or social collective' (Meindl, 1993: 101). As its name suggests, we can think of a leader's reputation (good or bad) as being something akin to influenza that can be passed on from follower to follower until everyone becomes infected. It is difficult to pinpoint exactly where the contagion originated. Suddenly it sweeps through a community, and often disappears just as unexpectedly. Social contagion highlights the interpersonal processes and group dynamics that underpin the widespread dissemination of charismatic effects among followers and subordinates.

The media are important contributors to these social construction and social contagion processes. Media accounts influence and shape the attributions that followers might give to a particular leader. They can also shape our general beliefs about what constitutes effective and ineffective, ethical and unethical leadership. These processes are illustrated to good effect in an empirical study, based on media accounts, conducted by Chen and Meindl (1991) of the career of People Express founder and chief executive Donald Burr. Burr's airline enjoyed a brief but highly celebrated heyday before encountering insurmountable financial problems and folding into Texas Air just five short years after it made its inaugural flight in 1981 in a blaze of publicity. The study shows how the press collectively constructed Donald Burr as an idealized representation of the American entrepreneurial spirit, infused with vision and inspiration in the manner of a pioneering evangelical preacher. They stuck with this image of the leader throughout the life of the company but made a marked switch – in the face of a sustained poor company performance – from celebrating the positive connotations associated with this image to revealing its negative connotations.

Chen and Meindl conclude that, contrary to popular wisdom, leaders do not control their own destiny despite the best efforts of public relations professionals. Brad knows this only too well from his time as a 'spin doctor'. Both the identity and influence of leaders depend to a large extent on the manner in which their followers perceive them. Leaders and followers are each subject to a range of forces beyond their direct control; prominent among these are the dynamics of the news industries that disseminate information about leaders to their followers and the wider society. The business media, in turn, are subject to a variety of internal and external pressures. They have to sell newspapers and advertising space and, therefore, have also to influence their readers and various other stakeholders. Consequently, they play to our hunger for personalized news in the belief that individual leaders control the fate of organizations rather than relational or structural forces. In constructing leader images, they match the leader's characteristics with the performance of the firm. Consequently, the CEO of a successful firm will tend to be depicted with positive personal qualities and vice versa.

The 'celebrity CEO' phenomenon takes full advantage of our tendencies to romanticize leadership (Guthey, Clark and Jackson, 2009). In an increasingly complicated and impersonal world, the public face of a charismatic and appealing CEO can prove to be a highly effective means for a company to build a symbolic link or brand with its various stakeholders, such as its shareholders, its customers, or its suppliers. A 'real' person supplies the human touch that cannot be provided by a mere logo. It is almost impossible to think about Richard Branson without also thinking about the Virgin brand and vice versa. Having a celebrity CEO at the helm can act as a double-edged sword, however. It is difficult to maintain confidence in an organization once the influential founder moves on, as The Body Shop found when Anita Roddick gave up control of the company. It's even more of a challenge when your founder goes to jail, as was demonstrated in a spectacular fashion with the imprisonment of Martha Stewart. Redemption can also be a powerful motivator, as witnessed by the impressive turnaround in Martha Stewart Living Omnimedia, Inc. since her release.

The romance of leadership theory is particularly strong in describing a tendency for followers to exaggerate the importance and influence of the leader in determining a group's or organization's performance. If things are going well, it's the leader's doing; if things are going badly, that is also the leader's doing. The theory also provides some useful insights into how this takes place, with its exposition of social construction and social contagion processes. Where the theory is not as strong is in explaining why this happens. The following two theories – psychoanalytic theory and social identity theory – provide pointers as to why followers might choose to construct leadership in the way they have been observed to do.

the psychoanalytic theories of leadership

When we addressed the question regarding leaders being born or made in the opening chapter, we pointed to the importance of our early years in shaping and defining our individual philosophies of leadership. Psychoanalytic theories of leadership take this observation several steps further.

Rooted in Sigmund Freud's psychoanalysis and Carl Jung's psychopathology, the psychodynamic approach highlights the centrality of our family of origin if we wish to understand our behaviour, whether as a leader or as a follower (Stech, 2004). A leader's style is heavily influenced by the models of leadership exhibited by parents, teachers, coaches and other adults during the maturation process from childhood, through adolescence, to adulthood. Most potent of these is the style of parenting, particularly that which happens very early in the impressionable years (Keller, 2003). An adult might choose to copy that parent's style or may opt for a diametrically opposite style. We often see someone who was raised in an authoritarian way consciously reject this approach in favour of a more *laissez-faire* approach. One is, however, struck when confronted with the actual challenge of raising a child by how those familiar patterns emerge – despite our best intentions.

The way in which we are raised also influences the way in which we choose to follow. If adults find themselves in a relationship with either an authoritarian leader or a leader with a more participative style, the reaction of the adult may be influenced by the way their authority figures – parents in particular – behaved and dealt with authority figures in the past.

Psychodynamically, we may react to a leader in either a dependent, a counter-dependent or an independent manner (Stech, 2004). We might become totally dependent on the leader for our livelihood and our emotional support. When we react in a counter-dependent way we react rebelliously, rejecting the directives of the leader. As an independent follower we will look at the leader's directive objectively, assessing whether or not it is reasonable and ethical, before choosing to act. It is this type of followership behaviour that responsible leaders actively try to encourage in their followers. Dealing with chronically dependent and counter-dependent followers presents two different sets of challenges that can prove to be gruelling and very painful to address for both parties.

In explaining why followers construct leaders in a dependent way, psychoanalytic theories of leadership point to two psychodynamic processes: projection and transference (Shamir, 2007). Projection is the process by which we attribute to another person our ideals, wishes, desires and fantasies. We see this tendency being demonstrated by diehard fans of pop stars, actors and models. Transference, on the other hand, is the process of responding to another person as if that person was one's mother, father or another significant person from early childhood.

Pyschoanalytic theories suggest that these processes are particularly salient during periods of crisis or threat. When people are confused, unsafe or helpless, followers can regress to early childhood patterns and behaviour. They become attached to leaders and idealize and obey them, not because of the leader's special characteristics but because the leader symbolizes a father, a mother, or some omnipotent figure. Citing Freud's writings on leadership (Freud, 1921), George Goethals (2005) suggests that strong male leaders, such as George Washington, have the ability to reawaken unconscious archaic images of the powerful male ('The Big Man') who ruled despotically over primitive human societies. Taking up Darwin's notion of the 'primal horde', Freud argued that the father or chief was a strong and independent figure who imposed his will on all other members of the group. Followers had the illusion that their leader loved each of them equally.

Drawing on accounts provided by undergraduate students of their experiences during a crucial meeting with the 'supreme' leaders of the organizations in which they worked during their six-month internships, Gabriel (1997) identifies four core fantasies about the leaders that emerge from their narratives: (1) the leader as someone who cares for his or her followers; (2) the leader as someone who is accessible; (3) the leader as someone who is omnipotent and omniscient; and (4) the leader as someone who has a legitimate claim to lead others. Against the backdrop of a predominant culture of narcissism, narcissistic personalities, expressed most acutely during adolescence, 'both claim to long for "strong leaders", and yet are unwilling to accept authority for any period of time' (1997: 339).

Leaders can also provide a means by which followers can reduce their level of anxiety and provide them with a measure of psychological safety. In order to meet these psychological needs followers, through the processes of transference or projection, will sometimes knowingly tolerate – and sometimes prefer and even create – 'toxic leaders'. Jean Lipman-Blumen notes that 'toxic leaders manipulate their followers' ordinary human needs and exploit their existential circumstances. They do this by creating illusions designed to allay the fears and address the human condition to which we all are heir' (2007: 3). By the same token, Lynn Offerman (2004) alerts us to the various ways in which 'toxic followers' might similarly lead their leaders astray.

Cult leaders such as Charles Manson, Jim Jones and David Koresh are held up as infamous prime exemplars of this form of deleterious leadership, which Micha Popper (2002) likens to a process of mass hypnosis in which followers lose their self and the ability to reason autonomously. We can also see elements of this process in more conventional leader–follower relationships. Brad's doctoral research, for example, examined why so many managers chose to follow such management gurus as Stephen Covey, Michael Hammer and Peter Senge. Lindholm (2002) extends this point to the general process of charismatic leadership, noting that if the charismatic leader is able to compel, then the follower must have a matching capacity for being compelled. We therefore need to consider what makes up the personality configuration of the follower, as well as that of the leader, if we are to understand charisma.

The psychodynamic approach to leadership is by no means a mainstream one within the study of leadership. Leadership scholars share the same general discomfort and reticence about working with the unconscious mind that psychologists tend to have. Critics point to the approach's origins in the clinical observation and treatment of people with serious difficulties, not those whom we tend to find in typical workplaces. The theory is also based on the subjective findings of clinical psychologists collected from individual case studies; it is not based on conventional scientific principles. In defence, Manfred Kets de Vries observes with typical irony, 'it's something of a paradox that, while at a conscious level we might deny the presence of unconscious processes, at the level of behaviour and action we live out such processes everyday all over the world' (2006: 4).

On the positive side of the ledger, psychodynamic theory does encourage an analysis of the affective relationship between the leader and follower. It encourages us to look to our past to identify deeply ingrained and recurrent patterns that might undermine our ability to become a fully effective and responsible leader and follower. It also asks the awkward questions about leadership that might provoke discomfort but nonetheless should not be left unasked. Goethals (2005) approvingly notes that it dares to suggest that perhaps people have a fundamental instinct to follow that is bolstered by a deep-seated 'thirst for obedience'. Taking this idea further, Cluley posits that 'the psychological distinction between leader and follower is an illusion, albeit a necessary illusion for the longevity of groups' (2008: 210–11). It gives the reassuring impression to groups of followers that leaders are more individual than they are in reality. Perhaps, then, another reason for the spectacular growth in leadership studies that we discussed in Chapter 1 could be attributed to our collective need to identify with a leader who is above the group and separate from its social psychology, someone we may look up to and believe in? How should leaders respond? Drawing upon James McGregor Burns, Gabriel (1997) helpfully reminds us that a key task for leaders, therefore, is to 'make conscious what lies unconscious among followers' (Burns, 1978: 40), by using power to achieve the ultimate test of leadership – the realization of collective purpose is in unleashing real and intended change (1978: 251).

the social identity theory of leadership

The third and final theory that emphasizes the process by which followers construct leaders is called the social identity theory of leadership. It proposes that the extent to which a leader is either selected or accepted by a particular group will depend on how 'prototypical' (i.e. representative) she or he is to that group (Van Knippenberg and Hogg, 2003). Hogg defines prototypicality as 'a fuzzy set of features that captures ingroup similarities and intergroup differences regarding beliefs, attitudes, behaviors and feelings' (2005: 56).

It draws upon the popular saying that 'like attracts like'. However, instead of the leader being attracted to a follower who shares a similar background and beliefs, and consequently brings a follower into his or her group, social identity theory highlights the reverse process, through which the leader is picked by followers or is chosen to be supported by followers precisely because he or she is most like them. When we talk about 'like' here, we mean how closely the leader represents the group's characteristics as well as its aspirations, values and norms. In a sense, leadership identity construction is a process through which the leader identity *and* follower identity are claimed and granted by both parties on an iterative and repetitive basis.

Prototypicality is not the only basis for leadership, however. People also rely on general and more task-specific schemas or stereotypes of leadership behaviours which have been dubbed by Robert Lord and his colleagues as 'leader categories' or 'leader schemas' (Lord, 1985). These will become particularly significant when we move our discussion on to consider the influence of culture on leadership in Chapter 4.

The importance of these stereotypes we hold about appropriate and inappropriate behaviour diminishes as group prototypicality becomes more important. That is, group membership becomes psychologically more salient. A group is psychologically salient if being part of it is important for someone as a basis for defining who they are, what they believe in, and how they function as an individual. This could be a gang, an Internet discussion group, a sports team, a fan club or a service club. While you might have a general view of what constitutes good or bad leadership, you will put up with leadership behaviour that is at odds with your ideals if belonging to the group is very important to you.

The way social identity theory is set up, the study of leadership begins with the group and not the leader. Assume you are observing a group of people, how does that group go about selecting and supporting an appropriate leader – nominal or otherwise? Social identity theorists suggest that this takes place in three broad phases (Hogg, 2005). First, a group member who is the most prototypical will appear to exercise influence over other group members. Second, because the most prototypical member is consensually liked by the group members (i.e. he or she is socially attractive), this will empower that person and enable him or her to influence other members. Eventually, that person will begin to be imbued with prestige and status. In the final phase of the process, group members will begin to attribute the success of their leader to that person's special personality and not because of their prototypicality. In this way a charismatic personality for the leader is constructed (Shamir, 2007).

By the same token, when the leader begins to fail to fully represent the group, to 'sell out' to other interests, what Krantz (2006) calls 'virtuous betrayal', followers might decide that this is due to personality defects in the leader. Consequently, they may decide to withdraw their support. In politics this is often the fate of populist leaders who come to power as a result of grassroots movements but, without the support of a political machine, lose the support of their original followers as they attempt to build a broader coalition of support with other groups in order to stand a chance of gaining or maintaining wider power. The spurned in-group may respond by selecting a leader who is more prototypical.

Social identity theory has been empirically tested in both laboratory and naturalistic field settings. For example, one laboratory study asked students to anticipate joining a group in order to discuss university resource allocation for undergraduate classes (Hogg et al., 2001). The salience of belonging to a particular group was manipulated in such a way as to make membership seem more or less important to the students. Participants were informed that their group was to have either an 'agentic/instrumental' (i.e. male stereotypical) norm or a 'communal/expressive' (i.e. female stereotypical) norm for how the discussion was to be conducted within their groups. Participants were also told that a leader had been randomly appointed – they discovered that the leader was either a male or a female. The study found that group salience would increase the perceived effectiveness of male leaders for those groups who had been assigned an agentic/instrumental norm and of female leaders for those groups with a communal/expressive norm. It would also reduce the perceived effectiveness of male leaders for groups with communal/expressive norms and of female leaders for groups with agentic/instrumental norms. In other words, the study found that when dealing with matters that count, leadership effectiveness depends more heavily on the match of the leader to the group prototype.

Social identity theory can be helpful in making sense of a number of contemporary leadership issues. For example, research has shown that in Western societies, demographic minorities (e.g. women and ethnic minorities' women) can find it difficult to attain top leadership positions because of what is widely described as a 'glass ceiling' (Stafsudd, 2004). As an aside, the glass ceiling has spawned a large number of problematic metaphors – brass ceiling, bamboo ceiling, concrete ceiling, glass closet and sticky floor to name a few – all of which could validly justify further research. If organizational prototypes (e.g. of speech, dress, attitude, interaction styles) are societally cast so that minorities do not match them well, then those minorities are unlikely to be endorsed as leaders under conditions when organizational prototypicality is more important – that is when organizational identification and cohesion are high. This might arise under conditions of uncertainty, such as when a company is under threat from a competitor or a potential takeover. This is an unfortunate tendency for a number of reasons, not least because it is often the case that, when a company is most in need of change, an outsider's perspective is what is most needed to lead that company out of its difficulties.

towards a general model

Each of these three follower-centric theories – the romance of leadership, and psychoanalytic and social identity theories – provides a useful insight into the process by which followers construct leadership. Boas Shamir suggests that if they are intertwined, we can begin to develop a general model of the construction of leadership by followers. Beginning with the individual, and drawing on a number of motivational theories, we need to understand that the follower has several unmet needs which a potential leader may or may not be able to fulfil. These are the need for clarity (e.g. what should we be doing? where are we going?), the need for meaning (e.g. what are we doing this for?), and the need for safety (e.g. will we be OK if we do this?).

Leaders are constructed in light of these unmet needs at the level of the individual and at the social level. Individuals construct leaders through the processes of attribution (e.g. they believe they are responsible for causing certain things); projection (e.g. attributing their ideals, wishes and desires to the leader); transference (e.g. responding to a leader as if they were a significant person from their childhood); and idealization (e.g. believing the leader can do no wrong). At the societal level, leaders are constructed through the twin processes of social information processing and social contagion.

Based on these constructions, leaders are selected and supported and their influence is accepted. This is by no means a static process. Construction is work that is always in progress. Leaders are constantly being assessed and compared to other leaders, real or imagined. Likewise, as Mary Uhl-Bien and Rajnandini Pillai (2007) have intriguingly argued, followers and leaders will also construct notions of followership. Followers will either reinforce or refine their constructions as new information comes to light, via direct or indirect interaction, either with themselves or with influential others who will report on these interactions. Sometimes, when leaders are seen to fail in a major way, followers will become so disenchanted and angry that they will be forced to demolish their constructions and seek an alternative leader. Because most of these theories have been preoccupied with explicating how leaders are created, the processes by which leaders are deconstructed, or if you like 'de-created', have remained relatively unexplored.

Follower-centric theories have sought to turn a lot of the conventional leader-centric research that was discussed in Chapter 2 on its head. They have shown that there is indeed much to be gained by starting our study of leadership with the follower and not the leader. In this regard they have provided a much-needed correction and counterbalance to the dominant preoccupations of leadership scholars. In fact we might even go so far as to ask, given the influence that followers can exert over leaders, why we might not consider the possibility of followers acting as leaders. Indeed, why not get rid of the leader–follower dichotomy altogether? It is to this possibility that we now briefly turn.

▬▬▬ followers as leaders: shared leadership

This approach is technically neither leader-centred nor follower-centred because it rejects the distinction between leaders and followers. Leadership is seen not as a role, but as a function or an activity that can be shared among members of a group or organization. Fundamentally, at the core of this approach is a belief that followers can and should be given their chance to lead, as it is not only the right thing to do but also the smartest thing to do. Traditional command-and-control, hierarchically-based organizations are seen as being no match for the flat, laterally-integrated network organizations in the context of a rapidly changing competitive global economy. People, as leaders or followers or whatever label one pins on them, are doing the flattening (Rost, 2008). Bligh (2011: 431) cites Visa founder Dee Hock as being emblematic in capturing the essence of this view when he remarks that 'in the deepest sense, the distinction between leaders and followers is meaningless. In every moment of life we are simultaneously leading and following' (Hock, 1999: 72).

We can think of the various theories which advocate that followers should act as leaders along a continuum. At the more conservative end of the continuum is the notion of 'co-leadership', which recognizes that leadership is rarely the preserve of one individual but frequently is exercised by a pair of individuals, a 'Number One'/'Number Two' combination such as a CEO and a CFO or a group of individuals such as a top management team (Alvarez and Svejenova, 2005). A good example of this type of leadership would be the triumvirate that collectively led Google.

Further along the continuum is 'shared leadership': the notion that the responsibility for guiding a group can rotate among its members, depending on the demands of the situation and the particular skills and resources required at that moment. Any member can lead the group for a certain period, during a key phase in a project, and then leadership can be passed on to someone else. For example, Joseph Raelin (2003: xi), in his book *Creating Leaderful Organizations*, argues with infectious passion that 'in the twenty-first century organization, we need to establish communities where everyone shares the experience of serving as a leader, not sequentially, but concurrently and collectively'. The principal task of senior management in this kind of organizational milieu is to produce the environment and the climate where followers can feel genuinely empowered to lead within and beyond the organization.

Even further along the continuum is the notion of 'distributed leadership' in which the team leads its work collectively by creating norms of behaviour, contribution and performance, and by supporting each other and maintaining the morale of the group (Day, Gronn and Salas, 2004; Gronn, 2002). This perspective complements, but does not replace, the perspective of leadership as an input to team processes and performance. However, a singularly zealous advocate of this approach, Jeffrey Nielsen, in his book *The Myth of Leadership*, 'makes the case for the end of leadership as we commonly know it – that is, rank-based management – and introduces a method for developing an organization into a true society of peers. I call this model the peer-based organization' (2004: x).

These theories tend to be more normative than descriptive. They talk about how things should be rather than how they necessarily are. However, case studies of exemplary practice are enthusiastically presented from companies as diverse as law firms, car manufacturers and IT service providers as evidence that shared and dispersed leadership are more than a gleam in the organizational theorist's eye. Though still a rarity, these forms of leadership do exist and can succeed.

At the more radical end of the continuum is the notion that the term 'leadership' might be profitably dropped as a useful means of understanding organizational behaviour. Alvesson and Sveningsson (2003b), for example, have shown through their empirical study of a research and development company that although senior and middle managers used the term 'leadership' freely to describe all manner of activities that were taking place within their organization, when pressed to expand upon and explain how leadership actually works, they were generally at a loss to do so. In light of this finding, and the general concerns they have about the inconsistency of definitions of leadership, coupled with our tendency to romanticize leadership, the authors concluded that perhaps we should seriously question the existence of leadership and, by association, followership as a distinct phenomenon. Instead we might probably be better to think of leadership as a hypothetical construct that has no empirical reality.

Because notions of shared and distributed leadership are attracting so much interest among leadership and organizational scholars as well as practitioners and consultants, we will devote a significant part of Chapter 5 to the topic. In that chapter we will also pick up on and expand upon the critically-oriented poststructuralist approaches to leadership that question many of the fundamental assumptions that leadership researchers have made about the existence of leadership as a distinct phenomenon. For now we want to close this chapter with an approach that recognizes the contributions of the follower-centric theories discussed above and seeks to integrate these with considerations of the role of the leader in constructing leadership. Indeed, it sees leadership as something that is essentially co-produced by followers and leaders.

followers as co-producers of leadership

The idea that leadership is a relationship based on a mutual exchange between leaders and followers is not new. Hollander (1958), for example, suggested that leadership is a two-way influence and social exchange relationship between leaders and followers. Messick (2005) describes leadership as a mutually beneficial relationship predicated on psychological exchange, in which leaders ideally strive to provide their followers with the following: vision and direction, protection and security, achievement and effectiveness, inclusion and belongingness, and pride and self-respect. Inspired by reading Herman Hesse's novel *Journey to the East*, Robert Greenleaf (1977) has famously encapsulated the lender's ultimate obligation to her or his followers with the idea that leaders should strive to become 'servant leaders'. He is not alone here. Along with 'guardian leader' and 'righteous leader', servant leader is one of the hallmarks of Islamic leadership, and has been for 1400 years. In return, followers ideally provide servant-leaders with: focus and self-direction, gratitude and loyalty, commitment and effort, cooperation and sacrifice, and respect and obedience. Of course, it is very rare that all of these needs are either met or even required by both leaders and followers.

It is unusual for there to be an explicit contract between leaders and followers but there may well be some form of implicit contract. While equilibrium is achieved between followers and leaders, leadership will be sustained. When it begins to become unbalanced, that is, leaders and followers are providing too little and/or taking too much, then the relationship ultimately has to be renegotiated. One of the most celebrated examples of leadership illustrates this principle in a dramatic fashion. The leadership produced by Ernest Shackleton and the 28 crew members of the *Endurance* expedition, when their ship was crushed in the ice floes off the coast of Antarctica, is held up by many as the apotheosis of leadership and its lessons have been widely imparted throughout boardrooms. At various points in the epic and perilous journey back to civilization, the leadership relationship became strained and occasionally challenged, but the numerous accounts of the voyage have shown how both Shackleton and his followers acted to preserve and strengthen the leadership relationship in the knowledge that this was vital to the survival of the group (Shackleton, 1999).

The best effort to date to model the co-production of leadership in a dynamic way is Leader-Member Exchange (LMX) theory which, based on repeated empirical observation, argues that leader–follower relationships evolve through three distinct phases (Graen and Uhl-Bien, 1995). At the initial 'stranger phase', interactions are largely formal, rule-bound and driven by self-interest rather than the good of the group. Some relationships never evolve from this stage. However, others may progress to a second phase, the 'acquaintance' phase – a testing phase in which the leader gives the follower the opportunity to take on more responsibility in return for inside information, friendship, and support. Assuming both the leader and the follower pass the test, the relationship becomes based more on mutual trust and respect and less on formal contractual obligations. At the final 'mature' phase, there is a high degree of reciprocity between leaders and followers; each affects and is affected by the other. Leaders and followers become tied together in productive ways that go well beyond the traditional hierarchically-defined work relationship towards a transformational leadership relationship.

LMX theory is intuitively appealing. Not only that, but research into LMX is proceeding with unrelenting vigour. Consistently for the past decade, in excess of 30 references appear each year in scholarly publications with LMX in the title. It accords with the experiences we have had both as followers and as leaders. It brings into relief the fact that differences exist in the quality of relationships that leaders have with individual followers. There are times when we have really got on with a boss and there are times when we haven't, and yet others seem to get on famously with that same boss. It also issues a cautionary note in warning leaders of the dangers of being selective in whom they choose to favour as this fosters divisive in-groups and out-groups within the larger group. Leaders are therefore encouraged to cultivate high-quality exchanges with all of their followers, recognizing that ultimately it always 'takes two to tango'.

Echoing the pioneering management thinker, Mary Parker Follett (1924), Keith Grint has noted that leaders can learn a lot about how to lead from their followers. He draws an intriguing parallel between the challenge of learning how to lead for the first time and the challenge of learning how to become a good parent, noting that 'in both cases, and counter-intuitively, it is the junior that teach their superordinates how to lead' (2005a: 104). In order to do this, open, honest and continual feedback is essential. Looking back on how we learned to become parents, we probably should have devoted more time and effort to trying to learn from our children instead of relying on more traditional sources, such as our parents, our friends or child-rearing books.

The parent–child metaphor, especially in light of our discussion of psychoanalytic theories of leadership, is potentially fraught with complications, not least because of its implicitly paternalistic or maternalistic view of leadership, which all leadership scholars worth their salt are trying to rid the world of. However, we think it's helpful here because it addresses the joint responsibility that leaders and followers have to open up lines of communication with each other. We need to create leadership relationships that are based on 'constructive dissent' rather than 'destructive consent' (Bratton, Grint and Nelson, 2004). This is a relationship in which followers are willing and capable of questioning and suggesting alternative courses of action in a way that does not undermine or personally attack the leader, and the leader is open and actively supportive of such efforts.

The movie, *The Queen*, provides a striking example of a highly celebrated moment when the roles between leader and followers were reversed. It is a fictional depiction of the behind-the-scenes turmoil within the Royal Family in the aftermath of Princess Diana's death. The Queen is stoically determined to follow protocol and to mourn the death privately and not bow to her subjects' desire, fanned by the media, for her to publicly acknowledge the death. In the end she acquiesces, making a public statement via television and by ordering the Royal Ensign to be flown at half-mast above Buckingham Palace. In a dramatically compelling fashion, we witness a liminal moment in which the followers are seen to lead the leader. A sub-plot in the film is, of course, the newly-elected Tony Blair's role in influencing the Queen to change her stance in the interests of preserving the monarchy's leadership in the longer term. One, of course, can't help musing at the end of the film whether Tony Blair himself may have lost sight of the principle of follower-led leadership when he made the decision to take the United Kingdom into the war in Iraq.

Perhaps Tony Blair and other besieged leaders might have derived some form of comfort from the lessons that Keith Grint distils in his (2001) book, *The Arts of Leadership*. On the surface, this book appears to be yet another conventional celebration of the heroic pursuits of well-known historical figures such as Horatio Nelson and Florence Nightingale, as well as business leaders like Freddie Laker and Richard Branson. From these accounts, Grint provides evidence not of their cumulative successes but of their propensity regularly and routinely to fail and make mistakes. What distinguishes them from leaders whom we have long since forgotten is the preponderance of their followers to consistently support and cover up for them. He poignantly concludes, 'the trick of the leader is to develop followers who privately resolve the problems leaders have caused or cannot resolve, but publicly deny their intervention' (2001: 420).

To date we have developed a reasonably robust understanding of the different types of leader, but we still tend to treat followers as an homogeneous entity. Collinson (2006) has noted that studies of leadership need to develop a broader and deeper understanding of followers' identities and the complex ways in which these selves may interact with those of leaders. His poststructuralist approach to studying leadership highlights how followers' identities may be more differentiated and contested within the workplace than is generally assumed. Collinson's own (2005a) empirical research has shown that leaders are often surprised by the unanticipated way followers have reacted to their plans. Followers are smarter and more cunning than they tend to be given credit for, whether it is in the way they appear to support, conform or resist.

Followers can play an equally active role in co-creating and promoting either good or bad leadership. In accounting for destructive leadership Padilla, Hogan and Kaiser (2007) indicate the pre-requisite of the three points of a 'toxic triangle' of 'destructive leaders, susceptible followers and conducive environments'. With respect to the 'susceptible followers' apex in this triangle, the authors distinguish between 'conformers', who comply with destructive leaders out of fear, and 'colluders', who actively participate in the destructive leader's agenda. Both types are motivated by self-interest, but their concerns are different. The distinction between these two types of follower and their motives is graphically displayed week-in week-out in the TV Series *The Sopranos*, the revisionist contemporary mafia drama that makes the psychodynamic struggles of its central protagonist, Tony Soprana, a compelling feature of its drama. Those wishing to pursue this line of inquiry should look to the book, *Tony Soprana on Management* (Schneider, 2004) (yes, it does exist!).

There is a well-worn saying that 'we get the leaders we deserve'. This is a statement that infuriates many of those we lecture to as it runs counter to the prevailing leader-centric wisdom. We believe, however, that there is much to be said for this statement as it encourages everybody to take an interest in, and play an active role in, producing the highest form of leadership we can. The follower-centred perspectives of leadership are helpful in this regard because, as Shamir notes, they enable us to 'reverse the lens' of leadership; they encourage us, as followers, to look not only at leaders, but also at ourselves and others as followers. In reversing the lens, however, 'it is important to examine not only how followers contribute to the construction of a leadership relationship, but also how they empower the leader and influence his or her behaviour and what is their contribution to determining the consequence of the leadership relationship' (Shamir, 2007: xxi).

Education needs to play a central role in promoting follower-centred development. To this end, Dennis Tourish and his colleagues propose that business schools should abandon their obsessive promises to produce transformational leaders and begin presenting an alternative and more realistic prospectus based on enlightened followership and the promotion of effective upward communication within organizations in order to create healthier and ethical organizations (Tourish, Craig and Amernic, 2010). What price on a competing volume to this book entitled *A Very Short, Fairly Interesting and Reasonably Cheap Book About Studying Followership* appearing within the next three years?!

conclusion

In this chapter we surveyed wide-ranging work done by those who have been curious about that other generally unheralded group of people when it comes to leadership, namely followers. We looked at various theories that have conceptualized followers to varying levels of significance, either as moderators or constructors, substitutes, or co-producers of leadership. This work has sought to provide a much needed counterbalance to the predominant lopsided focus on leaders held not only by academics but also by the general populace. We believe that this work creates a more holistic and complete picture of how leadership works or fails. Given its youthful and partially formed nature, follower-centred perspectives also provide plenty of scope for producing fresh and exciting new research. Finally, and most importantly, it encourages us to reflect and actively think about what we might change in our much rehearsed role as followers to co-create better and higher forms of leadership.

4

Cultural Perspectives on Leadership

One of the most important developments in the study of cross-cultural leadership in the past several years has been the recognition that this is a valid and appropriate field of study, rather than simply being seen as an adjunct to cross-cultural research, or to leadership research.

Dickson, Den Hartog and Mitchelson (2003: 748)

introducing context into leadership

In the previous two chapters we focused initially on the leader's role in creating leadership and then, to counterbalance this view, we looked at various efforts to understand and explain the role of the follower. We concluded at the end of Chapter 3 that it was more useful to think of leadership as something that is co-produced by leaders and followers, not losing sight of the asymmetrical power relationship that exists between them. We also recognized that leadership is something that is co-produced within a specific context.

The *Collins English Dictionary* defines 'context' in two ways. First, 'as the parts of a piece of writing, speech, etc., that precede and follow a word or passage and contribute to its full meaning'. Second, as 'the conditions and circumstances that are relevant to an event, fact, etc.'. It derives from the Latin noun '*contextus*', meaning a putting together, and the verb '*contexere*', meaning to weave, to braid. These are both useful and complementary ways of thinking about how context influences leadership. Leadership does not occur in a vacuum. The place where, and the time in which, leadership is created influence how the leaders and followers go about co-producing leadership. Osborn, Hunt and Jauch note that 'leadership and its effectiveness, in large part, are dependent upon the context. Change the context and leadership changes' (2002: 898).

Context also affects why leadership is done and for what purposes. Think about how you would approach leading a student protest compared to leading a memorial service for a family member. As Osborn et al. argue, 'leadership is embedded in the context. It is socially constructed in and from a context where patterns over time must be considered and where history matters' (2002: 798). How we have led in the past influences how we will lead today and tomorrow. In effect, by bringing context into the analysis we are suggesting that the 'when?' and 'where?' questions should be given a lot more prominence when we study leadership.

This is by no means a one-way process. In fact, as we saw in Chapter 2, a key task of leadership is to define the situation or context for the group in such a way that it motivates that group to pursue a certain goal. The 'management of meaning', as it is often referred to, is the process by which leaders attempt to align their interpretation of the situation (commonly called a 'frame') with their followers' interpretation (Bolman and Deal, 1997). The Shackleton example discussed in the previous chapter graphically illustrates this point. Other expeditionary groups may have decided that having your ship crushed in Antarctic ice floes was reasonably good grounds for accepting that the situation was hopeless. Through good leadership, the expedition was able to define it as an extremely difficult but hopeful situation.

As we saw in Chapter 3, situational and contingency leadership theorists have acknowledged context, albeit in a partial way, by building various independent variables into the leadership equation. In general, however, as Lyman Porter and Grace McLaughlin (2006) have concluded from their review of leadership research, context, like the weather, is talked about in polite conversation but rarely studied systematically. One of the reasons for this is that context is considerably tougher to pin down: it's invariably intangible yet all-encompassing and very difficult to measure. By contrast, it's much easier and more enticing to stick with real, live people, such as leaders and followers.

Those researchers who have highlighted organizational context in their leadership studies have also tended to acknowledge seven influential components: the goals/purpose of the organization (e.g. its strategy and mission); the composition of its people (e.g. its demographics and its capabilities); the organization's core processes (e.g. its technologies, policies and governance model); the state/condition of the organization (e.g. how successful it is); length of time (e.g. what stage it is at in its organizational lifecycle); its structure (e.g. size, hierarchy, degree of centralization and spatial distance); and finally, its culture/climate (e.g. its norms, values and ethics).

In 2009 a special issue of *Human Relations* was devoted to examining the role of context in leadership studies. The special issue encompassed two distinctive theoretical approaches – leadership psychology and social constructionism. With respect to leadership psychology, two of the co-editors concluded that:

> despite the encouraging trend of increased attention being placed on the context in leadership research, the vast majority of this research has focused on the influence of context on leadership or relationships between leadership and both individual and organizational outcomes. Relatively neglected has been the influence that individuals may have upon on the context. (Liden and Antonakis, 2009: 1596–7)

A notable exception is Schneider's attraction–similarity–attrition (ASA) paradigm, which highlighted the ways in which founding CEO characteristics typically result in the hiring of employees who share the same values as the leader (Schneider, 1987). In the editorial essay which accompanied the social constructionist articles within this special issue, Gail Fairhurst noted that: 'With a discursive and social constructionist view, a multi-layered and dynamic view of context is captured when we are able to determine how individual, dyad or group, organizational and socio-historical influences reflexively interrelate at particular moments in time. This becomes possible because discourse functions on more than one level' (2009: 1623). We will explore this discursive turn in leadership studies more fully in the following chapter.

In another encouraging sign that context is finally beginning to take its rightful place in leadership studies, *The Leadership Quarterly* in the same year published a special issue devoted to research into leadership processes within extreme contexts, such as 'trauma organizations' (e.g. hospital emergency departments), 'critical action organizations' (e.g. fire, search and rescue or disaster response teams), 'high reliability organizations' (e.g. normal police and fire operations, air traffic control and disease control organizations) and 'naïve organizations' (e.g. hotels suddenly subjected to a terrorist attack or a school hit by a tornado). The co-editors of the special issue defined an extreme context as 'an environment where one or more extreme events are occurring or are likely to occur that may exceed the organization's capacity to prevent and result in an extensive and intolerable magnitude of physical, psychological, or material consequences to – or in is close physical or psycho-social proximity to – organization members' (Hannah et al., 2009: 898). They noted that it was somewhat ironic that, even though most people readily associate the leadership as being epitomised by Bruce Willis and Arnold Schwarzenegger with situations when things get tough or people are in danger, leadership researchers have paradoxically shied away from extreme contexts such as these for conducting their leadership research. However, it's vital that we come to grips with the practice of leadership in these extreme contexts as, with the heightened threat of terrorism, the preponderance of extreme weather conditions engendered by long-term climate change, and our increased and rapid exposure to infectious diseases on a worldwide scale, these types of context will increasingly become less exceptional.

Culture and structure have received the lion's share of the attention from researchers as the most significant contextual influences on leadership. In this chapter we will focus our attention on culture. We will be looking at structure in the following chapter when we examine various ways in which organizational structure has or should be modified in order to promote an environment in which leadership becomes increasingly dispersed and distributed throughout the entire organization.

culture and leadership

In Chapter 1, we noted that defining leadership is an activity that is fraught with peril. In bringing culture and leadership together we are effectively asking for trouble as culture has been defined, debated and disputed to an even greater extent than leadership. As Mats Alvesson has wryly observed, 'culture is rather like a black hole: the closer you get to it the less light there is thrown on the topic and the less chance you have of surviving the experience' (1993: 3). This dire warning aside, we have found the linkage between leadership and culture to be one of the most intellectually satisfying areas to explore. It is also an area that the practitioners we work with find endlessly fascinating.

Leadership is essentially a cultural activity – it is suffused with values, beliefs, language, rituals and artefacts. Whether we look at a chief executive giving a speech at an Annual General Meeting or two rival gangs depicted in *The Wire* meeting to dispute the boundary of their home turf, culture mediates the ways in which a group of individuals come together to enact leadership. In light of this, it is surprising to learn that a great deal of leadership research either ignores or downplays the cultural dimension in favour of psychological and sociological dimensions.

The most vocal champion of culture and leadership has been Geert Hofstede, a Dutch academic whose work has attracted in equal parts admiration and critique. Hofstede defines culture as 'the collective programming of the mind which distinguishes the members of one group or category from another' (1991: 5). He notes that culture is something that is learned and not inherited. It lies somewhere between an individual's unique personality and human nature, and is likened to the 'software of the mind'. Hofstede identifies several layers of culture, in which the collective mental programming activities operate. At the inner core is the organization in which you work. The outer layer is the country or countries in which you live or have lived. The layers in between these two extremes include your social class, your generation and your gender, as well as your regional and/or ethnic and/or religious and/or linguistic affiliation. With respect to looking at the relationship between culture and leadership, most leadership researchers have been preoccupied by the organizational and national layers of culture.

▬▬▬ leadership and organizational culture

At a very simplistic level, organizational culture can be understood as 'the way we do things around here' (Deal and Kennedy, 1982). Its importance perhaps becomes most apparent to us when we are endeavouring to become a member of a group, such as when we start a new job. Somewhat ironically, however, we are invariably able to make the most sense of an organization's culture once we have left it and joined another organization.

Edgar Schein, the most influential thinker in the area of organizational culture, has more formally defined culture as:

> A pattern of basic assumptions that a given group has invented, discovered, or developed in learning to cope with its problems of external adaptation and internal integration, and that have worked well enough to be considered valid and, therefore, to be taught to new members as the correct way to perceive, think and feel in relation to these problems. (Schein, 2004: 9)

According to him, a key function of leadership is the creation, management, and sometimes even the destruction of organizational culture. Leaders do this through what he describes as primary 'culture embedding' mechanisms, such as role modelling; what they pay attention to, measure and resource; how they react to crises; and who they select, promote and reward within the organization. Schein also describes secondary mechanisms that leaders can work with in creating an organizational culture. These include such things as organizational design and structure; the stories, legends and myths they promulgate; rites and rituals (such as retirement and Christmas parties); the layout of the physical space in which employees work; and the Cartoon character, Dilbert's favourite perennial targets for ridicule – mission and vision statements (Adams, 1996). As the familiar cliché suggests, because 'actions speak louder than words' the secondary mechanisms which many managers associate with 'culture-building' activities are all for nought if they are inconsistent with the easily taken-for-granted primary mechanisms.

Inspired by Schein's thinking and that of other management gurus – and egged on by legions of consultants – managers wholeheartedly embraced the idea of organizational culture during the 1980s to the point where you were nobody unless you were working on creating a dynamic and innovative corporate culture. Practitioners tended to see culture as something that the whole organization 'had'. It was either a good or a bad culture and it had to be properly managed, from the chief executive all the way down to the shopfloor (Huczynski and Buchanan, 2006). In this regard, the interest in corporate culture closely paralleled the dramatic rise in interest in transformational and charismatic leadership described in Chapter 2. Unfortunately, most management consultants have concentrated on norms, values and heroes, and neglected rules, meetings and internal competition. When the consultants have gone, the organization is as transactional as ever and leadership is still stifled (Parry, 2009).

Academics, on the other hand, took a more circumspect view. They tended to think of organizational culture as something that was always in the process of being created, not exclusively by leaders but by everybody concerned with the organization. Moreover, it was perhaps naïve to think of the organization as having a single unitary culture with everybody pulling feverishly together in the same direction. Organizations were more likely to be either pluralistic in nature, made up of a number of loosely linked subcultures, or highly fragmented in that they were always in a state of flux with transitory subgroups coming together around specific issues, actively in conflict with each other (Martin, 1993).

Many academics (as well as employees) also took issue with the use of culture as just another means of exerting managerial control. While on the surface it was a kinder, gentler and more palatable control mechanism, the demands it made of employees – especially those working in 'high-commitment' organizations – were excessive and potentially immoral. The use of corporate culture as a form of normative control, especially among professional staff, is illustrated to chilling effect in Gideon Kunda's ethnographic (1992) study of an IT company called 'Tech' located in the Silicon Valley. In addition to the sinister effects of leading and managing through corporate culture, others have argued that, ultimately, it is an exercise in futility. As one commentator noted, 'most anthropologists would find the idea that leaders create culture preposterous: leaders do not create culture; it emerges from the collective social interaction of groups and communities' (Meek, 1988: 459).

While the reservations listed above about the limitations and dangers associated with leaders endeavouring to create and shape organizational cultures are well taken, we cannot ignore – and nor should we – the powerful influence that an organization's founder can exert on the dominant culture of an organization for good or bad. Following Schein's symbolic-functionalist line, if what the founder proposes attracts sufficient support from followers both within and outside the organization and is seen to work over the long term, then those values and assumptions will gradually become shared by the organization. They will also persist long after the founder has moved on.

Organizational culture is a remarkably resilient phenomenon. This becomes readily apparent when you try to lead change within it. This is one of the reasons why the first thing Brad does when he joins an organization is to track down a copy of its history. While these tomes do not tend to make for the most gripping reading material, you will be amazed how instructive they can be in explaining the present-day culture that permeates the place.

In one of our earlier books called the *The Hero Manager*, in which we featured nine of New Zealand's most successful chief executives, we were struck by just how much cultural leadership the founders were able to exert over their organizations when compared to those who had succeeded other chief executives (Jackson and Parry, 2001). Dick Hubbard, the founder of Hubbard's Foods, a cereal maker within New Zealand, is prototypical in this regard. Customers buy his company's cereal as much for his well-known stand on corporate social responsibility as for its nutritional value. Needless to say, Dick had a considerably tougher time exerting the same kind of influence in his role as the Mayor of Auckland and hung in for only one term as leader of this notoriously fractious council.

Interest in organizational culture reached its zenith during the mid-part of the 1990s. As Ian Palmer and Cynthia Hardy conclude, for academics it is now 'dead, dominant and deconstructed', whereas for practitioners it is a 'double-edged sword' that must be wielded with due care and attention (Palmer and Hardy, 2001). Initially held up as an antidote to the predominantly normative, functionalist and quantitative research that was being carried out on organizations, organizational culture provided a means to explore the 'soft side' of management and leadership. Culture has been subsequently absorbed into the mainstream. It is now firmly entrenched in the corporate lexicon and continues to generate impressive business for both global and local consultancies ready to provide a cultural audit, climate survey and cultural rejuvenation programmes, as well as executive coaching for leaders charged with the task of turning around companies with deeply entrenched and unhealthy corporate cultures.

With respect to exploring the relationship between leadership and culture, interest has shifted away from organizational culture towards the challenge of leading organizations with operations based in different national contexts. The increasing globalization of trade, finance, production and consumption presents a complex array of business challenges and opportunities which require an unprecedented level of intercultural competence and understanding.

cross-cultural leadership

Cross-cultural leadership refers to leadership in which a leader attempts to influence the activities and goals of a culturally diverse group by appealing to their systems of shared knowledge and meaning. Cross-cultural leadership recognizes the moderating effect that culture can have on leadership processes. It also seeks to discover the similarities and differences between cultures regarding what is generally considered to constitute appropriate and inappropriate leader–follower relationships.

Interest in cross-cultural leadership was initially prompted by the rapid expansion of a large expatriate workforce that had been driven to the far corners of an increasingly globalized world. These managers often experienced 'culture shock', as they set about trying to adjust their management and leadership styles to a different set of dominant norms and expectations in the host society. The expatriate's need to understand the fundamentals of intercultural interactions, combined with their sponsoring organization's need to successfully manage international assignments, drove the demand for cross-cultural leadership theory and skill development.

In response, a whole new genre of practical management guides has emerged which aim to provide helpful 'laundry lists' of specific cultural dos and don'ts, ranging from how to greet prospective business partners to how to properly conduct lunch. The highly successful *Culture Shock!* series of books is typical, with its promise to guide 'the reader through the mindscapes of a country's psyche – explaining the do's and don'ts, social customs and traditions, business and social etiquette'. Other books provide colourful case studies from a number of different national contexts which provide cautionary tales of the misunderstandings and transgressions that can occur when managers try to impose their ways of doing things in a foreign land (Hickson and Pugh, 2001; Hooker, 2003).

In one of the best exemplars of this genre, David Thomas and Kerr Inkson argue that in order to survive in an increasingly globalized business environment, managers need to develop their levels of 'cultural intelligence' (Thomas and Inkson, 2004). Cultural intelligence has three components which are linked in a virtuous cycle. First, it requires a knowledge of culture and the fundamental principles of cross-cultural interaction that goes beyond etiquette. Second, the culturally intelligent manager needs to practise 'mindfulness', that is, the ability to pay attention in a reflexive and creative way to cues in the cross-cultural situations they encounter. Third, based on this knowledge and mindfulness, the culturally intelligent manager has to develop a repertoire of behavioural skills which they can draw upon, depending on their reading of a situation. The authors suggest that this approach is superior to the 'laundry list' approach to cross-cultural leadership because, in building general as well as specific cultural intelligence, one can face new cultural challenges with increased confidence.

Another group of scholars has suggested that mythology provides one of the most important keys for understanding the nature, manifestation and dynamics of global leadership both within and across cultures. They suggest that myths need to be understood as 'the deep architecture' of culture that reveals 'fundamental patterns of thinking and acting and thus critical criteria in leading' (Kessler and Wong-MingJi, 2009: 2). For example, Wong-MingJi (2009) shows how several long established myths, such as the Yellow Emperor, the Eight Immortals and the Monkey King, memorably convey important Chinese leadership characteristics that include a holistic orientation, an ingenuity for problem solving, a hierarchical power, compassion for others and the ability to balance conflicts with a sustainable peace. Taking time to learn a nation's cultural mythology can assist leaders with navigating an increasingly interdependent global context in which place still holds a significant meaning for most people.

Perceptions of what it means to be a successful 'global leader' have changed, however. No longer are the 'geocentric globetrotters' who were transferred from country to country to manage foreign operations seen as being the exemplars of good global leadership. For example, Graen and Hui (1999) have argued that all leaders should strive to become 'transcultural creative leaders'. These leaders have the ability to learn how to transcend their childhood acculturation; respect very different cultures; build cross-cultural partnerships based on mutual trust, respect and obligation; actively engage in cross-cultural problem-solving conflicts; and to help construct new cultures based around projects, networks and transitory organizations.

cultural influences upon studying leadership

As we observed in the opening chapter, most leadership research has been conducted within the North American context. This creates two problems with respect to the validity and applicability of this research to cultural contexts elsewhere in the world. First, most of the work has been empirically tested within North American contexts. While there is a plethora of diverse cultural contexts within the North American context in which to observe leadership and test leadership theories, it does inevitably constrain the range of potential leadership contexts. To counteract this problem, North American researchers have either consciously sought out different ethnic groups to examine or they have teamed up with researchers from other parts of the world to conduct comparative leadership studies (e.g. Jung, Yammarino and Lee, 2009). Attend any management conference and you will come across a variety of papers in which a leadership instrument such as the Multifactor Leadership Questionnaire (MLQ) has been administered in two or more national contexts, with the differences and similarities presented within.

Widening the empirical net does not, however, address a second more profound problem. Namely, that the researchers themselves are products of a specific cultural context. The kinds of questions they tend to ask and the ways they go about answering them are influenced by their immediate cultural milieu. As Hofstede himself has noted, US management and leadership theories tend to focus upon the individual, privilege market processes and, as we saw in the previous chapter, emphasize the manager's needs and perspective at the expense of the employee's. The profound interest shown by American and other Anglo-Saxon countries in leadership is itself the product of an historical fascination with heroes and exceptional individuals (Den Hartog and Dickson, 2004). In contrast, European scholars endeavour to situate leadership in a broader social, legal and political context, taking a more critical line towards leaders and a more sceptical view of the desirability, let alone the possibility, of leadership.

Having worked in both European and North American academic contexts and now living in another part of the world, we are conscious of – and indeed endeavour to blend – the valuable insights that both of these academic traditions can bring to the table, even though these scholarly communities tend to talk past rather than with each other. However, living in another part of the world, we are also conscious that our understanding of leadership processes is still very geographically limited and skewed towards the West. Certainly, our experience of living and working in an explicitly bicultural country such New Zealand has exposed us to two quite culturally distinctive models of leadership – the indigenous Maori and the exogenous Pakeha (i.e. non-Maori) models. This has served to spark our interest in, and led us to appreciate the saliency of, just how culturally prescribed leadership processes are.

It is important, therefore, to try to become aware and understand the influence that values have in guiding the beliefs, assumptions and behaviours of the leaders we study, but also grasp how these guide what we choose to focus on when we study leadership and how we choose to study it. In the following section we will briefly review some of the key dimensions that have been consistently identified as ways of distinguishing different cultural groups at the societal level.

societal cultural dimensions that influence leadership

Undeniably the most influential global study of cross-cultural leadership is Hofstede's (1980) study of 100,000 IBM employees from 49 countries who participated in a survey questionnaire between 1967 and 1973. Twenty of the survey's 150 questions were used to create four value dimensions along which Hofstede compared the 49 national cultures. His work literally launched hundreds of cross-cultural studies, which aimed to replicate, extend or refute these sessions and to use these dimensions as the basis for comparing leadership differences and similarities. In their excellent overview of leadership and culture, Den Hartog and Dickson (2004) identify six dimensions (four proposed by Hofstede and two by others) that have been the most commonly proposed and studied.

Hofstedian dimensions

individualism/collectivism

According to Hofstede (1980), cultures characterized by individualism are closely knit social frameworks in which people are supposed to take care of themselves and look after their own interests and those of their close families only. In contrast, collectivist cultures are characterized by a tight social framework in which people will distinguish between in-groups and out-groups. In collectivist societies, leaders will be expected to keep the good of the in-group uppermost in their minds and will be judged by their ability to protect that group. Followers within individualist societies are more likely to tolerate leaders who look after their own interests and, in fact, are highly prized for their unique achievements.

In a similar vein, Schwartz (1999) has distinguished between societies in which people are expected to be either autonomous or embedded in the group. Autonomy is sought either intellectually, through the act of free thought, or affectively, through the independent pursuit of pleasure. In this regard, leaders would be judged according to the extent to which they are able to provide environments in which followers had a strong sense of belonging and cohesion or were able to encourage their followers to be able to think and express themselves and fulfil their dreams. These two leadership modes were illustrated to dramatic effect in the impromptu and widely celebrated 'kitchen debate' that took place between Richard Nixon and Nikita Khrushchev at the launch of the American National Exhibition held in Moscow in 1959.

hierarchy, status and power distance

Hofstede (1980) defined power distance as the extent to which a society accepted and embraced the fact that power in institutions and organizations would be distributed unequally. In cultures with a high power distance, authoritarian leadership and a more autocratic decision-making process are more likely to be accepted and expected. In more egalitarian cultures, followers will expect to have a greater say and so will tend to expect an open and more participatory style from their leaders.

In Hofstede's survey, many Latin American countries as well as Asian countries exhibited both high collectivism and a high power distance. This is evident in the relatively high respect that Asian students tend to accord their professors compared to Australasian students. The Anglo-Saxon countries, by contrast, were predominantly high in individualism and low in collectivism, along with the Scandinavian/German cluster of countries that exhibited slightly higher levels of collectivism. This difference was evidenced to Brad in the greater appetite that students from the Copenhagen Business School exhibited for group work compared to students from other business schools where Brad has taught. The Romance countries (e.g. France, Italy, Spain) along with Belgium and South Africa were characterized by high individualism and large power distances.

Another issue related to power and status arises from the question of whether status in a particular society should be based on achievement or ascription (Parsons and Shils, 1951). Achievement-oriented societies tend to accord status based on what people have accomplished. Ascribing cultures confer status on the individual because of their age, seniority or lineage. Within many of the Pacific Islands we can see the tension between ascribed and achievement-oriented norms manifest itself in the frustration that many formally educated younger leaders feel. They are anxious to be given the opportunity to lead so that they can apply their new-found knowledge and skills, yet have to defer to the traditional ascribed leadership of the tribal chiefs and elders.

uncertainty avoidance

This dimension describes a society's reliance on social norms and procedures to alleviate the unpredictability of the future. Leaders in countries with high levels of uncertainty avoidance will endeavour to ameliorate the threat of uncertainty and ambiguity by establishing formal rules, emphasizing their technical expertise, and showing little tolerance for deviant ideas and behaviours. If they wish to bring about change, leaders will have to do it within the existing system. Leaders in societies that are more accepting of uncertainty will, by contrast, have to be more flexible and willing to champion change by violating organizational rules and regulations (Shane, Venkataraman and MacMillan, 1995).

masculinity/femininity

This is the dimension over which Hofstede encountered most criticism because it covers too many topics and because of the semantic confusion it creates by alluding to gender (which is, in turn, a culturally produced construct). He argued that, in 'masculine' societies, the dominant social values stressed the virtues of assertiveness and toughness as well as the acquisition of money and material possessions. In 'feminine' societies, by contrast, values such as warm social relationships and quality of life are stressed.

The hero leader archetypes that a country holds up and celebrates will vary according to how masculine or feminine the dominant values are within that society. In more masculine countries, such as Japan, Austria, Italy, Mexico, Germany and the United Kingdom, heroic leaders will tend to be aggressive, decisive and highly visible. The hero in predominantly feminine cultures will be a lot less visible, seeking consensus and relying more on intuition. We can, therefore, appreciate that Margaret Thatcher and Nelson Mandela are, respectively, archetypal masculine and feminine political leaders.

other dimensions

linguistic/emotional

Two other means of contrasting dominant societal values also have considerable salience for the conduct of leadership. The first emphasizes language differences. The second emphasizes the role of emotions. Hall and Hall (1990) distinguish between societies that are characterized by 'low context languages', such as the Anglo-Saxon, German and Scandinavian societies, which emphasize the need to be direct, clear and explicit in communication, and societies with 'high context languages', such as the Japanese, Mediterranean, Latin American and Arabic societies, which are less direct, and more ambiguous and subtle. These are the societies that place a high premium on the ability to skilfully 'manage face' (Ting-Toomey, 1988), though in reality all leaders and followers should show a healthy concern for impression management, wherever they are located. Related to this issue, leaders who are concerned with how they present themselves should heed Trompenaars and Hampden-Turner's (1997) distinction between 'affective societies', in which people are encouraged to show their emotions, and 'neutral countries', where people are encourage to keep their emotions in check.

assumptions about human nature

When it comes right down to it, do you believe that most humans are fundamentally good or bad? Brad's grandmother was quite clear on this matter; she thought that everyone was basically decent with the exception of a few rotten apples. Kluckhohn and Strodtbeck (1961) have created a societal dimension to capture this value orientation. At one end of the dimension is the generalized assumption that 'human nature is good'. At the other end is the assumption that 'human nature is bad'. In those societies in which people are seen as being fundamentally good, leaders will rely more on building trust and being fair in influencing their followers. In those societies in which people are considered to be fundamentally flawed, leaders will seek to more closely monitor and directly control their followers.

After the publication of his original study, Hofstede acknowledged the existence of a fifth dimension of culture, which incorporated the distinctive philosophy of Eastern Asia (Hofstede and Bond, 1988). This dimension, which was originally labelled 'Confucian dynamism' but later renamed 'long-term versus short-term orientation', was found to be particularly significant for the Chinese culture. Long-term orientation cultures, typified by China, see truth as a relative phenomenon, have a pragmatic acceptance of change, and emphasize the value of perseverance, thrift, and saving for tomorrow. Societies with short-term orientations, on the other hand, such as the Anglo-Saxon countries, place great stock in absolute truth and have a high concern for normative rationality, quick results, and the need to live for today.

control orientation

Another persistent means by which cultures are contrasted by leadership scholars is to look at how societies view their relationship with the outside world. For example, Trompenaars and Hampden-Turner (1997) distinguish between 'internal cultures' and 'external cultures'. The former, typified by the United States, have a dominating and controlling attitude towards nature; the latter societies, typified by Middle Eastern countries, are more at ease with natural shifts and cycles of nature. In a similar vein, Schwartz (1999) describes 'mastery cultures' in which people are encouraged to master change and exploit the environment in order to achieve their goals. In these cultures, leaders need to be dynamic, competitive and strongly oriented towards achievement. Cultures at the opposing pole are labelled 'harmony cultures'. In these cultures, people are encouraged to understand and integrate with their natural environment, rather than change or exploit it. Leaders therefore need to take a more holistic view and try to understand the social and environmental implications of organizational actions.

the critique of cultural dimensions

While the Hofstede study has been hugely influential in our thinking about leadership and culture, it has been widely critiqued on several fronts. First, with respect to the design of the study, the research was based entirely on attitude survey questionnaires with too few questions asked of employees from just one company (Tayeb, 1996). Second, not all of the dimensions are well grounded in theory (e.g. masculinity/femininity and uncertainty avoidance) and several anomalies have been detected (e.g. Trompenaars and Hampden-Turner, 1997). Moreover, after 40 years there are grounds for thinking that these data are now outdated (Mead, 1994). For example, a study of students from 11 European nations using the same dimensions as those used by Hofstede revealed a significant convergence of national values, with gender becoming a more significant differentiator than national origin for masculinity, uncertainty avoidance and individualism/collectivism (Gooderham and Nordhaug, 2001).

Some scholars have subjected themselves to Hofstede's withering commentary by daring to criticize both his general approach and his specific research design. The most strident among these critics has been Brendan McSweeney, whose substantial critique and subsequently lively exchange with Hofstede in the pages of the journal *Human Relations* has probably done less to discredit Hofstede research strategies than it has to highlight the rhetorical strategies he employs to defend them. McSweeney could not possibly understand culture, Hofstede concluded in response, because he was an accountant, not an anthropologist, and unfamiliar even with the most basic sociological practice of statistical inference to boot (Hofstede, 2002; McSweeney, 2002a, 2002b).

Osland et al. (2000) have suggested that the Hofstedian framework is best viewed as a form of 'sophisticated stereotyping' because 'it is based on theoretical concepts and lacks the negative attributions often associated with its lower-level counterpart. Nevertheless, it is still limiting in the way it constrains perceptions of behaviour in another culture'. This weakness is made very apparent when we are confronted with 'cultural paradoxes', that is behaviour exhibited by an individual from a particular culture that violates our conceptions of what we think a particular culture is like. For example, how do we reconcile the fact that, while America is supposed to have one of the most individualist cultures in the world, Americans devote more time and energy to charitable causes than anyone else in the world? Osland and Bird (2000) suggest that if we want to become more competent intercultural leaders, we need to move beyond this sophisticated stereotyping by developing our abilities as cultural observers, so that we may purposely seek out disconfirming evidence that defies our cultural stereotypes.

Along these lines, Kanter and Corn (1994) caution us to avoid the temptation of committing a basic error when analyzing cultural behaviour. The 'fundamental attribution error' is the tendency to attribute our own behaviour to a particular situation but to attribute the other person's behaviour to their character. Commenting on research that they conducted of takeovers of American companies by foreign entities, they noted that the significance of cultural differences between employees and managers tended to be overstated. They concluded that:

> Cultural values or national differences are used as a convenient explanation for other problems both interpersonal and organizational, such as the failure to respect people, group power and politics, resentment at subordination, poor strategic fit, limited organizational communication, or the absence of problem-solving forums. Such differences are invoked as explanations for the uncomfortable behavior of others when people have limited contact or knowledge of the context behind the behavior. In the same way that it is dangerous to ignore the importance of national culture in management, it is just as dangerous to overstate its significance. (1994: 19)

Galit Ailon has provided perhaps the most intellectually challenging critique of the conventional cross-cultural paradigm to date (Guthey and Jackson, 2011). Performing what amounts to a postmodern and postcolonial reading of Hofstede's *Cultures Consequences* (1980), Ailon uses Hofstede's own dimensions to subject his work to a value-orientation test of its own design. By means of this 'mirroring' strategy, she raises concerns about the relationship between cross-cultural studies and the representation of the foreign 'other', about scholarly reflexivity, and about the supposedly objective nature of scientific research (Ailon, 2008). She concludes that scholars should devote more energy to examining the cultural politics of 'why and how difference comes to carry particular baggages of meaning by various kinds of global discourses, including cross-cultural research itself' (Ailon, 2008: 900). Her response to

Hofstede's trademark defence of his dimensions (Hofstede demanded 'Did she read my book or didn't she?' and 'Why me?') graciously extends her critique to herself, and concludes that 'we must become reflexive of how the things we say about "others" are often bound up with what we want to see in ourselves' (Ailon, 2009: 573; Hofstede, 2009: 571).

perceptions of leadership across cultures: the GLOBE study

Another major line of inquiry has sought to identify and delimit the shared prototypes or profiles of outstanding leadership that might be distinctive to specific national cultures. This has been done primarily by examining followers' perceptions of leaders' behaviour, values, attitudes and personality traits (Shaw, 1990), referred to generally as 'implicit leadership theories' (Schyns and Meindl, 2005). As we saw in Chapter 3, prototypes contain a set of attributes that define the essential characteristics of a category, for example, an effective business leader. The more closely a leader is perceived by followers to match the prototypical leader, the more likely the leader will be followed, at least at the outset (Lord and Mayer, 1991). The bottom line is that if someone looks, acts and sounds like a leader, then they must be a leader!

Exploring followers' perceptions of prototypical leaders throughout the world was the central quest of the Global Leadership and Organizational Behaviour Effectiveness research programme, memorably dubbed the 'GLOBE' study (House et al., 2002). The idea for GLOBE came to Robert House in the summer of 1991. Having reviewed a broad array of research into charismatic leadership that had been conducted in a wide range of cultural contexts, he had cause to believe that there might be a basis for believing that charismatic leader behaviour might be universally acceptable and effective. The GLOBE project provided him with the means to ascertain this on a grand scale. The project involved 127 investigators from 62 cultures. Between 1994 and 1997 data were collected from 17,300 middle managers based in a total of 951 organizations. Twenty-seven hypotheses were tested in the study, each linking culture to performance outcomes.

The GLOBE study identified nine major attributes of culture: future orientation, gender egalitarianism, assertiveness, humane orientation, in-group collectivism, institutional collectivism, permanence orientation, power concentration versus decentralization, and uncertainty avoidance. When quantified, these attributes are referred to as 'cultural dimensions'. For each of the nine dimensions, items were developed at two levels: societal and organizational. In addition, two measures were used. One tapped the participants' assessment of the extent to which their society or organization engaged in certain practices (i.e. as they *are*). The other tapped into their values relating to how things *should be* (Den Hartog et al., 1999).

Four of the nine dimensions were identified in Hofstede's landmark study, but were renamed. While the GLOBE project owed a great deal to Hofstede's work, it was by no means meant to act merely as a big budget remake. As House notes, 'we have a data set to replicate Hofstede's (1980) landmark study and extend that study to test hypotheses relevant to relationships among societal-level variables, organizational practices, and leader attributes and behaviour' (House et al., 2004: xxv).

The GLOBE project also identified six major global leader behaviours. The study found that there was a wide variation in the values and practices relevant to the nine core dimensions of cultures and a wide range of perceptions for what constitutes effective and ineffective leader behaviours. However, in all cultures, leader team orientation and the communication of vision, values and confidence in followers were reported to be highly effective leader behaviours. Perhaps not surprisingly, leadership attributes reflecting irritability, non-cooperativeness, egocentricity, being a loner, ruthlessness and dictatorial attitudes were associated with ineffective leaders. While some variation was found concerning participative leadership, the study found wide variation with respect to two major dimensions of leader behaviour: autonomous leadership and self-protective leadership.

Autonomous leadership is characterized by a high degree of independence from superiors and is reported to contribute slightly towards organizational effectiveness in Eastern European countries (except Hungary) and Germanic Europe countries (except the Netherlands). Self-protective leadership is characterized by self-centredness, status consciousness and narcissism. This type of leadership behaviour is seen to be slightly effective by managers in Albania, Taiwan, Egypt, Iran and Kuwait. These intriguing exceptions aside, one is struck overall by how little variation there appears to be in the ascribed values and practices of effective leaders between managers in the 62 countries surveyed.

The GLOBE project is unquestionably the single most ambitious leadership study to have ever been conducted. It is still, however, very much a work in progress. A second book has followed (Chhokar, Brodbeck and House, 2007), collecting documentary and quantitative summaries from 25 national societies as well as numerous publications aimed at academics and practitioners. As the editors of the first book humbly conclude, 'the wealth of findings provided in this book set the stage for a more sophisticated and complex set of questions' (House et al., 2004: 726). They acknowledge that, although the GLOBE findings have identified the various attributes of leadership, they have not identified the behavioural manifestations of such attributes. For example, it is clear from the study that integrity is a universally desirable attribute for leadership, but does it mean the same thing to a Chinese employee as it does to an American one and is it communicated the same way?

Critics of the GLOBE study have not been idle. Den Hartog and Dickson (2004) noted several areas in which this and other pan-national studies have been questioned. For example, the potential for this work to commit an 'ecological fallacy' has been raised. This is the tendency to ascribe what has been noted at one level (e.g. society) to another level of analysis (e.g. the individual). While the GLOBE participants actively endeavoured to address the 'levels of analysis' problem, a series of essays in the October 2006 issue of *Leadership Quarterly* showed that the study's measurement metrics and levels of analysis were still being actively debated (Dansereau and Yammarino, 2006; Dickson, Resick and Hanges, 2006; Hanges and Dickson, 2006; Peterson and Castro, 2006). Related to this is the problem of adequate sampling. In large, multicultural countries such as India, China and the United States, it is a daunting challenge to decide which sample would be the most representative. Doris Jepson supports this criticism of GLOBE in her (2009) case study of the German and UK chemical industries. She argues that an instrument like GLOBE cannot capture the dynamic nature of cultural interactions that often take place in several intersecting contexts, including not only the national context, but also the organizational, hierarchical, departmental and individual contexts.

Another fundamental problem associated with this type of cross-cultural survey is one of translation. How do we ensure that the respondents are interpreting the questions similarly? Even when we can provide re-translating checks and balances, we still have to be alert to cultural norms regarding the completion of questionnaires. Anne-Will Harzing (2006) notes that responses to survey questions are influenced by the content of the question and the response style, which is the tendency to respond to questionnaire items regardless of the item content. These response styles include acquiescence (ARS), middle response styles (MRS) and extreme response styles (ERS). For example, Hispanics and African Americans show higher ERS and ARS when compared to European Americans. On the other hand, Japanese/Koreans show lower ERS and higher MRS than US Americans.

Perhaps not surprisingly, given the amount of energy they have spent on the GLOBE project over the years, House and his colleagues have at times responded to such criticisms in a manner that would make Hofstede proud (Guthey and Jackson, 2011). Perhaps most notable was the engagement with George Graen that took place in the *Academy of Management Perspectives*, in which Graen described the GLOBE's research findings as the result of 'a large number of one-shot, self-reported, culturally biased survey studies' (Graen, 2006: 95), to which House and his colleagues responded by characterizing Graen as being 'careless' and underpublished to the point of being 'fictional' (House et al., 2006). The GLOBE authors did not respond quite so dismissively to Geert Hofstede's own criticism of their research. But when the *Journal of International Business Studies* hosted an exchange between them, both sides did their best to honour what appears to have become the established tradition of cross-cultural methodological mud-slinging (Hofstede, 2006; House, Javidan, Dorfman and De Luque, 2006). In his analysis of this clash of the cross-cultural titans – insightfully titled 'When elephants fight, the grass gets trampled' – Peter Smith pointed out that it was not at all clear now continuing this kind of statistical one-upmanship could contribute to a better understanding of the relationship between leadership and cultural context (Smith, 2006). It was fine for Hofstede and the GLOBE researchers to quibble over their quartiles, but at the end of the day the differences between their basic assumptions about how culture functions, and how we should study it, were not actually that significant. Meanwhile, such in-fighting about cultural dimensions and the proper statistical methods for measuring them could produce collateral damage by shutting down any meaningful discussions until a future date.

We believe that the GLOBE project represents a bold and ambitious step towards broadening the empirical net of leadership research but its theoretical base is still firmly rooted in American soil. We gain a great deal in methodological rigour but lose something in philosophical acuity. It's the quality of the questions the study generates that makes it useful, not the answers. House's intentions are unquestionably honourable when he states: 'Hopefully, GLOBE will be able to liberate organizational behaviour from the US hegemony' (House et al., 2004: xxv). However, we feel that, somewhat perversely, American supremacy in this field is being strengthened by this project, not challenged.

towards a more 'cultured' understanding of leadership

As one of the most accomplished cross-cultural leadership researchers over the past twenty years, Peter Dorfman has delineated four important caveats that he argues leadership researchers need to consider when applying a cross-cultural lens to leadership research (Dorfman, 2003). The first caveat is to not ignore significant differences within a country or culture, as well as significant differences between countries that are considered part of a country cluster. The pertinence of this caveat has been demonstrated to good effect in several studies conducted within New Zealand that highlight significant differences as well as similarities in leadership ideals and practices between the indigenous Maori and the exogenous Pakeha people (Holmes, 2007; Holmes et al., 2008; Pfeifer, Love and Jackson, 2006). In a similar vein, Ken has researched leadership practices within Islamic organizations based in Australia (Faris and Parry, 2011, in press). Recently, Sonia Ospina has performed a great service by raising the prominence of race and ethnicity as a new focus for mainstream leadership research (Ospina and Foldy, 2009: Ospina and Su, 2009). Noting that, despite the election of the first African-American president, the experiences of people of colour still tend to be treated as a 'special case', she forcefully argues that 'the field can – and must – learn from leadership studies that focus upon race-ethnicity as *particularly rich contexts* within which insights about the human condition as it pertains to leadership can be gained' (Ospina and Foldy, 2009: 877, original emphasis).

The second caveat Dorfman (2003) presents is that the expression of a cultural dimension within a culture may vary and seem contradictory at times. For example, how is it possible for followers to value in their leaders both humane and self-protecting behaviour? The third caveat is that individual differences will still exist in the adherence to cultural values and, as such, not all individuals will display the cultural values of their indigenous culture. Thankfully the world is richly populated with non-conformists who will either quietly or spectacularly defy their native culture's norms and expectations. *Vive la différence!*

Moreover, the world is becoming increasingly populated with people who have lived and worked in so many places that nobody, least of all them, know or frankly care where they are from. Guthey and Jackson (2011) point to the emblematic example of Carlos Ghosn, who is the Chairman of the Board, President and Chief Executive Officer of Nissan Motor Co. Ltd. He was born in 1954 in Porto Velho, Brazil, the son of French and Lebanese immigrants. He moved to Beirut at the age of 6, where he attended a Jesuit secondary school, and later to Paris, where he attended high school and university. He speaks Portuguese, French, English, and Arabic. He has held top executive positions on four continents, including Chairman and CEO of Michelin North American, and Executive Vice President of Renault in France. Now he runs a Japanese auto company. How do we characterize Ghosn's cultural background? Some sources call him French, others Lebanese. Many sources point towards the warm reception he has received in Japan, where he has appeared in the media in traditional garb and even graced the pages of a Japanese manga comic-book series called 'The True Life of Carlos Ghosn' (Prasso and Dawson, 2001).

It would not make sense to plot Ghosn's cultural influences on a pie chart in order to figure out what percentage of his leadership style is 'really' French, Lebanese, Brazilian, or even Japanese. He is a living, breathing example of what scholars of anthropology and globalization term 'creolization' (Stewart, 2007). This term refers to the process whereby cultures inevitably mix and mingle, creating new, unexpected and hybrid cultural forms, artefacts and identities. Marwan Kraidy argues that the 'hybridity' that results from this recombinant creation of new cultural forms amounts to nothing less than 'the cultural logic of globalization' (Kraidy, 2005).

The final caveat – and the one we think is most crucial for leadership researchers to consider – is that 'cultures are not static; they are dynamic and continually evolving' (Dorfman, 2003). In order to do this, Eric Guthey (2005) has observed that leadership and management researchers need to cross what he describes as the 'great divide' and address the occasional antagonisms between humanities-based cultural research and cultural research rooted in the social sciences, such as the GLOBE project, that has predominated in business schools.

Humanities-based perspectives help us to recognize that culture is all-pervasive and consists of all the forms through which people make sense of their lives and works – from opera to pop music to work organizations, leisure pursuits and the home (Guthey and Jackson, 2011). Each culture is not a separate domain, like economics and politics, as all human contact is culturally mediated. It may be funny, bizarre, disgusting and so on, but it can be understood only in its own context and on its own terms. Cultures are not discrete. We shift from one 'culture' to another. Cultures themselves change all the time through their own momentum and contact, through individual participants, with other cultures. Cultures are constructed by social groups. They are imagined through myths and folklore, manipulated by competing power elements and mobilized for particular ends. Humanities-based perspectives replace an 'essentialist' view of culture with a social constructionist conception of culture which stresses and values plurality, process and politics (Søderberg and Holden, 2002).

We will close this chapter by reviewing five recent studies that provide promising exemplars of how humanities-based leadership research can enrich our understanding of the relationship between culture and leadership. Each of these studies takes an 'emic' approach in that they attempt to understand the culture from *within* the culture they are studying (Triandis, 1980). Most of the studies we have reviewed in this chapter have been predominantly 'etic' in their approach. That is, they have attempted to generalize leadership theory by looking at cultures from outside the ones they are studying.

The first study by Andrew Jones (2005) advocates an 'anthropology of leadership'. Such an approach studies organizational leadership empirically at the conjunction between local culture schema and larger economic and cultural forces. Based on his ethnographic and documentary research of three companies based in the American South, Jones concluded that one of the key roles of the companies' leaders was to be both leaders and protectors of 'Southern' culture or, as he evocatively describes them, 'keepers of the tribe'. The leaders derived their influence from 'cultural capital', as authentic locals who grew up in the South, combined with their 'managerial capital' as global businessmen, derived from gaining MBAs elsewhere as well as global travel. His 'cultural theory of leadership' suggests that leaders can derive their leadership legitimacy and power from being 'local' and 'global' at the same time.

Using culture as a strategic symbolic resource is not something that is confined to senior managers, however. In *Global Ambitions and Local Identities* (2007), Gailit Ailon presents the results of a full year of detailed ethnographic research inside the pseudonymized 'Isrocom', the Tel Aviv headquarters of the newly merged company she calls 'Globalint'. She shows how the employees drew on the distinctiveness of their Israeli national identity to resist a merger between their company and an American company; the two were previously competing international organizations. On the basis of this insider perspective, Ailon concludes that national identity is best understood as 'a symbolic resource that is actively and creatively constructed by organizational members to serve social struggles which are triggered by globalization' (Ailon-Souday and Kunda 2003: 1073). In an ironic twist, the Israelis used Hofstede-inspired cross-national frameworks in defence of efforts on the part of American managers to integrate the company's management policies and practices.

A further irony is noted by Linda Sue Warner and Keith Grint that, despite most of the leading texts on leadership being American, these texts are virtually silent on the leadership dynamics of the 500 or so federally recognized American-Indian tribes who reside there (Warner and Grint, 2006). They note that significant differences exist between American-Indian and Western approaches to perspectives on leadership. American-Indian leadership has often been interpreted by non-indigenous observers as an inability to lead rather than a different ability to lead. Western approaches are often limited to positional authority, whereas American-Indian models are more concerned with persuading others to do something that they would not otherwise have done, not on the basis of position but by other means. Western approaches are more concerned with the individual leader. American-Indian models are more concerned with how different forms of leadership in different circumstance can serve the community rather than enhance the rewards and reputation of the leader.

Indigenous leadership research is not just a matter of different forms of leadership, it's also about how we go about trying to know it. Indigenous research, like indigenous leadership, requires taking the time for discussion, developing a consensus, and asking elders and spiritual advisers for consultation and guidance (Christensen, 1991). In New Zealand, Maori intellectuals are developing a distinctively Maori research paradigm, which is called 'Kaupapa Maori', in resistance to a Eurocentric colonial heritage and hegemony (Henry and Pene, 2001). 'Kaupapa Maori' literally means the Maori ways of doing, being and thinking, encapsulated in a Maori worldview or cosmology. Kaupapa Maori research, together with research conducted within other Asia-Pacific traditions, not only challenges Western research paradigms, it also critically examines the role of the academy as an implicitly Western institutional form that systematically excludes or marginalizes other ways of knowing.

Adding further fuel to this fire, Lesley Prince (2005) argues that the reasons why leadership remains a tantalizing enigma for Western thinkers and practitioners is the result of two interrelated presuppositions. First, our conceptions of leadership are located in a cultural framework of hierarchy and control that emphasizes outside direction and separation. Second, Western language codes leadership as a noun, and therefore views it as a separate object of study. By contrast, Eastern thought, notably Taoism and Zen, presents a view of leadership, and more especially the use of power, as a fluid set of interrelations coordinated with and within a natural order that is outside our immediate control but of which we are an intimate part.

Whereas for Western thinkers, leadership is about actively taking control, for Taoists it is about an engagement and accommodation with circumstances as they are. Prince concludes that:

> the difference in emphasis embodied by Taoism may be helpful in our attempts to understand leadership by moving away from codes, prescriptions and specifications much more towards a located and responsive social skill developed through doing rather than thinking – and emphasis on internal 'knowing' and experience rather than on external instruction. (2005: 106)

Using a striking metaphor, she provocatively invites Western leadership researchers to stop trying to eat the 'menu' of leadership and get on with eating the 'dinner'.

In the three years since the publication of the first edition of the book we have been struck by the upsurge in interest in Asian leadership by scholars based within Asia and beyond. This is reflected in the greater than anticipated interest that was generated by the first Exploring Leadership and Learning Theories in Asia (ELLTA), held in Penang, Malaysia, in February 2011. We envisage that Asia, and to a lesser extent Africa and Latin America, will provide the new frontiers for leadership scholars. In addition to increasing geographic representation within the leadership research community, which up until now has been spatially restricted, we look forward to more emically-oriented leadership research of the kind we have described above to complement the preponderance of etically-oriented research within the field of cross-cultural leadership.

towards global leadership

The quest to define a good universal model of global leadership, that is leadership which brings individuals together from diverse national and cultural contexts in a productive and ethical way without any one group dominating, has attracted considerable interest from a number of leadership scholars (Link, Corral and Gerzon, 2006). This quest has become an urgent one in light of the widespread recognition that global problems – such as global warming, intractable famines and global epidemics – have outstripped the capacity of existing institutional leadership structures. Good sources for this kind of thinking are the biennial collection of essays published in the *Advances in Global Leadership* series (e.g. Mobley and Weldon, 2006) as well as the Global Leadership Network (www.globalleadershipnetwork.net). Along similar lines, the Leadership Trust, based in Ross-on-Wye in the UK, holds an International Worldly Leadership Summit (worldlyleadership.org).

In endeavouring to adapt to this globalized world, cross-leadership scholars like the many executives they study might consider looking to the burgeoning field of global leadership for inspiration. Beechler and Javidan have observed that:

> the cross-cultural leadership literature (CCL) simply ignores the notion of global leadership (GL) and makes no effort to connect to it, even though it acknowledges the reality of global responsibilities for many executives. The field of global leadership seems relatively more aware of the CCL literature but only makes passing reference to it and certainly makes no attempt to bridge the divide or even define and contrast the two constructs. (2007: 15)

While CCL with its predominantly psychological approach is focused on relationships among individuals within the boundaries of an organization, GL focuses on broader relationships between the leader and a wide range of stakeholders both within and outside the global organization.

Several members of the GLOBE study have refocused their attention on the challenge of developing global leadership, which they define as 'the process of influencing individuals, groups, and organizations (inside and outside the boundaries of the global organization) representing diverse cultural/political/institutional systems to contribute toward the achievement of the global organization's goals' (Beechler and Javidan, 2007: 4). To assist this, they have developed an inventory for assessing a manager's 'Global Mindset'. The Global Mindset Inventory measures leaders according to their levels of: 'global intellectual capital' (i.e. general knowledge and a capacity to learn, cognitive and cultural acumen), 'global psychological capital' (i.e. an openness toward differences and a capacity for change), and 'global social capital' (i.e. an ability to build trusting relationships with and among people who are different from oneself) (Javidan, Teagarden and Bowen, 2010).

conclusion

In this chapter we highlighted the role of context in creating leadership, most particularly the influence of culture in enabling and constraining various forms of leadership. A challenge and opportunity for the future is a greater realization of the role of context in operationalizing leadership. This is an opportunity for leadership scholars as much as for practitioner understanding. The relationship between culture and leadership has been investigated in the context of the organization, with a view towards improving organizational performance by leading and managing the organization's culture. Assuming that an organization can be said to possess a distinct and unitary culture, a number of academics have expressed doubts about the real influence that leaders can or should exert on forming – let alone changing – culture. Others have suggested that the leader is the *only* person who can have an influence.

The other major thrust has been in understanding societal variations in culture, and the influence these have on desired and actual leadership values and behaviour. The relatively new yet growing field of cross-cultural leadership seeks to help managers to become more effective leaders within and between the diverse cultural contexts they inhabit in an increasingly globalized business environment. The growing interest in leadership research throughout the rest of the world has revealed contributions as well as limitations in the applicability and relevance of the predominantly American-based research to other national and local contexts. Others have argued that it is not just the specificity of the cultures being explored but also the culturally-specific way in which they have been explored that has limited our ability to understand the full range and depth of leadership practices throughout the world. Yet others have begun to develop and advocate normative models of global leadership that recognize and honour cultural difference but can also enable the human race to confront the very serious and increasingly complex global problems that we all share in common.

5

Critical and Distributed Perspectives on Leadership

Concertive control evolved from the value consensus of the company's team workers to a system of normative rules that became increasingly rationalized. Contrary to some proponents of such systems, concertive control did not free these workers from Weber's iron cage of rational control. Instead, the concertive system, as it became manifest in this case, appeared to draw the iron cage tighter and to constrain the organization's members more powerfully.

J.R. Barker (1993: 408)

So far, we have developed a focus on the leader, then on the followers, and after that on the cultural differences between different societies of leaders and followers. Now we need to examine leadership as the 'glue' that holds all these people together within those 'societies'. New views from the Humanities have looked at leadership from the perspectives of Plato and Tolstoy and early Islam. Recent articles in *The Leadership Quarterly* have covered Islamic leadership in Western society and even Xenophon's education of Cyrus in Ancient Greece. All these scholarships involve alternate perspectives on this leadership glue that holds different societies together. However, for the moment, the literatures that we will cover are the critical perspective on power, co-leadership, distributed leadership, leaderless workgroups and team leadership. These are critical perspectives because they challenge the traditional orthodoxies of leadership and following. They challenge the hegemonic view that leaders are the people in charge and followers are the people who are influenced. The critical perspectives make the claim that leadership is a process that goes on between all people and that all people can be involved in leadership, almost in spite of their formal position.

▬▬▬ critical perspectives on power

Most of what leaders can accomplish is as a result of their utilization of power. Power is axiomatic of leadership. Leaders use their power to influence others. An understanding of power and leadership can be achieved through critical discourse analysis (Fairclough, 1992; Phillips, Sewell and Jaynes, 2008). This is not so much a methodology as an approach to the study of discourse and power in organizations. It seeks first to identify the nature, level and impact of power relations between people, and then attempts to clarify and understand the process by which powerful, individual people contribute to the institutionalization of beliefs.

For example, political leaders in just about every country in the Western world will alternate between the use of terms like 'asylum seeker' or 'illegal immigrant' or 'political asylum seeker' or 'refugee' or 'political refugee' or 'potential terrorist' when discussing people who attempt to cross their borders without due process. These terms are just one example of discourse. The terminology that is used, especially when it is produced with either a certain vitriol or a certain sympathy, and reinforced over and over, can influence the perceptions and therefore the actions of whole nations. Because these politicians are influencing followers, they are exercising power. Therefore, they are exercising leadership. History has shown many times over how leaders can institutionalize beliefs within entire nations. The ways that power is exercised can be illuminated with the help of critical discourse analysis.

Elsewhere in this book, when we write about power, we are normally referring to the *behavioural* view of it. This approach presents management's authority as being relatively automatic, its legitimacy sanctioned through the hierarchy and rules within an organization and exemplified by their leadership roles. This relates to what we might usually call positional power.

The *political* view of power (Linstead, Fulop and Lilley, 2004; Hardy, 1994) argues that it is woven into what we take for granted and the rule systems that appear to constitute the 'natural' running of day-to-day procedures. This view includes a consideration of hidden agendas and people's behind-the-scenes activities. We can see this in virtually every organization that we are involved in. Power is usually wielded for personalized objectives (for personal benefit), rather than for socialized objectives (for the greater good).

For Foucault (1977, 1980) power is *relational*, becoming apparent when it is exercised. The focus of interest is on 'how' power is exercised instead of on 'who has power' or 'where power resides'. Viewed this way, power becomes part of a process rather than what people do. The emphasis is clearly on 'leadership' rather than the 'leader'.

Whichever way we might view power, Mumby and Clair (1997) would argue that there is a level of asymmetry in power relations between dominant and subjugated actors. This asymmetry determines how strongly the institutionalized belief is held – refugees (deserving pity) might become illegal immigrants (warranting sanctions) and soon after they will become asylum seekers (dividing ideologies and loyalties). Institutionalized beliefs and resulting practices can become ubiquitous or 'total'.

Goffman (1961) coined the term 'total institution'. Its driving characteristic is the power of incarceration, rules and surveillance. Goffman dealt with what people did do, not what the designers of their institutions would have them did do. Institutions are 'total' when they surround the person at every turn. They cannot be escaped. Thus, total institutions are organizations that contain the totality of the lives of those who are their members.

Stewart Clegg (2006) says that, as such, people within total institutions are cut off from any wider society for a relatively long time, leading to a closed and formally administered existence. Whereas total institutions are usually thought of in terms of prisons and mental asylums, where members are incarcerated against their will, they can also include organizations that are founded on voluntary inclusion, such as a professional army, boarding school, or monastery.

Clegg also suggests that several types of organization can be a total institution, including organizations dedicated to a specific work task, such as vessels at sea or even remote company towns. Clegg and his colleagues have identified several characteristics that define total organizations:

- Each member's daily life is carried out in the immediate presence of a large number of others.
- Members are very visible – there is no place to hide from the surveillance of others.
- Members tend to be strictly regimented.
- Life in a total organization is governed by a strict, formal and rational planning of time.
- People are not free to choose how they spend their time – instead it is strictly prescribed for them.
- Members lose a degree of autonomy because of an all-encompassing demand for the interpretation of rules.

Ken worked for almost a decade in a factory that had all these characteristics. He managed to leave and get back to a university before insanity took complete control. Goffman (1961) argued that total institutions demonstrate in a heightened and condensed form the underlying organizational processes that can be found, albeit in much less extreme cases, in more normal organizations. Clegg (2006) argued the converse perspective. He said that up to a point, almost all organizations exhibit the characteristics of a total institution. For 40 hours per week, almost all workaday organizations are total institutions.

Let's try to summarize the critical perspective on power. Because (our) lives are institutionalized, power is omnipresent and ubiquitous. The administration of that power controls these institutionalized lives. The administration of that power is axiomatic of leadership. The administration of that power can be understood better with the help of critical discourse analysis, which is the study of the relationships between discourse, texts and action within the context of institutions. It is critical because it studies the way social power abuse, dominance and inequality are enacted, reproduced and resisted by text and talk within our social and political context. As the old saying goes: 'If you are not a socialist at 20, you don't have a heart. If you are not a capitalist at 40, you don't have a brain.' Whether compassionate socialist or dispassionate capitalist, you are concerned about the abuse of power and inequality – either you are a victim or you are creating victims. These are leadership concerns.

co-leadership

Co-leadership, a concept first coined by Heenan and Bennis (1999) in their book *Co-leaders: The Power of Great Partnerships*, is described as two (or more) leaders in vertically contiguous positions who share the responsibilities of leadership. Brad Jackson, Dale Pfeifer and Bernadette Vine (2006) studied the co-leadership phenomenon by focusing on four leaders in one organization, who were regarded by others as being transformational. With the use of discourse analysis, they explored an interaction between the four leaders and their followers for evidence of both co-leadership and the communication behaviour that Berson and Avolio (2004) associate with transformational leadership, namely careful listening, careful transmitting and open communication. 'Careful listener' and 'careful transmitter' are not terms or constructs we would normally use, especially where they imply a sender–receiver or transmission model of communication (which we would challenge). Instead, their aim was to explore these communication styles in the authentic communication of transformational leaders. The use of discourse analysis allowed them to examine a real workplace interaction rather than just relying on what people reported as occuring. Leaders lead through what they say and what they do, so studying the words of those leaders – their discourse – enables researchers to examine how people *do* their leadership.

One major concern is that most studies will focus on a pair of individuals (a leader and a follower), otherwise known as a dyad. In response, many contemporary scholars will then adopt a critical perspective by examining a leader's influence over a group of multiple followers/ organizational processes. However, as signalled by the currently popular shared leadership paradigm, focusing on multiple leaders may also be important. Of concern too is how leadership studies will define a generic set of leader behaviours and their effect on followers, but will fall short of clearly identifying exactly what those behaviours are. As Alvarez and Svejenova suggest when referring to the wider field, leadership studies 'mostly focus on the personal characteristics and psychology of executives rather than on their actual behaviour and their activities in performing the tasks prescribed by their roles' (2005: 3). They go on to suggest that studies of leadership are too often lacking in context. This call is echoed by numerous scholars advocating that we need to determine a better understanding of precisely how leadership manifests in specific contexts in order to give a deeper understanding of how leaders' behaviour impacts on the leadership process.

There is a growing debate within leadership studies over whether or not leadership should be regarded either as an individual or as a shared activity. When suggesting that leadership is a shared or group-level activity, an individual might step forward to lead or step back to follow, depending on the moment and the skills and knowledge required (Pearce and Conger, 2003). Fletcher and Käufer (2003) have noted that shared approaches to leadership question the individual-level perspective, arguing that it focuses excessively on top leaders and says little about informal leadership or larger situational factors.

shared transformational leadership

We believe that co-leadership makes an important contribution to the leadership literature, although it currently lacks empirical analysis. Transformational leadership, on the other hand, has gained widespread attention and significant validation, as we have already explained. Not that we are intentionally overemphasizing transformational leadership, but several influential leadership scholars have made references to transformational leadership as a shared process. Burns (1978), widely regarded as the father of transformational leadership, wrote of the existence of *webs* of potential collective leadership. He suggested that individual leaders are likely to merge with others in a series of participant interactions that will constitute collective leadership. In his work on transformational leadership in teams, Bass (1998) notes that transformational leadership can be shared among the team members. However, substitutes for leadership may evolve that will help support the team's higher levels of achievement. Additionally, Avolio and Bass (1995) argued that transformational leadership theory can be considered as a multilevel construct and the type of individualized relationship that a leader builds with each follower can also emerge among team members. Hence, the notion of the co-leadership of transformational leadership has been around for a long time. It has just not figured prominently on research agendas.

However, Kellerman and Webster have cautioned that: 'The prevailing scholarly winds have now shifted so much in favor of collaboration – in contrast to hierarchical decision-making and organizational structures – that the challenge for researchers has become one of guarding against excess' (2001: 493). We must be careful not to overestimate the degree to which transformational leadership is shared between members of a team (Locke, 2003). What we would argue here is for a special case of shared leadership that acknowledges the importance of both hierarchical authority and collaboration. This is important because, as Kellerman and Webster suggest, collaborative leadership between team members is not necessary – and does not necessarily work – in all circumstances. However, to counter this, evidence suggests that groups make better decisions than individuals (Elkin, Jackson and Inkson, 2004). What we have noted is that leaders often do collaborate, but not with all organizational members. Instead they collaborate with their closet allies, who also usually hold leadership positions within the organization. As always, the consensus is lacking and the jury is still out. As well as providing a definition for co-leadership, Heenan and Bennis describe co-leaders as 'truly exceptional deputies – extremely talented men and women, often more capable than their more highly acclaimed superiors' (1999: 6). CEO–COO–CFO, president–vice-president, chancellor–vice-chancellor, prime minister–deputy prime minister, and managing director–artistic director are among the leadership partnerships or top management teams featured by many organizations, explicitly dividing leadership roles between more than one leader at the top of an organization. These structures, in executive suites, political organizations and public institutions, give traction to the argument that leadership is often engaged in by more than one leader.

Heenan and Bennis also suggest that we seem to continue to be mesmerized by celebrity and preoccupied with being 'Number 1'. However, this belief overvalues the contribution of the general or CEO or president and depreciates the contributions of subordinates. 'The genius of our age is truly collaborative,' they write. 'The shrewd leaders of the future are those who recognize the significance of creating alliances with others whose fates are correlated with their own' (Heenan and Bennis, 1999: viii). Whether it is Ralph Norris and David Turner at the Commonwealth Bank or Michael Luscombe and James Strong at Woolworths, we have seen many examples of how the combination of CEO and Chairman of the Board makes a better leadership team than just the sum of their two characters.

When things go very well for a publicly listed company, the CEO gets the leadership kudos and financial reward, and rightly so. The CEO will often pay homage to the support of the Chairman in those dark hours when insecurity or doubt had started to creep in. Similarly, when happily reporting to shareholders at annual general meetings, the Chairman will invariably pay homage to the dedication and leadership of the CEO. Indeed, this co-leadership occurs much more than we, the public, see in the media. We may witness it occasionally in the business pages of the newspapers and in business shows on television, but in reality this co-leadership dynamic is constant and unrelenting. It has to be.

By contrast, a corporate failure often correlates with a breakdown in that relationship between CEO and Chairman. We have seen many times in our research that when a CEO and Chairman lose sight of their shared destiny, then the leadership of the company falters, and company performance is damaged irreparably. In yet other case studies, CEOs have confided to us in quiet moments that the relationship between a CEO and a union leader is critical to the success or failure of the organization. Granted, this particular example of co-leadership is less relevant in New Zealand and the United States than in the UK or Australia, and in many other countries. However, the point is well made that co-leadership takes on many and varied guises. When it comes to leadership, an old cliché may well ring true: 'two heads are better than one'.

Although co-leadership has yet to undergo rigorous testing, several scholars suggest that it improves leadership effectiveness (Alvarez and Svejenova, 2005; Heenan and Bennis, 1999; O'Toole, Galbraith and Lawler, 2003; Sally, 2002). Upper Echelons Theory, conceived by Hambrick and Mason (1984), gives us some insight into why this might be. This theory suggests that leadership is an important ingredient of organizational performance. However, the complexity of organizations makes it improbable that one leader alone will be able to exert a huge influence over all members of the organization. A co-leadership structure makes this more likely, helping to fill the gap between the top-tier leader and the rest of the organization.

Hambrick also argues that strategic leadership occurs in an environment embedded in ambiguity, complexity and informational overload.

An important responsibility of top-level organizational leaders is enabling the organization to adapt to this complex environment (Boal and Hooijberg, 2000). The skills required to negotiate this increasingly complex environment successfully are extensive and may be too broad to be possessed by one leader (Alvarez and Svejenova, 2005; Storey, 2004). Moreover, collaboration at the senior leadership level improves the success of the strategic organizational partnership (Huxham and Vangen, 2000), allowing top corporate managers adequate time to pay attention to different aspects of the leadership task, including day-to-day operational activities and long-term strategy.

The notion of co-leadership has a long way to go, and will be a fertile area for research for years to come. As this discussion suggests, we believe that further scholarly exploration of co-leadership is important for gaining a deeper understanding of the transformational leadership phenomenon.

distributed leadership

From the outset, let us say that this is a complex topic. Under the heading of 'collective leadership', Tamara Friedrich and her colleagues (2009) came up with 55 propositions to illustrate the number of contextual and intervening variables within their framework for understanding collective leadership. Collective leadership and distributed leadership are also referred to as 'dispersed' leadership. The terms vary slightly, but in effect are saying much the same thing. What this body of literature is dealing with is a departure from the notion that leadership and followership reside within clearly distinguishable persons. Instead, the notion is that leadership – like power and like information – can be moved between people at differing levels of the organizational or societal hierarchy.

Parry and Bryman (2006) have identified five strands to the writing on distributed leadership. First, Manz and Sims (1991) and Sims and Lorenzi (1992) developed an approach which specifies the advantages of a type of leadership that was expected to supersede the 'visionary hero' image of leadership. They developed the ideas of SuperLeadership and Self Leadership. One feature of SuperLeadership is the quaint eccentricity that it is always written as one word with a large L in the middle. A keynote feature, however, is the emphasis that is placed on 'leading others to lead themselves', or at least to demonstrate more leadership themselves. 'Self-leaders' are those people who act on their own through self-discipline and self-behaviour modification. They are high on the attributes of self-awareness and self-consciousness. These are allied concepts and both are associated with the manifestation of effective leadership. Self-awareness involves the extent to which an individual's attention may be focused internally on certain aspects of oneself. It involves having a knowledge (and awareness) of self, including a knowledge of one's interests, aptitudes and limitations, as well as leadership ability, logically. Self-consciousness is a more acute sense of self-awareness, often pre-empted by the attention of others. Indeed, it involves the additional realization that others are similarly aware of you.

Second, Kouzes and Posner (1998) argue that credible leaders develop capacity in others and have the capacity to turn their 'constituents' into leaders. Bass and Avolio (1990) have referred to 'constituents' as 'associates'; other terms are 'co-workers' or, simply, 'followers'. The great Boas Shamir, speaking at the annual leadership conference at Lancaster University in late 2005, suggested that we think of followers as 'co-producers' rather than 'recipients' of leadership. He also reaffirmed that we should be looking at what is 'going on' between people in terms of leadership, rather than adhering to either a 'leader-centric' or a 'follower-centric' dichotomy. Whichever way we articulate it, quite simply, it is all about the other people you work and interact with. For Kouzes and Posner (1998), the issue is not one of handing down leadership to these other people, but of liberating them so that they can use their abilities to lead themselves and others. Ken's research has supported this proposition (Parry and Proctor-Thomson, 2003). Leadership capability is inherent within many of us and can indeed be trained (Parry and Sinha, 2005). However, the crucial issue here is that the organizational systems must be made less bureaucratic in order to liberate that leadership potential. One acronym that executives use is RAMPP – reports, approvals, meetings, policies, procedures. If RAMPP is minimized, then the leadership that is inherent within all workers can be freed up. These two strands signal a change of focus away from heroic leaders, who normally reside in the upper echelons of organizations, and towards teams as repositories of leadership.

The third expression of the dispersed leadership tradition can be seen in the suggestion that there should be much greater attention paid to leadership processes and skills, which may or may not reside in formally designated leaders. There is much written about leadership skills. Even special editions are devoted to the topic. The problem is that a great deal of it relates to the formally designated leader – in other words, the manager. Hosking (1988, 1991) conceptualized leadership in terms of an 'organizing' activity and spells out some of the distinctive features of leadership in terms of such a perspective. For example, she identified 'networking' as a particularly notable organizing skill among leaders, in which the cultivation and exercise of wider social influence are a key ingredient. But such a skill is not the exclusive preserve of formally appointed leaders. Indeed, it is the activity of networking and its effects that are critical to understanding the distinctiveness of leadership. The grounded theory method provides insights into the social processes of leadership. Parts of those social processes are activities or skills that leaders undertake. However, the lie of the land is still shrouded in fog, and the nature of the dispersal of leadership remains unclear.

In a similar vein to Hosking, Knights and Willmott (1992) advocated greater attention to what they called the 'practices' of leadership. This emphasis means looking at how leadership is constituted in organizations, so that in their study of a series of verbal exchanges at a meeting in a British financial services company, they show how the chief executive's definition of the situation is made to predominate. Unfortunately, the distinctiveness of this research, and Hosking's (1991) investigation of Australian chief executives and of much leadership research coming out of North America, is marred somewhat by a focus on designated leaders. As a result, it is difficult to disentangle leadership as a skill or activity from leadership as a position. However, the potential implication of these ideas is to project an image of leadership as much more diffuse and dispersed within organizations than would be evident from the tendency for leadership to be viewed as the preserve of very few formally designated leaders. The point here is that demonstrating leadership makes you a leader, and not the other way round.

A fourth expression of distributed leadership is Gordon's (2002) distinction between a dispersed and traditional leadership discourse. By using observation and critical discourse analysis within an organizational setting, Gordon asserts that the deep power structures of organizations serve to maintain traditional notions of differentiation between leader and follower, with low levels of sharing power and information. This high differentiation adversely affects the behaviour of team members. Further, Gordon asserts that organizations frequently have surface-level or espoused empowerment, but serve to maintain domination at the deep structure levels. The surface-level empowerment includes the discourse of empowerment, the flattening of hierarchy, and the act of delegation. However, the deep power structures are represented by such things as seating arrangements, intimidating language, deference, implied threat, offensive humour, and the allocation of rewards – among many others. By so doing, the deep power structures serve to reinforce pre-existing leadership relativities, in spite of the rhetoric and discourse of the distribution of power that those in senior positions would have followers believe.

By contrast, Collins (2001b) asserts that level 5 leadership, a combination of humility and fierce resolve, will enhance leader credibility and achieve genuine empowerment and the motivation of followers to achieve optimum performance. Level 5 leadership is pitched at the individual level of analysis. However, it seems to reflect a more genuine attempt at distributing leadership and overcoming the effect of deep power structures, whether implicitly or explicitly. Clearly, more research is needed into the concept of level 5 leadership and also into the impact of deep power structures upon the distribution of leadership.

A fifth expression of distributed leadership, according to Parry and Bryman (2006), is leadership within the context of e-commerce (Brown and Gioia, 2002) or an advanced information technology environment (Avolio, Kahai and Dodge, 2001). The technology associated with e-commerce and with advanced technology systems, also called Group Support Systems (GSS; Sosik, Avolio and Kahai, 1997), provides particular challenges for leadership. On the one hand, senior managers are able to get information to large groups of followers quickly and in a large volume. On the other hand, group members can access large amounts of information independent of their leaders. In effect, managers will lose much control over this information flow and the power that goes with it. Avolio, Kahai and Dodge (2001) conclude that in some settings, people can observe and model others for how they should interact. By doing this, technology becomes part of the social transformation in the organization, and in turn, part of the leadership process. In other settings, other leaders may view the technology as a cost-effective way of controlling employee behaviour through a constant monitoring of deviations from standards. This latter style of leadership is likely to generate a very different social system from the former, and quite possibly a negative emotional contagion. This latter style resonates with the notion of the total institution and reads much like Gordon's issue with deep power structures that reinforce the existing allocations of power and influence.

Brown and Gioia (2002) found that the e-commerce environment was characterized by speed, ambiguity and complexity. They agree with Avolio et al. (2001) that not only is leadership influenced by this context, but it is also integrated with and even defined by it. To Brown and Gioia, leadership is not solely a set of characteristics possessed by an individual, but an emergent property of a social system, in which 'leaders' and 'followers' share in the process of enacting leadership. The notion here is very clear: that effective leadership depends upon multiple leaders for decision-making and action-taking. With the interest of people like Bruce Avolio, John Sosik, Brown, Gioia and others, the future of this research is assured. Once again, the key to success lies in distributing leadership across the population and not concentrating it within the workloads of a few.

Much more research is needed into how the process of leadership is operationalized in the e-commerce environment. One reason for this need is that the speed and depth of change in this area of life continues unabated. Whether it is a global financial crisis or an erupting volcano, you know that the real leaders are the people with control over the technology. You doubtless get the point here. The other reason is that we have only just touched the surface of our knowledge about how leadership can or should operate in this brave new world. Processual research is needed. Questionnaire-based research is unlikely to achieve the level of insight and depth of understanding that are required. In these five sets of writings, we can see an alternative perspective that emphasizes the importance of recognizing the need for leadership to be viewed as a widely dispersed activity which is not necessarily lodged in formally designated leaders.

leaderless work groups

In a similar vein, there exist literatures on self-managed work teams, self-directed work teams and leaderless work groups. A milder version of this concept is that of 'semi-autonomous workgroups'. In these situations, much of the responsibility and authority usually invested in a manager's position is turned over to the team members.

Most of the research on these self-managing teams was done in manufacturing industry or process work. Certainly, it was undertaken within an organizational or business environment. Team members usually have similar backgrounds, namely of trade or technical experience. They also usually take turns performing the various tasks and thus generate flexibility and a degree of job enrichment. The tasks undertaken by self-managing teams are usually of a day-to-day administrative nature, and include setting work schedules, dealing directly with external customers, setting performance targets, and conducting training (Gordon, 1992). Many of the larger-scale or 'visionary' aspects of leadership are not part of their scope of activities. Therefore, much of the higher-level or 'macro' aspects of leadership still have to be undertaken by the external leadership role, specifically the senior manager. Consequently, we could conclude that it is difficult to do away with a person in the primary leadership role. In other words, an organization or work unit must always have someone 'in charge', even in a so-called leaderless workgroup.

In a sense, we are really just discussing one aspect of organizational structure rather than a leadership issue in organizations. Notions of authority, accountability, span of control, unity of command and such like still have to be taken into account when organizing any workgroup. However, it is the issue of what is 'going on' between people that really determines the nature of the leadership that is represented in that group of people.

Having said that, great improvements have been reported in self-managed work teams. The research has mainly been in the form of various types of case study. Examples include the work of Banker et al. (1996), Cohen and Ledford (1994), Cordery, Mueller and Smith (1991), and Pearson (1992). Research into leaderless workgroups and self-managed work teams has diminished in recent years. Methodologically, there is the potential problem that most of the research is self-reported. The empirical evidence varies greatly and the self-report nature of many write-ups throws doubt on the extent to which leadership really has been dispersed within workgroups. To be sure, self-managed work teams and leaderless workgroups may well be an effective way to achieve manufacturing output. However, perhaps the most telling insight comes from Barker (1993).

Barker researched self-managing teams. His fascinating work is genuine ethnography, with no inherent bias towards the organization. It is no longer new research but it is class work and class work is ageless. He provides an ethnographic account of how an organization's control system evolved in response to a managerial change from hierarchical, bureaucratic control to 'concertive' control in the form of self-managing teams. Members developed a system of value-based normative rules that controlled their actions more powerfully and completely than the former system. Concertive control evolved from the value consensus of the company's team workers to a system of normative rules that became increasingly rationalized and normalized. In spite of the newly delayered and empowered environment, people began to develop their own norms, rules, and expectations of each other. They also developed their own hierarchy and formal leadership roles. These emergent structures were even more powerful than before because they had been developed by the workers themselves and not imposed from above. In effect, they could not be escaped. Contrary to the beliefs of some advocates of such systems, concertive control did not free these workers from bureaucratic control. Instead, concertive control appeared to draw the 'iron cage' of bureaucratic control even tighter to constrain organizational members even more powerfully.

To the literature on self-managing teams, Barker (1993) has added the concept of concertive control. Perhaps one leadership outcome of the creation of self-managed teams is to create more powerful normative control over co-workers. If that is what is intended as a leadership outcome, then self-managed teams are successful. Perhaps a critical management theorist would say so. However, such an outcome flies in the face of much of the contemporary literature on the processual nature of leadership. After all, leadership is meant to empower workers and create innovation rather than impose more powerful control mechanisms. Perhaps self-managing teams have the opposite effect from what is normally expected by contemporary notions of 'leadership'. Perhaps self-managing teams actually inhibit innovation and empowerment. Certainly, they appear to reduce individual discretion through the impact of concertive control. If so, a conclusion might be that people may need *some degree* of self-leadership (or self-management), but *in addition* they might continue to need the more traditional formal leadership role in order to achieve the expression of the 'visionary' and macro aspects of leadership.

Ironically, since Barker's was published, we have seen a reduction in the volume of new literature on self-managed teams. This is not to say that this represents the end of the story – far from it. We do however need to work out what we are really trying to research in this field. There is the opportunity for more ethnography to reveal how and why these phenomena operate. Just as concertive control emerged, so might other very illuminating constructs also emerge.

Our sense is that the leaderless workgroup is really just an oxymoron. Humans still need direction, control, rules, hierarchy, predictability, routine, and so on. Any work unit must have a person in the primary leadership role. In other words, there must be an appointed manager. The issue at stake is the extent to which leader*ship* can be distributed among the various people who constitute that group. If that leadership is distributed effectively, one starts to move from group to team. This brings us on to the matter of team leadership.

team leadership

Theoretical and conceptual discussions about team leadership abound, and many of these overlap with discussions about 'shared' leadership (see, for example, Pearce and Sims, 2000). The notion of team leadership measures leadership as a group-level construct, and looks at leadership 'by' the team rather than 'of' the team or 'in' the team. However, research into team or shared leadership is still scarce. One exception is Avolio et al. (2003) on the validation of the Team Multifactor Leadership Questionnaire (TMLQ). Another is Mayo, Meindl and Pastor's (2003) social network approach. Although this latter work is about the process of social network analysis and its value as a research tool, rather than an actual report on a completed research project, the possibilities are opened up for researchers to pick up this ball and run with it. Social network analysis is useful for understanding the dynamics of shared leadership in work teams for three reasons. First, shared leadership is a relational construct and would benefit from a relational approach such as social network analysis. Second, the unit of analysis is the relation and not the leader or follower. Third, the essence of leadership is influence, and social network analysis examines the nature of influence networks.

Shamir and Lapidot (2003) adopted the perspective of shared leadership as a reciprocal influence process among multiple parties in a systems context. They examined the narrative surrounding certain critical incidents in a military environment to test for the form and effect of those reciprocal influence processes. Data that were gathered included questionnaire responses, group interviews, and individual interviews. They provided a fascinating insight into the notions of collective power, leader (in this case 'commander') vulnerability, shared values, and shared identity. Narrative analysis provides huge scope for research into leadership. Boje's (2001) text is the best insight into these methods. He proposes a range of methodologies by which narrative analysis can be undertaken.

One problem with research into team leadership is that people have an intrinsic fear of the notion of leadership by a team, rather than leadership by an individual or individuals. For example, this fear can be represented by potential research questions like 'How does a board of directors demonstrate leadership?' When gripped with this fear, the natural reaction is to think that the board is a collection of people and it is those individuals who demonstrate leadership. Therefore, team leadership is little more than multiple individual leaderships represented concurrently. After all, people will come and go from the board, so the 'board' will be changed every time there is a change in membership. On the other hand, the team, namely the board, will still be providing leadership even though the membership of the team changes. It is a little like a winning sporting team that stays ahead of the competition. For various reasons, including injury and loss of form, individuals will be replaced from time to time, but the team will still lead the competition over time. The team, in effect, demonstrates leadership.

Therefore, the challenge for the research mindset is to distinguish individuals on the board from the collective entity itself. The research question is about how the collective entity demonstrates leadership, and NOT how individuals behave. We have used the 'board' as one example. Other examples of leadership teams might include sporting teams, as we have said, or political parties, societal groupings, fashion designers, and even companies demonstrating market leadership.

Brad Jackson's (2001) work on management fads and fashions, utilizing dramatistic inquiry and fantasy theme analysis, is one such example. He researched management gurus, but if the subject of the inquiry is the fad or fashion, and not the person, then the new direction of the research becomes a very exciting insight into team leadership. This is a hugely fertile direction for leadership research to take in the near future.

The conclusion to be drawn thus far is that everyone can display leadership. Such an outcome reduces the role of formal leaders. Groups cannot do without a formal leader, but team leadership reduces the pressure on the formal leader to produce all the leadership. However, before we get too carried away with models of distributional leadership, Grint (2005a) offers us some grounds for caution. He notes that some forms of distributive leadership may be attractive to people who are inhibited by idiosyncratic leaders or being suffocated by stultifying bureaucracies. Even so, simply wishing away leadership, 'the big pink elephant' as he colourfully characterizes it, may result in some grossly ineffective and inefficient organizations that can become susceptible to takeovers by authoritarian leaders.

Moreover, distributed leadership can also generate the means by which liberal democratic societies can be destabilized by small and unrepresentative groups or even individuals. By way of a graphic example, Grint brings us smack bang up to date with a sobering and trenchant account of the rise and persistence of the hydra-like terrorist group, al-Qaeda. Grint concludes that distributed leadership presents us with a serious paradox: 'it provides something of a blueprint for making us face the terror of the pink elephant, for *inhibiting* authoritarian leaders, but it also provides terrorists with a blueprint for *cohabiting* with what seems to be leaderless authoritarianism' (2005a: 145, original emphasis).

conclusion

In this chapter we have looked at more critically-oriented perspectives of leadership. They all share a common concern with the concentration of power in the hands of a few nominal leaders as well as a general dissatisfaction with the hierarchical, top-down models of leadership that have dominated conventional leadership thinking since time immemorial. These leadership thinkers attempt to develop alternative, either more 'leaderful' or 'leaderless' leadership models which enable followers to take on leadership responsibilities either at the top of the organization, through co- or shared leadership models, or throughout the organization, via the creation of dispersed leadership models. While there is plenty of support for these post-heroic or anti-heroic normative modes of leadership, there is still – as yet – a paucity of empirical models of organizations that have successfully created and sustained distributed models of leadership over the longer term.

This is not to denigrate in any way these well-meaning theorizing efforts, but it does give one pause for thought as to the viability and, indeed, desirability of these alternative models. We remain continually impressed by the influence that leaders at the top of an organization can have, either for good or bad. We tend both to overestimate and to underestimate the influence that these leaders' hold over their followers. After all, it is the followers who get the work done and ultimately decide whether or not an organization will either succeed or fail. That being said, leaders continue to play an important role in influencing followers' beliefs about whether or not a goal is worth pursuing and whether or not they have the ability to achieve that goal successfully. Our stance, therefore, is not to turn our backs on hierarchical forms of leadership simply because we do not trust or like hierarchy. We remain more concerned with the ends of leadership rather than its means. This is why we still continue to find ways of invigorating the existing leader-centric models of leadership and to refine and bolster follower-centric models of leadership by means of maintaining a healthy democratic counterbalance.

6

Leadership with a Higher Purpose

The concept of 'leading beautifully' brings our attention to that often un-articulated, but nonetheless powerful aspect of how leaders embody their role. Leading beautifully speaks to a quality of being – one honed trough the development of self-mastery, and quickened through the congruence of one's acts with their 'measured' expression. It also alerts us to the possibility of a leader's goals being directed towards the best of human purposes.

Ladkin (2008: 40)

▬▬▬ introduction

The ways in which we study leadership must involve much more than just how one person gets other people to follow their lead. If we restrict our implicit theory of leadership to mere following, then *everything* becomes leadership. Of course, if everything is leadership, then nothing is leadership. This is far too trite an approach to what we all speculate is a much more complex topic. Let us provide an example that is often cited in popular press writings and tutorial-room discussions about leadership (Ciulla, 1998). That example is the leadership of Adolf Hitler. Steve Kempster and Ken Parry have a standing bet on how long it will take before Hitler gets mentioned in a leadership programme. The record is 10:15a.m. on Day One. It is amazing. The one person who always gets mentioned in conjunction with leadership is Hitler, yet he reflects all that is immoral and bad about leadership. To those people who believe that Adolf Hitler was a leader, Ken asks for the aspects of his leadership that they will adopt for themselves. 'What parts of Hitler's leadership will become part of your leadership?' Would they adopt the dramatic histrionics of the mass rally? Would they copy the brutal bullying and extinction of those who disagree? Would they exploit a desperate and hungry population and ultimately lead them towards an even more catastrophic destiny? Would they adopt the lies and hubris, and the resultant vilification of a 'common enemy'? Does the end really justify the means? You doubtless get the point. People start to question whether Hitler was a leader or just a tyrant. Hitler certainly got people to follow him, but there must be more to leadership than just getting people to follow. Hitler is hardly a role model for leadership training courses today. I am aware of no such courses on 'How to be an Adolf Hitler for your organization'. If Adolf Hitler was a leader, and if Adolf Hitler demonstrated leadership, then 'anything goes'. We really must look past charisma and delve into the motives of the leader. We must also look past leader behaviours and into the heart of the leader. We really need to have an insight into leadership for a higher purpose. This process has already begun, but it has still a long way to go.

Purpose is so fundamentally tied up with leadership that it is almost invariably subsumed or taken for granted by leadership scholars. Kempster, Jackson and Conroy (in press) argue that there has been too little discussion on the nature of purpose and its relationship with leadership and this has profound implications for practising managers. The fundamental 'leadership for what?' question is probably the most important yet also the most difficult question to answer. In this chapter we will examine three leadership theories that directly address the moral potential of leadership and the quest for a higher purpose: ethical leadership, authentic leadership, and spiritual leadership. To varying degrees these theories seek to address some of the limitations and shortcomings of transformational leadership (a primary focus of Chapter 2) that were identified in the previous chapter. In their comparative analysis of these three theories, Brown and Trevino (2006) note that they all share a concern for others that is rooted in altruism, they foreground the integrity of the leader, and they highlight the importance of role modelling. However, they do differ by virtue of their varying disciplinary roots and approaches and what they choose to place right at the heart of effective leadership: ethics, honesty, or spirit. While these three leadership theories share a great deal in common, the last part of the chapter will highlight a growing but disparate group of leadership scholars who privilege the long-suppressed aesthetic experience of leadership and look to the arts, not the social sciences or the humanities, for enlightenment and inspiration in their quest to promote leadership for a higher purpose.

leadership and ethics

The moral goodness of leaders has been a topic of analysis for centuries. Most prominent philosophers have at some point expounded on the ethical and moral obligations of leaders from Plato to Confucius to

Machiavelli to Carlyle (Grint, 2011). Ciulla and Forsyth (2011) have highlighted the three main moral facets to the ethics of leaders and those philosophers who have written most forcefully about these: the ethics of *what* a leader does or the ends of a leader's actions (John Stuart Mill); the ethics of *how* a leaders does things or the process of leadership (Aristotle); and the moral reason of *why* leaders do things (Immanuel Kant). Ciulla (2005) pithily encapsulates these three moral facets into her definition of an ethical and effective leader as 'someone who does the right thing, the right way, and for the right reasons', adding that leaders might be pillars of virtue in one or two of these areas but wrong in one or others. This is definitely a case, to paraphrase Meatloaf, of 'Two out of three *being* bad'!

In the past decade, the moral character and the ethical practices of the organizations that they lead have become an increasing concern for leadership researchers in the aftermath of the global financial crisis and earlier well-publicized corporate scandals. Ethics has also become a central preoccupation for leadership educators smarting at accusations that the MBA and other business programmes have been inadequate in instilling a fundamental ethos as well as the basic principles of sound ethical business practice. In fact, the argument goes, business schools are at least partially responsible for these corporate scandals and financial malpractice with their one-dimensional view of the world which promotes financial greed above all else. Responding to these charges business schools have promptly incorporated ethics into their curriculum, usually in conjunction with their leadership courses. They have also funded chairs in ethical leadership and centres that promote ethical, responsible, or integral leadership. Business cases that highlight ethical dilemmas in strategic leadership have also been become much more prevalent, most notably in the Harvard Business School case collection.

In an extensive review of leadership definitions Ciulla (1998) noted the strong normative element that permeates how leadership is conceptualized. In America in particular, leadership is a 'morally laden social construction' and the leader is someone who reflects what people in a certain place and time think they *should* be like. Of course, leaders' ethics are no different from those of the broader populace: although Price (2000) notes that leadership, by virtue of its peculiar cognitive challenges, can induce and maintain a leader's belief that he or she is somehow excepted from the moral requirements of the rest of us. However, as leaders quickly find out when their ethical transgressions are discovered, because of the public nature of their work, because of the level of trust that is bestowed upon them, and because their actions impact upon so many more people, they are often held to account for a higher level of ethical and moral standard than followers.

In recognition of these higher levels of expectation, a number of scholars have sought to distinguish 'ethical leadership' as a higher form of leadership. In seeking to bolster the moral foundation for transformational leadership, Bass and Steidlmeier noted that the ethics of leadership rests upon three pillars: '(1) the moral character of the leader; (2) the ethical legitimacy of the values embedded in the leader's vision, articulation and program which followers either embrace or reject; and (3) the morality of the processes of social ethical choice and action that leaders and followers engage in and collectively pursue' (1999: 182). Brown, Trevino and Harrison highlight the moral management dimension of the leader's work, which is aimed at influencing followers' ethical and unethical behaviour. They note that:

> Moral managers make ethics an explicit part of their leadership agenda by communicating an ethics and values message, by visibly and intentionally role modelling ethical behavior, by using the reward system (rewards and discipline) to hold followers accountable for ethical conduct, by the demonstration of normatively appropriate conduct through personal actions and interpersonal relations, and by the promotion of such conduct to followers through two-way communication, reinforcement and decision-making. (Brown et al., 2005: 120)

The salience of the role modelling of ethical leadership draws on social learning theory (Bandura, 1997) to emphasize the 'trickle-down' effects of both ethical and unethical leadership behaviours upon the ethical behaviour evinced by groups and individuals lower down the organizational hierarchy (Mayer et al., 2009). These modelling effects are by no means irreversible, however. An intriguing qualitative study of the City and County of Denver, Colorado, showed how, through various interventions, including making ethics visibly stand out from the everyday business and introducing a formal ethics programme, leaders were able to emerge from a major ethical scandal to become hailed as a model of organizational ethics (O'Connell and Bligh, 2009).

In parallel with this recent interest in the ethics of leadership has been the emergence of the field of leadership and fairness, which draws upon organizational justice research. In a special issue of the *European Journal of Work and Organizational Psychology*, the co-editors noted that 'most research in leadership and fairness is about the main effects of leader distributive, procedural and especially interactional fairness and supports the conclusion that leader fairness is associated with more desirable follower affective/evaluative responses and behaviour' (Van Knippenberg and De Cremer, 2008: 174). Similarly, we have witnessed a growing interest in the relationship between trust and effective leadership between leaders and followers (Burke et al., 2007); the practice of 'responsible leadership' by senior leaders in order to build social capital among diverse and often competing stakeholders in organizations by identifying and promoting the common good (Maak, 2007); and the role of leadership in either promoting or constraining corporate social responsibility (CSR) (Waldman, Siegal and Javidan, 2006).

It is clear that, in addition to the field of philosophy, ethical leadership has, in the past decade, received increasing attention from leadership scholars trained in psychology. Terry Price and Joanne Ciulla, at the Jepson School of Leadership Studies, have brought their philosophical training to bear on the ethics of leadership to significant effect. They note that psychologists generally provide rich descriptions of leader behaviour but tend to rest these on narrow and somewhat simplistic characterizations of ethical concepts. Philosophers will have a more sophisticated understanding of ethical concepts but will have generally not grounded these in a thorough empirical analysis of how leaders actually behave in practice. Moreover, psychologists tend to focus upon *explaining* leadership while philosophers are more generally concerned with *understanding* it (Ciulla, 1995). As in Chapter 4, when we examined the relationship between culture and leadership, one can readily appreciate the benefits of a similar interdisciplinary effort being deployed to tackle the question of what constitutes ethical leadership practice. The same argument could be applied to the field of authentic leadership, to which we now turn.

authentic leadership

Authentic leadership has assumed an important position among strength-based leadership approaches as a potential solution to the challenges of modern leadership. While authentic leadership research only developed a coherent focus in 2003, it has since attracted considerable theoretical attention and continues to figure prominently in practitioners' treatment of leadership. Ladkin and Taylor (2010) note that it has provided the focus for three special issues of academic journals: *Leadership Quarterly* (2005/1), the *Journal of Management Studies* (2005/5) and the *European Management Journal* (2007/2). Authentic leadership has also provided the inspiration for numerous popular books and articles (e.g. George, 2003; Goffee and Jones, 2005). The following is an abridged account of an extensive review of authentic leadership conducted by Caza and Jackson (2011).

Luthans and Avolio's (2003) chapter on authentic leadership development is generally credited with being the starting point of the research programme on authentic leadership. This programme is usually described as the union of Avolio's interest in full-range leadership (e.g. Avolio, 1999) with Luthans' work on positive organizational behaviour (Luthans, 2002). Authentic leadership theory can be seen as a part of the growing popularity of positive perspectives throughout the social sciences, including psychology (Seligman and Csikszentmihalyi, 2000), organizational studies (Cameron, Dutton and Quinn, 2003) and organization behaviour (Luthans, 2002). Consistent with this, authentic leadership scholars have explicitly recognized their intellectual debt to the humanistic values of psychologists such as Rogers (1963) and Maslow (1968) as important influences upon the development of this new positive perspective on leadership (Avolio and Gardner, 2005).

The most important influence on the development of authentic leadership theory most likely emerged from the post-charismatic critiques of transformational leadership (Michie and Gooty, 2005). The response to these concerns by the leading theorists of transformational leadership was to draw a distinction between 'authentic' transformational leaders and 'pseudo' transformational leaders (Bass and Steidlmeier, 1999). They noted that 'to be truly transformational, leadership must be grounded in moral foundations' (1999: 181). In this reformulation, leaders who are not morally and ethically sound may exhibit influence and charisma, but they are only pseudo-transformational. Authentically transformational leaders are distinguished by their personal moral character, the admirable values that comprise their agenda, and the ethical means they use when interacting with others.

Authentic leadership theory makes distinctions between three types or levels of authenticity: an individual's personal authenticity, a leader's authenticity as a leader, and authentic leadership as a phenomenon in itself (Shamir and Eilam, 2005; Yammarino et al., 2008). These three types of authenticity are argued to be hierarchically inclusive, thus you cannot be an authentic leader without being an authentic person and authentic leadership is not possible without the intervention of an authentic leader (Gardner, Avolio and Walumbwa, 2005). Harter (2002) emphasizes the origins of the term in ancient Greek philosophy and describes two components of authenticity: knowing one's true self and acting in accord with that true self. Kernis (2003) defines authenticity as consisting of four components: a full awareness and acceptance of self; an unbiased processing of self-relevant information; action consistent with the true self; and a relational orientation that values openness and truth in close personal relationships. Combining these two views, authentic leadership scholars define authenticity as having clear and certain knowledge about oneself in all regards (e.g. beliefs, preferences, strengths, weaknesses) and behaving consistently with that self-knowledge (Gardner,

Avolio, Luthans et al., 2005; Ilies, Morgeson and Nahrgang, 2005). In describing the characteristics of authentic leaders to our classes, we have found it easier to provide powerful counter-exemplars of 'inauthentic leaders'. David Brent, from the original *The Office* TV series reigns supreme – showing his photograph anywhere in the world communicates this instantaneously!

Given the four behaviours required of authentic leaders, 'authentic leadership' is then defined in terms of the consequences of those behaviours. It is 'a pattern of leader behavior that draws upon and promotes both positive psychological capacities and a positive ethical climate, to foster greater self-awareness, an internalized moral perspective, balanced processing of information, and relational transparency on the part of leaders working with followers, fostering positive self-development' (Walumbwa et al., 2008: 94). Several potential sources of authentic leadership have been proposed, and these can be broadly grouped into environmental factors and individual differences. The environmental factors include facilitative support, particularly through established norms of authenticity (Chan, 2005), a positive organizational context (Avolio et al., 2004), role models (Gardner, Avolio and Walumbwa, 2005) and direct intervention through training (Avolio and Luthans, 2006). Among the individual differences that have been singled out in creating authentic leadership, personal history is particularly important (Gardner, Avolio and Walumbwa, 2005). Authentic leaders' interpretations of the events in their past are predicted to create a personal meaning system (Goldman and Kernis, 2002) based on specific leadership moments or 'triggers' that will shape their approach to leadership (George and Sims, 2007).

The hypothesized effects of authentic leadership are extensive and varied, offering potential benefit to leaders, to their organizations as a whole, and to individual followers. For themselves, authentic leaders are predicted to experience more positive emotions (Chan et al., 2005), improved well-being (Ilies et al., 2005), and greater leadership effectiveness (Eigel and Kuhnert, 2005). For groups and organizations the most discussed benefit is fostering a more positive culture or climate (Woolley et al., 2007). However, the most dramatic benefits proposed to arise from authentic leadership are those for individual followers. Behaviourally, followers of authentic leaders are predicted to exert greater effort, engage in more organizational citizenship behaviour and enjoy better work performance, improved well-being, and increases in psychological capital (Avolio et al., 2004; Avolio and Luthans, 2006; Gardner and Schermerhorn, 2004; Ilies et al., 2005).

To explain the many benefits that are expected to arise from authentic leadership, authors have pointed to the importance of attitudinal change and the changes in the relationships that followers have with their leaders and their organizations, such as a greater identification with the leader and the organization, improved communication between parties, and the imitation of positive role models (Gardner, Avolio, Luthans et al., 2005; Ilies et al., 2005).

Despite the many important theoretical predictions associated with authentic leadership, and the topic's considerable popularity among academics and practitioners, surprisingly little empirical research has been conducted to date. Caza and Jackson (2011) noted only seven published research reports, with only four of these subject to peer review. Authentic leadership has only been measured at the individual level and has almost exclusively concerned followers' attributions of leader authenticity. There is obviously a lot more scope for empirical exploration.

In the past decade, authentic leadership has seized the popular imagination in a way that few other leadership ideas have. This is evident in the business media and through our interactions with managers in the MBA and the executive development classes that we teach. Many people seem taken with the idea of authenticity and are keen to learn more about it. In part, we suspect that authenticity's appeal derives from its face validity and common-sense value. After all, who would advocate for inauthentic leaders? However, we believe that the source of the appeal goes deeper still. Authentic leadership resonates with a widespread disillusionment about the performance of business, political, and religious leaders. Authentic leadership seems to provide a ready answer to concerns about the intentions and morality of these leaders. This combines with managers' fears and concerns about their own leadership ability to make the notion of authenticity particularly appealing. As the well-worn cliché runs, authentic leadership is an idea whose 'time has come'. It is a powerful response to the entrenched scepticism and suspicion towards established leaders and it accords with a general desire for selfless, enlightened leadership. In fact, somewhat ironically, the most encouraging sign for the future of authentic leadership theory may be in the intensity of the critical response it has provoked (e.g. Caza and Carroll, in press; Collinson, 2011; Ladkin and Taylor, 2010).

the spirituality of leadership

The spiritual dimension of leadership has long been understood at least implicitly but has not widely recognized or become a central preoccupation. For example, Bass's original (1985) notion of transformational leadership included the role of enabling followers to transcend their interests above the day-to-day transactional concerns and to take inspiration from emotional appeals to a higher spiritual level of interest. Indeed, Hicks (2002) has noted that there are a number of characteristics of leadership that resonate in the mainstream literature which have a spiritual tone to them. These characteristics include self-actualization and self-awareness, authenticity, the management of meaning, emotion and passion, intrinsic motivation, wisdom, discernment, courage, transcendence and interconnectedness – as well as the more traditional leadership subjects of morality, integrity, values, honesty, and justice.

However, in the past decade 'spirituality and leadership' has emerged as a distinctive field for leadership research. Fernando (2011) notes that the label 'spirituality and leadership' generates 335,000 hits on Google Scholar, with articles ranging from education, healthcare, psychology, and management disciplines. He also notes that the 'spiritual' element of spiritual leadership has been largely shaped by theory, measurement, and construct development from the more established workplace spirituality field (Mitroff and Denton, 1999). This field originated and developed almost exclusively in the West (particularly in the United States), within a mostly Judaeo-Christian tradition. Conceptualizing the proper role of religion has been the focus of debate within the workplace spirituality discourse (Dent et al., 2005). The same division is reflected within the fledgling spiritual leadership discourse. Several scholars argue that spiritual leadership can and should be directly linked to religion (e.g. Benefiel, 2005; Fernando, 2007; Hicks, 2002; Kriger and Seng, 2005), whereas others (e.g. Giacalone et al., 2005) consider that spiritual leadership should be viewed from an exclusively non-religious perspective.

According to Fry (2006), spirituality is one of several basic needs that individuals need to satisfy. The purpose of spiritual leadership is to 'tap into the fundamental needs of both leader and follower for spiritual well-being through calling and membership, to create vision and value congruence across the individual, empowered team, and organization levels ... to foster higher levels of employee well-being, organizational commitment, financial performance, and social responsibility' (Fry and Cohen, 2009: 266–7). In what is still the predominant theory of spiritual leadership, Fry (2003) posits that leader values, attitudes and behaviours, which essentially are covered comprehensively within the extant leadership literature, will generate outcomes via the intrinsic motivation of followers. Further, he notes that intrinsic motivation is a factor of followers' needs for spiritual survival. Those needs are met through being understood and appreciated, and by a feeling that life has meaning for them and that they can make a difference. In one sense, it could be argued that followers' needs for spiritual survival are merely a reiteration of Shamir's (1992) self-concept theory of motivation blended with Pye's (2005) sensemaking and Smircich's (1993) management of meaning theory. On the other hand, and more realistically, Fry's theory is a comprehensive examination of how these more recent leadership concepts come to have their ultimate impact upon outcomes such as organizational performance. Several writers have suggested that there needs to be greater integration between spirituality within the main-stream leadership discourse (Fry and Cohen, 2009; Reave, 2005; Smith and Rayment, 2007). Most specifically, the linkage between authentic leadership (Avolio and Gardner, 2005) and servant leadership (Greenleaf, 1977) is seen as being ripe for exploration. Indeed, servant leadership is often treated synonymously with spiritual leadership (Sendjaya and Sarros, 2002). Daft (1999) presented four underlying precepts of servant leadership: service before self; listening as a means of affirmation; creating trust; and nourishing followers to become whole. All of these are based on the notion of connectedness, a key concept within spiritual leadership (Fernando, 2007).

Workplace spirituality is frequently asserted to provide greater mean-ing at work, superior ethical practices and greater effectiveness and profitability (Fernando, 2011). As with authentic leadership and serv-ant leadership, however, empirical investigation has lagged well behind theoretical development. They are also confined to the North American and European research settings. In a rare case study of the leader of a multinational corporation based in Sri Lanka, Fernando, Beale and Geroy (2009) found that the spirituality of leadership moves a leader from transactional leadership and on to transformational leadership and then past that on to a transcendental level of leadership. Transcendental leaders grow beyond their own ego towards a higher influence in order to comprehend an extraordinary, spiritual presence in their lives. In this sense they are more than just socialized leaders, because they sacrifice themselves in the service of their collaborators, even at the expense of their own interests. It is indeed leadership with a higher purpose. The spirituality of leadership is characterized by a high internal locus of control and is perceived to be extremely effective.

On the other side of the coin, Tourish and Tourish (2010) have provided a timely critical poststructuralist perspective on 'spirituality at work'. They noted from their empirical study that some managers will attempt to use the notion of spirituality as a novel tool that will help them to gain more compliance from an otherwise non-compliant work-force. The Tourish argument is that spirituality is how we choose to live our lives, and work is work, and the two should be kept separate. In particular, managers (leaders) should never use 'spirituality' as a cunning ploy with which to deceive workers (followers) with hypocritical counterfeit piety. Effectively, the accusation parallels inauthentic leadership. It is important, therefore, to distinguish the notion of the spirituality *of* leadership from leadership using spirituality as a technique with which to wield more power over followers.

▬▬▬ pragmatic leadership

The trenchant critique of transformational and charismatic leadership described in the previous chapter combined with the emergence of ethical leadership, authentic leadership, and spiritual leadership during the first decade of the twentieth century have taken the field into what Parry and Bryman (2006) describe as 'post-charismatic' and 'post-transformational' leadership realms. Storey (2004) has suggested that transformational and charismatic leadership were very much constructs of the late twentieth century. The technology of the time and the prevailing management orthodoxies were enthralled by the heroic visionary individual leader being able to transform corporations and the perceptions and motivations of people who worked within those corporations. And yes, it was mainly 'corporations' that dominated the discourse, and not 'communities' or 'societies'. The increasingly distributed nature of leadership, combined with concerns regarding narcissistic and pseudo-transformational leaders and the shadow or 'dark' side of charisma, has spurred on the quest for a major reconceptualization of leadership for organizations (Fullan, 2001).

Against this backdrop, Mumford and Van Doorn (2001) went 'back to basics' by proposing a theory of pragmatic leadership which would confront the shortfalls of the transformational, transactional and charismatic approaches, without throwing out the potential influence that might be exerted by individual leaders or small groups of individuals irrespective of the historic period. To this end, they engaged in a historiographic case study of Benjamin Franklin. Not only were the theory and conceptualization of the research problem post-transformational, but the research methodology was as well. They chose a case study for which there were considerable data. Not only that, but the figure in question was sufficiently historical that subjective attributions about the moral authenticity of his leadership – normally a potential weakness in research – had probably lapsed.

From their study, they concluded that pragmatic leaders would exercise influence by identifying and communicating solutions to significant social problems, meeting the practical needs of followers, working through elites in solution generation, creating structures to support solution implementation, and demonstrating the feasibility of these solutions. Franklin utilized these tactics to achieve, among other things, the establishment of subscription libraries, the municipal police department, the volunteer fire department, road paving and lighting, and the University of Pennsylvania. These leadership tactics might seem little more than organizational politicking. Certainly, the political process of leadership – that of working through elites and communicating solutions to a wider fraternity of people – is necessary. We would contend further that while it is indeed necessary, this is not sufficient. After all, organizational politics for its own sake is inauthentic and self-serving leadership. We might also contend that Franklin's strategy is what we would now call the triple bottom line or corporate social responsibility, or an earlier version of 'frequent flyer points', by demonstrating to people the personal financial benefit that they could accrue by climbing aboard his visions.

Pragmatic leadership tells us that the pragmatic leader will understand the implicit theories of followers and work within the context of those theories. Pragmatic leaders will also have a keen understanding of what motivates followers and how to meet those needs. In addition pragmatic leadership has a keen sense of the identity of followers and a respect for that identity. The pragmatic leader has a keen general sense of the lived experience of followers and makes that experience a satisfying one for them. Leaders within our large bureaucracies could well benefit from a keen appreciation of pragmatic leadership. Political leaders probably do have an innate insight into pragmatic leadership (we hesitate to call it 'rat cunning') and the effective implementation of good policy probably reflects pragmatic leadership. Further theoretical refinements to pragmatic leadership by Mumford et al. (2008), as well as several mixed methods studies of historical figures (Bedell-Avers et al., 2009) and business leaders (Ligon, Hunter and Mumford, 2008), might be the harbingers of the revival of leader-centred theories of leadership in the post-transformational and post-charismatic leadership era.

aesthetics and leadership

Most of the theories and concepts that we have reviewed in this book have focused either on instrumental explanations of leadership (i.e. 'how does it work?' and 'how can we make it better?') or, to a lesser extent, on ethical understandings (i.e. 'what is the right way?' and 'how should a leader be?'). An aesthetic approach to leadership, however, focuses upon the sensory experience and the felt meanings that are produced by and guide our interactions and decisions (Hansen and Bathurst, 2011).

The aesthetic approach to leadership deliberately examines the tacit dimension of leadership, an area that we rarely talk about but one that is more influential than we would care to admit when we make sense of or try to enact leadership (Taylor, 2002, describes this as 'aesthetic muteness'). Of course we know that you are a thoughtful and discriminating judge of leadership – that's why you bought this book. However, even you may have thought at one time about not voting for someone just because they did not 'look right' or you found their voice to be grating or because they simply had no dress sense!

Aesthetic approaches to leadership do not seek to replace conventional approaches to leadership but rather to complement and supplement the more mainstream approaches to leadership. Instrumentality, ethics, and aesthetics are all necessary elements that inform leadership practice (Guillet de Monthoux and Statler, 2008). Those who conduct research into leadership draw their inspiration from the more established field of organizational aesthetics. Antonio Strati (1992) led the way by pointing out that the core of aesthetics – empathic knowledge, feelings and intuition – was central to management science (see Barnard, 1938, for example). However, these aspects of organizational life had been subsequently removed from the picture by an overwhelming preoccupation with rational practice and technical understanding. It is time that we put these back where they belong (Hansen, Ropo and Sauer, 2007).

One important implication when we bring the aesthetic lens to bear is that we need leaders who are endowed with aesthetic abilities in addition to the technical and ethical abilities that are so highly prized (Dobson, 1999). Drawing on a compelling case study of the *a capella* maestro, Bobby McFerrin, Ladkin (2008) suggests, as we saw in the chapter's opening quotation, that we should be developing leaders who are able to 'lead beautifully'. She identifies three aspects that contributed to Bobby McFerrin's 'beautiful' leadership style that resonate with classical philosophical conceptions of the beautiful (most notably Plato and Plotinius). These were mastery of the self and the context; expressing the self through forms which are congruent with one's overall message and purpose; and attending to a 'beautiful goal' towards which one is leading. In a similar vein, Ropo and Eriksson (1997) and Ropo, Parviainen and Koivunen (2002) have promoted the need for leaders to develop 'bodily knowledge' in addition to cognitive knowledge or affective influence, which is the usual focus for leadership development. Bodily knowledge is a type of tacit knowledge, derived from demonstration and learning-by-doing, and is conceptually similar to a 'sixth sense'. Just as the conductor of an orchestra might have a 'feel' for the music, the leader within an organization should develop a 'feel' for what other employees are sensing and experiencing.

There is the possibility that aesthetic approaches to leadership might be misconstrued as only being relevant to artists or artistic organizations given the strong reliance on the arts for exemplars. But this is by no means the case. For example, Bathurst, Jackson and Statler (2010) have illustrated the relevance of this approach to leadership in conditions of uncertainty and crisis using the case of Hurricane Katrina's impacts on New Orleans in 2005. Drawing on the aesthetic philosopher Roman Ingarden (and armed with the benefit of hindsight), they show how the leadership in that context could have been very different and so much better. They conclude that:

> Human creativity has an important role to play in disaster situations, even if those catastrophes begin with natural events like typhoons and hurricanes. How we respond to the events can be guided by astute and aesthetically-attuned leaders. The ability to confidently make instant judgments and to offer rationales that rouse the public's imagination are tools that the aesthetically-aware leader is able to use by being sensitive and responsive to the moment. (2010: 325)

The aesthetic lens has something valuable to contribute to a number of leadership theories, most obviously charismatic leadership, impression management and authentic leadership (Ladkin, 2008). With respect to the latter theory, Ladkin and Taylor (2010) note that the widely publicized incident involving Hillary Clinton breaking down in tears during the Democratic primary election shows that authenticity has an embodied, aesthetic dimension. They go on to argue that the way in which the leader's 'self' is embodied is a critical determinant of the experience of authentic leadership, noting that 'although it may be obvious, for the purposes of our argument, it is important to point out that it is the leader's body, and the way in which he or she uses it to express their 'true self', which is the seemingly invisible mechanism through which authenticity is conveyed' (2010: 65). They highlight how the system of method acting developed by Constantin Stanislavski uses the somatic sense of self (i.e. the body) to contribute to the feelings of authenticity, and how, through engaging with somatic clues, leadership can be performed in a way which is experienced as authentic, both to the leaders and their followers. They close by inviting researchers to investigate empirically how leaders who are widely considered to be 'authentic' actually experience themselves at a somatic level of awareness.

In concert with this, there is a need to better understand how followers make aesthetically-based assessments of their experiences with leaders. For example, it is remarkable how reliable naïve viewers (i.e. children!)

have been found to be in predicting electoral success in US elections (Antonakis and Dalgas, 2009) just by viewing candidate photographs and how good looks can be at predicting CEO success (Rule and Lambady, 2008, 2009). Moreover, in an experimental study, Nana, Burch and Jackson (2010) were surprised to discover how much information was derived from portrait photographs of CEOs previously unknown to MBA students and how willing they were to form collective opinions – many of them quite sophisticated – regarding the effectiveness of the leader that was being portrayed.

sensemaking and the art of leadership

A number of scholars have attempted to distil the essence of leadership – to integrate all those messages and mottos and mantras down into one overarching message. As we have already noted, Smircich and Morgan (1982) stated it was the management of meaning. Bass and Avolio (1990) argued it was transforming the hearts and minds of followers. In Ken's PhD research some years ago, he found that the essence of leadership was in enhancing the adaptability of people to the turbulence and uncertainty of change (Parry, 2004). Karl Weick (1995) and Annie Pye (2005) said the essence of leadership was sensemaking. All these people were saying much the same thing, but the last essence has resonated the longest with us.

Sensemaking is when people understand the vision and are not just following a plan; it comes from face-to-face personal contact, not from distant impersonal contact; it comes from delegation, not control. Sensemaking enables people to act and not just react; it also enables them to take risks and not just avoid risk; to initiate change and not just to accommodate it. Yes, sensemaking is the essence of leadership.

This sensemaking can be achieved through *science*. The science of sensemaking about leadership is extremely noteworthy because it has formed the basis of the vast majority of leadership research for many years. It has come from experimental research, from quantitative content analysis, from questionnaire-survey research. Strongly influenced by psychology and economics, it has given us structures and equations and models and structural equation modelling. Science has given us a huge amount of sensemaking. But it only goes so far.

Given the increased expectations placed upon leaders to foster creativity and innovation within and beyond their organizations, an increasing number of leadership commentators have argued that we should be looking not just to the sciences but also to the arts to help us make sense of and develop leadership. Most persuasively, in his book *The*

Arts of Leadership, Keith Grint (2001) has observed, 'if we abandon the infinite quest for scientific certainty and seek out the philosophical, fine, martial, and performing arts, we might go some way to resolving the most perennial of human questions: what is leadership?' Effective leaders, he argues, need to develop and learn from an ensemble of arts.

From the philosophical arts, Grint suggests that leaders can learn to create a compelling sense of identity for their organization (i.e. who are we?); from the fine arts they can learn to forge a powerful strategic vision for the organizations they lead (i.e. where are we going?); from the martial arts they can learn to develop smart organizational tactics (i.e. how will we achieve this?); and from the performing arts they can learn to communicate persuasively to their followers the organization's identity, its strategic vision, and its tactics.

Sensemaking can be achieved through verbal techniques such as metaphor and analogy. You have already read about how the use of metaphors helps us to make sense of the nature of leadership. Similarly, metaphors can help leaders to convey meaning to followers. The Chief Executive might call himself the 'Chief Enthusiasm Officer', as does a colleague in Brisbane who is CEO of one of the biggest retail food companies in the country. Peta Fielding, from the Burleigh Brewing Company, has 'Chief Entertainment Officer' on her business card. The marketing plan could be a 'sure bet' or it could be 'Russian roulette'. We use them all the time. We could and should use them more to ramp-up the usefulness of most 'management-speak'.

Sensemaking can also be achieved through the use of humour. Humour is another art form. It brings out all the paradoxes, ambiguities and ironies associated with mixed messages, and in so doing resolves them in the hearts and minds of followers. Refreshingly, research by people like Avolio, Howell and Sosik (1999b) supports this point. Hughes and Avey (2009) also found that transformational leaders who use humour generate higher trust and affective commitment from their followers. Humour is a sensemaking activity. The use of humour helps make leadership more effective.

Sensemaking can be achieved through dance as well. Peter Cammock (2002) captured the essence of leadership that future leaders will need to recognize and master when he stated:

> Leadership is a dance, in which leaders and followers jointly respond to the rhythm and call for a particular social context, within which leaders draw from deep wells of collective experience and energy, to engage followers around transforming visions of change and led them in the collective creation of compelling futures.

Sensemaking can be achieved through another art form, that of poetry. For example, Japanese haiku poetry can convey extraordinarily complex messages in one 17-syllable three-line poem. Try it out for yourself – 5 syllables, 7 syllables, 5 syllables – three lines of poetry. Rick Brenner uses Haiku to teach project management. This one highlights the problems associated with expedient solutions:

Our project was late
So we added more people
The problem got worse

This one came from work Ken did with a government agency and reflects the sort of cynicism and scorn that are so often triggered by organizational change:

We want leadership
Must have self-managed work teams
Try again next year

You can find many examples on the Internet. You can also have fun with them. You can combine humour with haiku and double the leadership impact. They embody a powerful sensemaking. They are leadership. OK, we are not so conceited or superficial as to suggest that the leadership challenges that face senior managers can be condensed into a three-line poem. We are simply saying that poetry is one way that the art of leadership can be understood and conveyed to an audience of followers. Sensemaking art forms such as these could and should form the basis of future studies of leadership.

Sensemaking can also be achieved through visual art. Inspired by the power of art to communicate and challenge thinking, Brad and Erin Griffey, an art historian colleague from the University of Auckland, mounted an exhibition entitled 'The Power of Portraiture', which featured 40 commissioned oil paintings of New Zealand leaders from a wide range of fields and historical periods. They were surprised and struck by the power that these 'virtual' and 'hybrid' leaders could wield over those who attended the exhibition and how much debate and discussion these paintings generated (Griffey and Jackson, 2010). The visual representation and consumption of leadership is a field of inquiry that we have only just begun to explore and one that is ripe with possibility.

We know how a good frame can transform an otherwise lifeless painting into a virtual masterpiece. Hence, the notion of framing can help us to transform mere words into a persuasive argument. Indeed Gail Fairhurst (2011) holds that the ability to create powerful frames is one of the most important tasks for leaders and shows how they can develop this ability.

This sensemaking of leadership can also be achieved through song. On August 28, 1963, when Martin Luther King uttered these famous and rhythmical words, 'My country 'tis of thee, sweet land of liberty, of thee I sing: Land where my fathers died, land of the pilgrims' pride from every mountainside let freedom ring', he stirred the hearts of a nation. He was telling the story of America to the American people. He was bringing their attention to an issue that needed resolution. He was 'dramatizing an appalling condition'. By simply reciting those words he was sensemaking and generating a following. Jay Conger (1991) has drafted probably the best explanation ever written about the inspirational leadership impact of the 'I have a dream' speech and other rhetorical techniques that leaders can use.

The rhythm and harmony of song, and not just the lyrics, can also generate a following. Usually, it is the rhythm or the 'riff' that draws our attention to a song. It is only when we are following the sound of the music that we can then understand the lyrics. All too often these will have a powerful message, one that can generate sensemaking and commitment to a cause. However, it is the music that we follow. It is the music that is a form of leadership. 'So what?' I hear you ask. Well, in our organizations we get many lyrics and not much riff. We get speeches and emails and reports and strategic plans and KPIs (Key Performance Indicators). We get very little that makes our feet tap and then makes us want to take notice of the lyrics. Just as we study leadership and organizations through the lens of drama, so too can we study organizations and leadership through the lens of song. We believe that this is a hugely fertile direction that leadership research can follow.

But we still need more. We need more than just having the topic and the interest and the research heritage. We also need people who can think like an artist or a musician or an actor *and* also think like a leadership scholar. For many years leadership research has been driven along by people who think like a psychologist or a sociologist or an economist or a business manager. They have done great work and created great insights, but we need more. The era of an artistic and dramatic genre of leadership research has begun. We are continuing to see a need to move away from the investigation of the cause→effect challenge of leadership as science, and move on towards the cause→affect→sensemaking of leadership as art. In particular, we are looking now at leadership as drama.

Just like actors in movies ... as a leader, you play a part (it might be the CEO part); you have a role to play (it might be a good guy or it might be a bad guy or it might be a change agent); you have a script (it might be the address to the board or the off-the-cuff chat to employees); you have a costume (it might be the business suit, but this will vary depending on the screenplay); you have an audience (employees or media or board members or other managers); you have a plot (it might be high drama or it might be a farce or it might be black comedy); you have a setting (it might be the committee meeting or the corridor); you have an emotional impact on the audience (it might be arousal or pride or surprise or disappointment or apprehension) ... and finally, you have the sensemaking that you want the audience to take away. Hopefully it will be a profitable production. This is leadership.

We will have to rehearse as well. You might be able to generate the same vitriol and anger as Jack Nicholson did in *A Few Good Men* when you say, 'You can't handle the truth!!' But if people think you are just trying to be Colonel Nathan Jessop, or trying to imitate Jack Nicholson, you will lose credibility and following. Be your authentic self as you live out the role, the script, the costume, the plot, the audience, the emotional impact, and the sensemaking. Yes, leadership is drama. Our challenge is to study leadership from the perspective of the social construction of leadership as drama. Dramatism and dramaturgical analysis have been around for many years. Burke (1975), Turner (1974) and Goffman (1959) were the creators of this field of scholarship, but its incursion into leadership scholarship is more recent. Starratt's (1993) book initiated travel into the area of leadership as drama. Gardner and Avolio (1998) conducted a dramaturgical investigation of the charismatic relationship, which is of course a prominent manifestation of leadership. This is an extremely fertile direction for leadership research.

metaphors of leadership

Michael Michalko (2001) has written that metaphors dominate the discourse of geniuses. The thought and talk of people with very high IQs are dominated by metaphors and analogies. We should remember that the craft of the wordsmith is central to the effectiveness of managers in their leadership role. Keith Grint would probably say that the craft of the wordsmith is central to enacting the performing art of leadership. Elsewhere Ken has also provided more detail about the role that metaphor plays in leadership (Parry, 2008). The basic message is somewhat deductive: sensemaking is leadership; metaphor is sensemaking; therefore metaphor is leadership.

Rosener (1997) and Calás and Smirich (1997) looked at leadership through the lens of gender stereotyping and concluded that mainstream leadership literature has traditionally been couched in masculine terms and that leadership can be interpreted as seduction. This proved to be a very powerful metaphor for leadership that still resonates today, most especially in postgraduate seminars. As we write, a new book is being launched which is entitled *Metaphors We Lead By* (Alvesson and Spicer, 2011). Drawing on in-depth studies of managers who are actively engaged in trying to 'do' leadership, the book features six metaphors for the leader: as gardener, cosy-crafter, saint, cyborg, commander, and bully.

We will end this chapter by briefly discussing three metaphors of leaders that Ken uses a lot in his teaching. There are parenting, schooling, and captaincy. When we do this we are doing more than just engaging in the art of word games. These metaphors help us make sense of the leadership challenge that managers face. These metaphors are supported not just by fifty years of research, but also by the implicit ideas that so many clients and students have brought to us in executive development and teaching courses we have conducted.

leadership as parenting

Those of us who are parents realize that we are charged with a grave responsibility. A responsibility ... I hear you say ... a grave responsibility? Is there another kind? Parenting is the gravest of responsibilities. We develop our children from a state of complete dependency, through ever-increasing levels of independence and autonomy, until ultimately they are fully independent and self-reliant adults. We are role models for them. We must provide the information and resources they need to be able to grow and develop. We must develop and train (in other words, educate) them. We must provide the knowledge they need to make sense of the otherwise confusing state of affairs that constitutes growing up. We must provide a healthy and safe environment for them. We must protect them from violence and harassment. They are a reflection upon us as parents.

Exactly the same responsibility confronts the challenge of leadership in our society more broadly. OK, take away the nappies and baby stuff, but the role of leadership is the same thing as parenting. Let's take organizational leadership as an example. As leaders, we develop followers from dependency to autonomy – let's call that empowerment, for want of a less 'faddish' term. We are role models for our employees. We have a legal responsibility to provide the information and resources to enable people to do their jobs. We also have a legal responsibility to provide a healthy and safe environment for employees. We must provide developmental opportunities and knowledge. The culture of the workplace is an eye into the leadership of that workplace. Yes, leadership is like parenting.

⬤ leadership as schooling

Schooling develops children through adolescence into adulthood, just as leadership develops followers from dependence to autonomy. Schooling involves conformity and control as well as knowledge and independence. So too does managerial leadership in organizations. Schooling involves teaching, training, mentoring, developing. So too does leadership. Schooling has a hierarchy and structure. So too does leadership. Schooling involves rewards as well as punishments. So too does leadership. Yes, leadership is like schooling.

⬤ leadership as captaincy

We use the dual metaphor of captaincy of a sporting team and captaincy as a military rank. The captain of a sporting team is a role model on and off the field, as is the leader. The captain of the sporting team ensures teamwork on the sports field, as does the leader. The captain of the sporting team enacts the game plan, as does the leader. The military captain provides for the welfare and morale of the troops, as does the leader. The military captain fights the good fight, as does the leader. The military captain puts her or his welfare before that of the troops, as does the leader. Yes, leadership is also like captaincy.

The aim of this book is certainly not to trudge through the history of leadership research. Conventional textbooks perform that task well enough. However, having said that, the student can observe a transition over time in the progressive maturity of the world of leadership research. Initially, researchers asked the general question, 'Who is the leader?' As the answers to that question became progressively more problematic, scholars had a nagging doubt that perhaps they were asking the wrong question. As a general rule, they began to ask another question: 'What does the leader do?' The interrogation of this question was extremely fruitful, but the nagging doubts came back. It then began to become apparent that there was much more to leadership than certain people doing certain things. There were higher purposes at stake and there were dramas unfolding. Consequently, it seemed other questions were needed. Today, the contemporary research questions revolve around something like: 'What is going on?' It is this larger processual question of what is going on, as certain people do certain things that have a leadership impact upon other people, which must be teased out and unpacked by researchers.

conclusion

In this chapter we looked at a series of related efforts to rehabilitate and invigorate leadership in response to widespread concerns that were brought into dramatic relief by the number of corporate and political scandals that had erupted in the first part of the twenty-first century. Five rapidly growing areas of leadership scholarship were examined which have sought to respond to the shortcomings of mainstream leadership research and practice: ethical leadership, authentic leadership, spiritual leadership, pragmatic leadership, and aesthetic leadership. The chapter closed with a consideration of how the artistic ways of knowing and, perhaps even more significantly, the artistic imagination might energize and improve our understanding and our practice of leadership. 'Everybody take your places, let the play begin ...'.

7

Conclusion: Take Your Lead

Leadership should be aimed at helping to free people from oppressive structures, practices and habits encountered in societies and institutions, as well as within the shady recesses of ourselves. Good leaders liberate. Further, we can liberate leadership thinking itself from its narrow instrumental confines, so it may reconnect with ideals.

A. Sinclair (2007: vx)

introduction

The term 'research and development' or 'R & D' is often used to capture that set of activities aimed at identifying and testing new products or services. With respect to the leadership field, 'research' activities have sought to understand better what constitutes good and bad leadership and, in light of this knowledge, to make recommendations about how we might promote better leadership. Much of the book has been taken up with explaining to you the range of activities that have been undertaken under the 'research' umbrella. 'Development' activities supposedly take into account that knowledge and create ways in which leadership might be better understood more widely by practitioners and improved through a variety of learning processes and interventions which will be described in this chapter.

As we saw in Chapter 1, leadership development has and continues to be big business. It has been fascinating to see that, throughout the recent economic recession, the investment in leadership development has not fallen off all that significantly. Prior to this there was an unwritten rule that, at the first sign of a financial downturn, the leadership development budgets should be the first to go. Our personal experience, as well as that of others whom we know in this field, suggest that interest in developing leadership is even greater now, particularly the kind which is geared to 'leading through difficult times'. Quite naturally, though, those who do invest in leadership development have become much more interested in getting a better handle on their return on this investment, which has prompted some researchers to call for a more evidence-based and scientific approach to leadership development in terms of its theorization, its empirical inquiry, and its evaluation (Day, 2011).

Given the continued interest in developing leadership, it seems ironic that conducting scholarly research into leadership development is generally considered by many leadership researchers to be a low priority. Relatively few leadership researchers concentrate in this area – the bigger prize is gaining fresh insights into understanding how leadership works. As we have seen in the preceding six chapters, there is still active debate and disagreement about what leadership actually constitutes. This fundamental problem has led Barker (1997) to pose the important yet embarrassing question, 'How can we train leaders if we do not know what leadership is?'.

Some of the more astute leadership researchers have attempted to exploit potential synergies between research and development activities. These activities create opportunities to engage with leaders who are participating in their programmes. These leaders help to research questions, research priorities, and act as sources of data. They also become primary audiences for leadership research, acting as initial sounding boards before research findings are more widely disseminated. This type of synergistic R & D model is the one that has been developed at the New Zealand Leadership Institute (Carroll and Levy, 2010; Carroll, Levy and Richmond, 2008) and now practised by a number of the other leadership centres throughout the world that we have listed in the Appendix.

A critical element in this R & D strategy is an engagement by senior undergraduate and postgraduate students in leadership projects that are connected to leadership development activities. Along these lines, if this book has done what it was supposed to do and your desire to research leadership has been reinforced (rather than weakened), we would strongly encourage you to think about how you might become more familiar with the leadership development field in general and also become aware of and, if possible, make some connection with leadership development activities that might be taking place in your immediate vicinity. For example, Steve Kempster turned his PhD research into the LEAD programme for SME managers, which was independently validated to increase sales by 10 per cent and to increase the gross value added (GVA) per employee: this in turn attracted £10 million in investment from the British government to improve the leadership of SME managers across the north of England.

If you are considering a longer-term career in the leadership field then it is very likely, given what we have said about investment priorities, that you will have to spend some time learning the ropes and becoming an active player in leadership development. Very few leadership researchers do not engage in any form of leadership development. Leadership development provides an invaluable means for escaping the ivory tower and becoming plugged into the experiences and preoccupations of leaders from the private, public and not-for-profit sectors, as well as a useful means for road-testing new theories and findings with a view towards receiving a 'reality check'.

For these reasons, we will primarily focus this chapter on the 'development' side of the R & D equation. We will briefly look at the range of activities that generally constitute leadership development. We will also consider some of the problems and limitations associated with conventional leadership development that have been raised by various commentators. Related to this, we will discuss some of the recommendations that have been made about how the still very nascent field of leadership development should evolve in the future.

We will close the chapter by considering what you might wish to make the next step of your own leadership research journey, by sketching out some of the areas you may wish to take a look at.

developing leaders

In his review of the evidence regarding how leaders learn to become leaders, Doh (2003) makes the point that, even if we can learn to lead, it does not mean that leadership can be taught. It is possible that the process of learning is simply too complex, unconscious, or non-replicable to teach. His review suggests that some leadership can be learned and some aspects of it can be taught. Jay Conger (1992) illustrates this conundrum to graphic effect in his overview of the leadership development process from his book, *Learning to Lead*. He notes:

> The development of leadership ability is a very complex process. It starts before birth, with a prerequisite of certain genes that favor intelligence, physical stamina, and perhaps other qualities. Family members, peers, education, sport, and other childhood experiences then influence the child's need for achievement, power, risk taking and so on. Work experiences and mentors shape the raw leadership materials of childhood and early adulthood into actual leadership by providing essential knowledge and behavioral skills. Opportunity and luck are the final determinants of who gets the chance to lead. (1992: 33)

With respect to the ways in which leaders learn about leadership, most individuals will readily acknowledge that leadership is something that is largely and primarily learned through experience. Unfortunately, there are no short-cuts when it comes to experience, although more than a few popular business book writers have endeavoured to claim this is possible. Experience is not something that can be speeded up, but it's clear that some experiences can be managed in such a way that leaders can gain more insight and knowledge (McCall and Lombardo, 1988). Several studies have shown that learning from experience is affected by the amount of challenge, the variety of task or assignments, and the quality of feedback that is received by the participants.

Challenges that are given to developing leaders need to enable each participants to experience success as well as failure (assuming the person accepts responsibility for this). These challenges should not engender excessive stress and strain. It is especially beneficial for managers to have some early experience with a wide variety of problems that will require different leadership behaviours and skills. However, it is also important for developing leaders to be able to stick with a task or project long enough to see and reflect upon the consequences, favourable or otherwise, of their actions. Too often in this fast-paced world we will have to move on before we have had a chance to see the real and lasting impact of our work as leaders – good, bad, or negligible. Useful feedback about a leader's behaviour is seldom provided within operational assignments, and even when this is available, it may not result in learning due to a combination of a lack of time and reticence on the part of the leaders and followers to either give or receive feedback.

on-the-job leadership development

With respect to the kinds of leadership development activity that can be used to facilitate learning relevant leadership skills on the job, Yukl (2002) identifies the following seven activities as being the most widely used.

- *Multi-source feedback* (e.g. '360-degree' feedback and 'multi-rater' feedback such as the MLQ that we discussed in Chapter 2)   This tends to be expensive, time-consuming and better suited to large organizations rather than small ones. A relatively recent innovation, the jury is still out on how effective this form of feedback really is in developing leadership.
- *Development assessment centres*   Traditionally geared to selection and promotion decisions, there has been a growing interest in using these centres to develop managers. As with multi-source feedback, development centres are expensive and time-consuming and their effectiveness has not been established in the literature.
- *Developmental assignments*   These cover being assigned to specific projects, different parts of the organization, or suppliers or customers

of the organization. Job rotation is a process by which managers are assigned to work in a variety of different functional sub-units of an organization for periods of time varying from six months to three years. There is a danger here that people can be moved too quickly, with insufficient time to see the consequences of their actions or reflect on the experience. Staying in the position too long can also lead to boredom and lost opportunities for more meaningful development.

- *Action learning*   Individuals or teams will conduct field projects on complex organizational problems requiring the use of skills learned on formal training sessions. The emphasis is on developing cognitive and interpersonal skills rather than technical knowledge. The effectiveness of action learning is dependent upon the type of project, the composition of the team, and the type of coaching required.

- *Mentoring*   This is a relationship in which a more experienced leader helps a less experienced protégé. Mentors provide a psychosocial function (e.g. acceptance, encouragement, etc.) as well as a career-facilitation function (e.g. sponsorship, protection, exposure, etc.). The success of formal mentoring programmes is probably increased by making participation voluntary, by providing mentors with a choice of protégé, by explaining the benefits and pitfalls, and by clarifying the expectations, roles and processes of mentor and protégé to both parties. In the UK's LEAD programme, Steve Kempster calls these mentors 'grey wolves'. These are managers who have established their credentials over a sustained period of time and are happy to share their experience with up-and-coming leaders (Kempster, 2006).

- *Executive coaching*   This has experienced a rapid increase in popularity. Coaching is usually provided to a high-level executive by either a successful former executive or a management consultant. It has several advantages over formal training programmes: convenience, confidentiality, flexibility, and more personal attention. However, it is very expensive and good coaches are hard to find.

- *Outdoor challenge programmes*   These involve physical activities performed by a group of people in an outdoor setting. Participants are given a sequence of increasingly challenging activities that require mutual trust and cooperation among group members. The Leadership Trust, based in Ross-in-Wye in the UK, has done a great deal in pioneering and refining this method.

formal leadership training and education

Most leadership training programmes are designed to increase generic skills and behaviours that are relevant for leadership effectiveness and advancement. The old pattern (affectionately referred to as 'sheep dipping' in the trade) of selecting mostly 'fast-track' managers for leadership training and providing it only once or twice during a manager's career is gradually being replaced by a series of leadership training opportunities that are available to any manager in the organization at appropriate points in her or his career (Yukl, 2002).

It's important to recognize that you cannot *train* leaders. You can, however, help to develop certain behaviours and skills that can assist individuals in leading others. Training in interpersonal communication skills, presentation skills, decision-making skills, and facilitation skills can be very helpful. But all of these are merely the means to an end. Many leaders have gotten by without fully (or, in some cases, even partially) developing these skills. What's really important here is the ability to keep on learning from your experiences. Education can play a part in this as it can provide us with new and challenging ways of looking at and conceptualizing our and others' experiences. But, like training, it's better treated as a means rather than an end to leadership development. It also needs to be situated in a planned and integrated model of leadership development (Cacioppe, 1998).

A large variety of methods are used for leadership training. When we design leadership training programmes, we tend to bring together a blend of instructional approaches that will take into account the different learning preferences of those individuals participating in the programme and a need to keep the learning process dynamic and engaging. We especially find that mixing short 'lecturettes' and small-group and large-group discussions – combined with experiential exercises, case studies, and role modelling – tends to work most effectively with a wide range of audiences. The case studies can take both a written and visual form but are generally more effective when they are directly relevant to the participants' experience and are processed initially in small groups and then debriefed in large groups. Role modelling can either involve guest speakers who have successfully led not-for-profit organizations or encompass role-playing in typical leadership situations. Other teaching methods that we have found to be useful include psychometric tests, site visits, and participant role plays and presentations.

In the past when we have attempted to develop leaders, we have tended to focus our attention on cognitive understanding (i.e. *knowing* leadership). To a lesser extent we have also devoted some effort and attention to developing a behavioural understanding of leadership (i.e. *acting* leadership). However what we really need to understand and foster are the emotional aspects of leadership (i.e. *feeling* leadership). Frequently, when you look at leadership failure, it comes down to emotional issues and not cognitive behavioural ones. Most specifically, does the leader have sufficient emotional toughness or resilience to survive the tough times? The notion of 'emotional intelligence' (EI) that has been popularized by Daniel Goleman has something important to offer leaders in that it brings into consideration the emotional realm that the leadership field has sorely missed. Goleman (1998) has argued that having high levels of emotional intelligence is important to leaders because these will enable them to better adapt to different situations, especially crises; such levels also allow them to better understand their own emotional needs and those of their followers. In addition, through stronger self-regulation, emotionally intelligent leaders can prove able to maintain a positive frame of mind even when many around them are experiencing strong negative feelings about the same situation.

In addition to developing our understanding and facility with the emotional dimension of leadership, a rapidly growing and very committed group of consultants and academics has taken a growing interest in applying the burgeoning field of neuroscience to leadership. Ringleb and Rock note that the purpose of what they have dubbed 'NeuroLeadership' is to improve 'leadership effectiveness within institutions and organizations by developing a science of leadership and leadership development that directly takes into account the physiology of the mind and the brain' (2008: 3). Neuroscience encompasses the fields of social cognitive neuroscience, integrative neuroscience, and neurobiology and genetics. In assessing the contribution that neuroscience can bring to the development of authentic leadership, McDonald (2009) concludes that the three-way integration of neuroscience, genetics, and leadership research might finally help us to settle the age-old question concerning the degree to which leader are born versus made that we tackled in the opening chapter. Stay tuned for further developments.

With respect to selecting the most appropriate training programmes, you should look for a programme that has stood the test of time. Avoid programmes that emphasize the latest and greatest techniques. Leadership is an ancient art – in truth, not that much has changed despite what the hype suggests. So, it is important to ask: what kind of a track record does this programme have? Can you talk to alumni of the programme from both the recent and more distant past? To what extent has the facilitator had a stake in the development of the programme? Have they just been booked in to lead the session? Is the programme based on good-quality empirical research?

the problem with leadership development

As we saw in the opening chapter, leadership development has become a multibillion global industry. Grint (2007) provides estimates of between \$15 and \$50 billion annually for the world. Despite these staggering sums, many commentators argue that this is not sufficient given the range and scope of the leadership challenges faced by humanity. For example, Jay Conger asserts that 'most would agree that to seriously train individuals in the arts of leadership takes enormous time and resources – perhaps more than societies or organizations possess, and certainly more than they are willing to expend' (1992: 73).

Surprisingly, given the amount of money that is invested in leadership development, very little has been done to evaluate the impact of this investment (Dvir et al., 2002). Much of what has been written has been generated by trainers or consultants who will often have a vested interest in promoting their particular leadership programme or intervention. The research that has attempted to do just this has by no means been definitive in its evaluation of the effectiveness of leadership development. Moreover, it has not been able to isolate which types of leadership development are most effective.

In general, individuals who participate in leadership development programmes tend to be clearer and more positive about leadership development programmes than the organizations that sponsor them. Most corporate leaders who are responsible for management and leadership development programmes see these as an act of faith: it is better to do the development work than risk the consequences of not doing it.

Researchers have long highlighted the need for more empirical studies that will examine managerial leadership development (Brungardt, 1996; Collins, 2001a; Day, 2000; Lynham, 2000), but still these calls have remained largely unheeded. Transformational leadership is also represented strongly in published work on leadership development. For example, a (2005) study conducted by Ken and Paresha Sinha found that the display of transformational leadership by people in leadership positions increased with two days' interaction and three months' application back at work. Using a quasi-field experiment they found increases in all five transformational leadership behaviours and contingent reward behaviour, and decreases in the display of passive transactional leadership behaviour as a result of the training. Followers put in an increased amount of observable extra effort. Goal-setting was also found to be a particularly effective learning intervention method.

Virtually all the work on leadership development has been conducted at the individual level of analysis. More specifically, it has looked at how to increase levels of leadership skills within individual leaders. There is a major need for research into how to develop the processes of sharing leadership, either as co-leadership or in a more distributed form, as we discussed in Chapter 5. There is also a need for research into leadership development at a collective level either within a team or throughout an entire organization. The full range of methodologies is available here. There are opportunities for questionnaire research, as always. This work could be complemented by more experimental work. There are opportunities for work on assessment centres by human resource management researchers. There is also wide scope for more case studies of an ethnographic nature.

Of course, training people to be better leaders will be all for nought unless the environment within which they operate is conducive to allowing that type of leadership to flourish. Another (2003) study conducted by Ken, this time with Sarah Proctor-Thomson, showed quite clearly that the leadership displayed by individuals is strongly moderated by the culture, climate and bureaucratization of the work environment. Moreover, Boyce, Zaccaro and Wisecarver (2010) have found that the level of organizational support tends to reduce the magnitude with which a propensity for self-development on the part of a leader was translated into actual self-development activities. Leadership training and development will continue to fall short of expectations and ultimately reinforce the status quo if the deep power structures within existing leadership hierarchies continue to constrain rather than enable progressive forms of leadership (Gordon, 2002).

This tendency is powerfully exemplified through the widespread promotion and adoption of leadership competency models and frameworks. As with management competencies, which were widely adopted a decade or so prior, leadership competencies attempt to isolate those ideal behaviours that are critical for leaders to possess in order to engender leadership effectiveness. Leaders are duly measured for the extent to which they have mastered individual competencies with the assistance of targeted training. While the use of competencies might have provided a measure of reassurance to both organizations and managers, their widespread application may in fact prove to be ultimately counterproductive when it comes to fostering genuine leadership development. Leadership competencies are by their nature partial, static, individualistic, context-free and, ultimately, controlling (Carroll, Levy and Richmond, 2008). Drawing on a musical metaphor, Bolden and Gosling (2006: 160) note that 'we should encourage people in leadership roles to not only develop their music reading and basic playing skills (i.e. competencies) but also their interpretation, improvisation and performance abilities (i.e. emotion, intuition, moral judgement, experience, and so on)'. By way of a direct alternative, Carroll et al. (2008) propose a 'leadership-as-practice' approach to leadership development which emphasizes the everyday, localized, collective, 'nitty-gritty' nature of leadership through the lens of those who are engaged in creating it rather than the objective, rational, individualistic perspective of the expert.

developing leadership for the future

Almost all leadership development activities are aimed at those who occupy or are about to occupy formal leadership roles. If we recognize that leadership is co-produced, would it not make sense to extend leadership development activities to include followers as well as leaders? Day (2000) has helpfully distinguished between a 'leader development' orientation, which focuses on developing the individual capabilities of leaders (i.e. building 'human capital'), and 'leadership development', which focuses on developing reciprocal relations and commitments (i.e. building 'social capital'). Currently, far too much emphasis is being placed on the former rather than the latter (Drath, 2001). In a review of five global surveys of leadership development practitioners, McCallum and O'Connell (2008) detected a marked 'tilt' in favour of developing human capital development competencies. Consequently, critical social capital development activities, such as creating an open-systems organic mindset that values boundary crossing and appreciating the relational nature of leadership as well as network building and storytelling skills, are being neglected. An unlikely source of social capital development for future leaders has been identified as online computer games such as *Guild Wars*, *EverQuest* and *World of Warcraft* (Reeves, Malone and O'Driscoll, 2008). Perhaps we should be more tolerant of the amount of time our children spend at the computer – they are developing their leadership capability, after all!

It is important to recognize that what is generically referred to as leadership development is, in fact, leader development (Bolden, 2005; Iles and Preece, 2006). Jones (2005) notes that current leadership development programmes can perpetuate leaders' self-preoccupations through their emphasis on 'self-development', 'self-awareness', and 'self-improvement' at the expense of understanding their followers.

A key challenge for effective leadership development should, therefore, be to develop a more sophisticated understanding of what it means to be a good follower as well as a good leader. We have developed a reasonably robust understanding of the different types of leader, but we still tend to treat followers as an homogeneous entity. We therefore need to find a way of thinking about leadership development which 'views the identities of followers and leaders as inextricably linked, mutually reinforcing, and shifting within specific contexts' (Collinson, 2006: 187).

In contrast to our traditional orientation towards leader–follower relations, which considers relations from the standpoint of individuals as independent, discrete entities, this 'relational' view of leadership starts with processes and views persons and leadership as things that are made through these processes (Hosking, 2007). Leadership development and training should not only include both leaders and followers, it should also actively blur the leader–follower divide, generate a collective understanding, and resist the temptation to impose top-down, predefined models of leadership in favour of bottom-up, locally generated content. In this regard we need to create more 'cultured' leadership development programmes.

Andrew Jones (2006) has raised some interesting anthropological questions about the nature and purpose of leadership development programmes across cultures. In evaluating a number of the world's most prestigious leadership development programmes, he argues that, in addition to the work of 'developing individual leaders' to make their sponsoring organizations more effective, the leadership development process also serves an important role as a context for organizations and cultures to confront and (attempt to) resolve social and economic conflicts affecting the larger society as well. Drawing on the language of symbolic anthropology, he sees leadership development programmes as sites of 'ritual process' through which executives will grapple with moral and ethical matters through self-reflection. In other words, leadership development programmes frequently provide an opportunity for leaders to work through leadership issues which are well beyond the organizations that they are immediately associated with and which have footed the bill for the programme.

In conducting the post-mortem for the financial meltdown that was precipitated in 2008, a portion of the blame has been laid at the door of business schools and the manner in which leadership is taught in them. Despite the tendency for business schools to trumpet the distinctive way in which they educate and develop global leaders, critics argue that the type of leadership that is being taught is a far too narrow, top-down, 'heroic' form aimed at creating maximum value for the shareholder to the exclusion of other stakeholders (Tourish, Craig and Amernic, 2010). This has had paradoxical and unfavourable results. For example, Gabriel (2005) has observed that 'the structure, ideology and ethos of MBA programmes are fundamentally opposed to an education of leaders'. Likening the MBA classroom to 'the playing fields of Eton', he concludes that 'the MBA experience is one for educating followers rather than leaders – committed followers, obstinate, hardened lieutenants perhaps, but not generals' (2005: 147).

In her provocatively entitled (2007) book, *Leadership for the Disillusioned*, Sinclair talks about her own struggle to make her teaching more impactful and more liberating. She now incorporates three principles into all of her leadership teaching. First, reflection has become the basis for learning to become a better leader. Each student is encouraged to dig deep into their own history, investigating their own path as leader and follower. Second, learning comes from direct experience. The class itself becomes the primary source of leadership learning. Finally, leadership theory is used as a body of ideas and concepts which are to be examined critically in light of the participants' experiences, but also on ethical and moral grounds. This is something to which we would both strongly subscribe. Indeed, we hope the book you are currently reading has presented the various leadership theories in such a way that it has encouraged you to engage critically with these theories and not take them as gospel. At the end of the day we judge the quality of a leadership theory by the quality of the questions it creates in our minds rather than by the quality of the answers it gives.

Sinclair's approach to teaching leadership is backed up by another leading leadership educator, Keith Grint, who has suggested that we can fruitfully return to Aristotle's division between *techné* (skills), *episteme* (knowledge), and *phronesis* (wisdom) in an effort to understand whether or not leadership can be taught and, if so, why some aspects seem so difficult to teach. He concludes that although leadership educators may be able to teach skills and knowledge directly, wisdom, which is fundamentally important to leadership effectiveness, is something that can be achieved only through learning from experience. In light of this, we should be concentrating on the construction of opportunities to lead rather than on the selection of leaders, the construction of competency frameworks, or the use of formal lectures. He underlines his argument by closing his paper with the poem by Piet Hein called 'The Road to Wisdom', which reads as follows: 'the road to wisdom – well, it's plain and simple to express: err and err and err again but less and less and less' (Grint, 2007: 243).

A corollary of this approach is that 'perhaps the first step is for those involved in the education of leaders to acquire more humility concerning the limits of their experience' (Grint, 2007: 18). This is something that Ken and Brad have had no trouble getting to grips with. Our family, colleagues, and students have certainly made sure of that!

developing future leadership researchers

This book has attempted to give you a quick, yet reasonably comprehensive idea of the range of things that leadership scholars are interested in researching as well as some indication as to *how* they go about researching these phenomena. We hope that at least one and perhaps a number of the areas we have reviewed has sparked your interest and got you thinking about how you might want to become more involved in studying leadership.

Ideally, of course, we hope you are feeling like us: slightly overwhelmed by the range of possible leadership topics that you'd like to study. If this is the case, then you're well on your way to becoming a leadership scholar. With respect to coping with this feeling, the wisest advice Brad ever received from one of his earlier mentors was to draw up a notional 20-year research programme with three columns. The first column will be for those projects you want to pursue within the near future (i.e. within the next 1–3 years). The second column will contain those projects you want to work on in the medium term (say 3–10 years). The third column will hold those projects that you want to get to in the longer term (i.e. 10–20 years). Of course, you are never likely to reach any of these in the third column, but at least you will have the feeling that you haven't dropped them.

With respect to which leadership topic you might choose to focus on in the near future, consider thinking about a leadership issue that has affected you personally, whether it is something that has happened to you as a follower or as a leader. This might be something that has happened to you in a direct, face-to-face leader–follower relationship or something you have observed in the media or read historic accounts of. Usually, if a fundamental spark of interest is generated – either through annoyance or anger, or through respect or admiration – it's a good sign that you might be on to something. In our preliminary conversations with students who are thinking about doing leadership research, we will talk to them about their experiences and listen carefully for cues as to what moves them personally. Invariably, this is manifested in their speech speeding up or an increased animation in their voices.

For example, an Indonesian student whom Brad supervised talked about his experience working for a manager who had been brought in to run the planning department in which he worked. In a very short time, thanks to the manager's inspiring leadership, the department changed from being a very slow, moribund, and sleepy outpost of the company to becoming a dynamic, vibrant, and growing concern that many people were queuing up to join. This student was mystified because within three months, despite this remarkable turnaround, his manager was unceremoniously fired. Brad encouraged the student to go back to the company as a researcher to find out what had happened from the perspective of a number of observers within and outside the company. The thesis provided the student with a number of invaluable lessons regarding the finer arts of upward leadership, as well as longer-term survival strategies within complex organizations.

Once you have some idea of the topic or research problem you want to focus on, it's time to think about how you might go about researching it. A useful exercise here is to think about how each of the perspectives we have discussed in this book – either leader-centric, follower-centric, culturally, critically or ethically-oriented perspectives – might look at and position your research problem. There is a tendency, in the interests of expediency, to pigeonhole a research problem too early on in the process, to take the most obvious lens on the problem either because it's the one you are most familiar with or because everybody else is doing it. If you take this line you are more than likely to prematurely shut out some potentially creative options which might, in the long run, yield fresher and ultimately more profound insights into your problem. Ken has always found enjoyment and value in researching non-traditional or innovative research methods and research topics. For example, there is an emerging and ongoing interest in wisdom in leadership. This topic requires further research. Also, some theoretical constructs require further empirical research. The spirituality of leadership is one of these.

Brad recalls, having decided that he was going to focus on management gurus and what lay behind their extraordinary appeal, that he 'tried on' many different research methodologies as you would try on pairs of shoes in a shoe store. In this case he veered dangerously close to Imelda Marcos territory. A useful technique in this regard is to generate numerous different 'proto' projects, dissertations, or theses in the manner of film directors generating 'movie pitches'. It was in the course of generating one of these prototypes that he discovered, in one of those all too rare 'ah-ah' moments, that the peculiarly named Fantasy Theme Analysis was tailor-made for getting at what he wanted to examine in his thesis. The next challenge, of course, was to persuade his sceptical supervisor that this method was the way to go.

With respect to coming up with a research design, that is working out who you will approach and with what means, it is extremely useful to look at model pieces of empirical work. In this book we have tried to give you a flavour of the range of research methods that is used in leadership research by providing brief descriptions of sample empirical studies. These have included questionnaire surveys, laboratory experiments, document analyses, discourse analyses, and participant observation. We would advise you to track down some of the studies we have referred to and examine in detail how they designed their empirical research projects and how they structured their accounts of them. You can learn a lot from both their successes and their failures. Sometimes, merely replicating what they have done in your own empirical context can prove to be a sufficiently valuable contribution to leadership knowledge.

To this end, we would strongly advise you to conduct a small pilot study to experiment with a particular method before launching head-long into a major study. One thing you will appreciate very early on is that conducting original research is a lot trickier than you imagined before you embarked upon it. You will quickly gain a greater appreciation for the research that has been done. On a more positive note, it's a lot more personally rewarding than you could ever imagine.

Essentially, our best advice is to determine your research problem fairly early on in the process but to give yourself plenty of time to choose from a variety of ways in which you might go about investigating the problem. Be prepared to read widely and explore more than a few blind alleys. Remember, no exploration is ever wasted. It is still likely to serve you well in the future, especially when it is time to defend your work.

In terms of which areas of leadership research are likely to be 'hot' in the next five or so years, Avolio, Walumbwa and Weber (2009) have highlighted the following eight future issues which they suggest warrant particular attention by leadership scholars: conducting more mixed methods leadership research; determining the causal mechanisms that link leadership to outcomes; assessing and developing leadership using evidence-based strategies; examining strategic leadership as a process and person; producing more theoretical work and research focusing on the follower as a prime element; developing global mindsets among leaders; conducting leadership research in cultures that are under-represented such as Muslim cultures; understanding how shared leadership evolves and develops will be a focus in face-to-face and virtual environments. This is quite a useful and comprehensive list. We would nominate only four additional issues that we believe will also become more of a priority for both further theoretical and empirical research: complexity leadership theory; the linkage between leadership and identity; the relationship between leadership and governance processes; and understanding the sources as well as the prevention of destructive leadership.

The good news, as we said at the outset, is that there has never been so much interest or support for doing leadership research. You will have no trouble explaining to a potential research participant why your research is important or significant. Besides, everyone wants to talk about leadership. It's something that we all have an opinion on and most people are keen to share these opinions. Research subjects will therefore invariably be keen to assist you as long as you respect their busy schedule and, of course, their privacy.

The privacy issue highlights one of the challenges that are particularly salient to leadership researchers. When talking to leaders, it is sometimes quite difficult to determine what they really think about a particular aspect of leadership. There will be a tendency either to want to tell you what they think you want to hear about leadership or to convey a good impression about their leadership. Because we live in a society that places such great stock in being an effective leader, it is difficult for leaders to talk about where they might come up short. Somewhat perversely, it might be more acceptable to admit to one or two weaknesses as a manager, but never as a leader. Of course this is less of a problem for followers, many of whom will freely lay most of their personal woes and injustices at the foot of their leader.

Moreover, there is high potential for confusion about whether a subject is talking about how they would *ideally* like to lead or be led or about how they do *actually* lead or are led. Of course, the higher you go in the organization, the more this is likely to be the case – simply because the stakes are so much greater. Exposing how one leads has the potential not only to adversely affect the reputation of the leader, but also the reputation of the company or organization they lead. Of course, the leader's and the company's reputation can be considerably enhanced if a favourable portrayal of leadership can be conveyed. To counter this problem, considerable investment needs to be put into building sufficient levels of trust with research subjects to enable the researcher to get at these issues.

The pressures exerted by thesis submission, publishing, or promotion deadlines mean that researchers often do not have the luxury of time to conduct this kind of deep research. One response is to focus on leaders at the lower levels within a company, where access and cooperation might be more readily secured. This is why there is a relative dearth in senior-level leadership research, one that sorely needs to be addressed.

Another response to time pressures is to select research methods that are comparatively efficient, reliable, and widely accepted. For this reason, surveys and laboratory experiments continue to be the preferred research methods of choice for many leadership researchers rather than ethnographically-rooted, participant observation which requires considerably more time and presents greater risks. It's also why so much leadership research is conducted either on students or within the university or other educational settings. Those who are willing to spend the time, look further afield and take risks are rewarded by the fact that invariably their studies will become heavily cited and respected because they have endeavoured to get in among those who practise leadership and management in a more than superficial way. Good examples of these types of studies would be Rosabeth Moss Kanter's *Men and Women of the Corporation* (1977), Robert Jackall's *Moral Mazes* (1988), Gideon Kunda's *Engineering Culture* (1992), and Tony Watson's *In Search of Management* (1994).

With respect to writing up your research and disseminating to others your hard-won and precious leadership knowledge, we suggest that you again 'look and learn' from the more experienced and seasoned researchers who can provide you with exemplars to work from. To this end, we have dared to compile in the Appendix a list of 'Ten Leadership Books That You Should Read Before You Die'. Read these books not only for what they say about leadership but also for *how* they write about leadership. In a similar way to musicians, actively try to mimic these styles. They will start to rub off on your own writing.

Another tip: when you track these books down in your library, look either side of them on the shelf and grab four or five of their less famous neighbouring books to flick through their contents, introductory and concluding chapters. You'll be amazed by what you will discover. You will also start to see some recurring themes that will give you the confidence that you are starting to 'get' leadership. In our age of instant access to knowledge provided by electronic database searching technology, we have lost the art of semi-random browsing which spending real time in libraries still affords, yet students and academics now rarely take advantage of this.

Undertaking any kind of undergraduate or postgraduate study is like serving a form of apprenticeship. To be honest, in academe, the apprenticeship is effectively a life sentence because you can never truly master your subject – especially when it is something as nebulous, as contestable, and as fascinating as leadership. The academics we most admire are those who still consider themselves to be students. They are as excited and as mind-boggled by their subject as they were when they started out on their studies, as hopefully you are right now. Their research, their teaching, and their service activities all work together to help them become more accomplished students of leadership. Every waking moment of their day presents them with an opportunity to learn something more about leadership, for which they are constantly grateful. Be warned, though: like the infamous 'Hotel California', you can check in any time to study leadership but you can never check out.

conclusion

Looking back to what we said we wanted to achieve in this book under the heading 'Should You Buy This Book?' we hoped that, if you were already a university student studying leadership or perhaps contemplating studying leadership as part of a senior undergraduate or a postgraduate course, it might provide you with an excellent base from which to proceed. You should have gained a 'quick and dirty' feel for what gets studied within leadership and how it gets studied. It's possible, of course, that the book might have confirmed your worst suspicions about the field of leadership being 'fuzzy and flaky' and you have firmly decided that it is not for you. In that case, your investment in this book has been a sound one.

If you are on the verge of starting a project, dissertation, or thesis on leadership we hope that you not only have an even better handle on the various ways that you might go about doing this, but that you also feel affirmed in your choice to join the field of leadership studies. We hope we have encouraged you to select a research problem that is not only important to you personally but also has some general significance that we can all benefit from. We would urge you here to be creative and innovative in your research design and to take risks with your research, but to heed well the lessons of experience that your supervisors will pass on to you.

Because this is such a young and growing field, you have every opportunity to play an active role in building knowledge about leadership and making your mark. In this regard you are by no means alone. We would therefore strongly encourage you to join the groups of leadership researchers and developers we have listed in the Appendix. Come to the conferences and get involved in reviewing and writing for leadership journals, both for practitioners and academic audiences. On the local front, either find or found a local special-interest group that shares your passion and fascination for leadership.

If you are not currently engaged in a formal programme of study but have always had an interest in leadership, we hope you have been encouraged or perhaps even inspired to 'promptly march down to your nearest seat of learning and sign up for a formal programme to find others who have already decided to make that fateful leap'. While our tongues are firmly implanted in our cheeks when we make this statement, we do want to underline the well-worn cliché that 'there is no time like the present' to pursue your studies. We both embarked on our doctoral studies in our mid-thirties when families and careers were at their most demanding, yet we have never once regretted taking that step. It opened up a whole new world of learning for us, which, in this book, we've striven to share with you.

Finally, for those of our academic colleagues who are not involved in leadership research or have always been mildly suspicious of it, we hope that reading this book will have served to at least partially allay your suspicions and may have even whetted your appetite to explore leadership studies even further. In our wildest evangelical dreams, we speculate that a few of you may have come to the realization that you are, after all, already doing leadership research and are now willing to 'come out of the closet'. To you we say 'Be brave' and 'Amen'. There will be those who, as a result of reading this book, might have become scandalized by what passes for leadership research and are now moved to shut down all leadership research centres forthwith. To you we say: 'Catch you later'.

Appendix: Resources for Studying Leadership

▬▬ ten very useful leadership reference books

Antonakis, J., Cianciolo, A.T. and Sternberg, R.J. (2004) *The Nature of Leadership*. Thousand Oaks, CA: Sage.

Bass, B. and Bass, R. (2008) *The Bass Handbook of Leadership: Theory, Research and Managerial Applications* (4th edn). New York: The Free Press.

Bryman, A., Collinson, D., Grint, K., Jackson, B. and Uhl-Bien, M. (eds) (2011) *Sage Handbook of Leadership*. London: Sage.

Collinson, D., Grint, K. and Jackson, B. (eds) (2011) *Major Works in Leadership* (vols 1–4). London: Sage.

Goethals, G.R., Sorenson, G.J. and Burns, J.M. (2004) *Encyclopedia of Leadership* (vols 1–4). Thousand Oaks, CA: Sage.

Khurana, R. and Nohria, N. (eds) (2010) *Handbook of Leadership Theory and Practice*. Boston, MA: HBS Publishing.

Marturano, A. and Gosling, J. (eds) (2007) *Leadership: The Key Concepts*. Oxford: Routledge.

Northouse, P.G. (2010) *Leadership: Theory and Practice* (5th edn). Thousand Oaks, CA: Sage.

Wren, T., Hicks, D. and Price, T. (eds) (2004) *The International Library of Leadership*. Cheltenham, UK: Edward Elgar.

Yukl, G.A. (2010) *Leadership in Organizations* (7th edn). Upper Saddle River, NJ: Prentice-Hall.

▬▬ ten leadership books you should read before you die

Bass, B.M. and Avolio, B.J. (eds) (1994) *Improving Organizational Effectiveness through Transformational Leadership*. Thousand Oaks, CA: Sage.

Burns, J.M. (1978) *Leadership*. New York: Harper & Row.

Gardner, J.W. (1990) *On Leadership*. New York: The Free Press.

Greenleaf, R.K. and Spears, L.C. (2002) *Servant Leadership: A Journey into the Nature of Legitimate Power and Greatness* (25th anniversary edn). New York: Paulist Press.

Grint, G. (2005) *Leadership: Limits and Possibilities*. New York: Palgrave Macmillan.

Harter, N. (2006) *Clearings in the Forest: On the Study of Leadership*. West Lafayayette, IN: Purdue University Press.

Heifetz, R. (1994) *Leadership Without Easy Answers*. Cambridge, MA: Harvard University Press.

Kouzes, J.M. and Posner, B.Z. (2007) *The Leadership Challenge* (4th edn). San Francisco, CA: Jossey-Bass.

Ladkin, D. (2010) *Rethinking Leadership: A New Look at Old Leadership Questions*. Cheltenham, UK: Edward Elgar.

Sinclair, A. (2007) *Leadership for the Disillusioned*. Crows Nest, NSW: Allen & Unwin.

And of course...

Jackson, B. and Parry, K. (2011) *A Very Short, Fairly Interesting and Reasonably Cheap Book About Studying Leadership*. London: Sage.

seven leadership journals worth monitoring

International Journal of Leadership Studies
Journal of Leadership and Organizational Studies
Journal of Management & Organization
Journal of Organizational Behaviour
Leadership
Leadership & Organization Development Journal
The Leadership Quarterly

four associations with a leadership focus

Academy of Management (AOM)
http://www.aomonline.org/

International Leadership Association (ILA)
http://www.ila-net.org/

Network of Leadership Scholars List Serve
LDRNET-L@aomlists.pace.edu

Social Science Research Network (SSRN)
http://www.ssrn.com/

▬▬▬ nineteen leadership research centres worth investigating

Banff Centre Leadership Development
http://www.banffcentre.ca/departments/leadership/

Bristol Centre for Leadership and Organisational Ethics (Bristol Business
    School)
http://www.uwe.ac.uk/bbs/research/bcloe/index.shtml

Center for Creative Leadership
http://www.ccl.org

Center for Leadership Studies (University of Binghamton)
http://cls.binghamton.edu/

Center for Public Leadership (Harvard University)
http://www.ksg.harvard.edu/leadership/

Centre for Leadership Studies (University of Exeter)
http://www.leadership-studies.com/

Foster Centre for Leadership and Strategic Thinking (University of
    Washington)
http://www.foster.washington.edu/centers/leadership/Pages/leadership.
    aspx

Fuqua/Coach K Center of Leadership and Ethics (Duke University)
http://www.leadershipandethics.org

Institute for Innovative Leadership (University of Nebraska)
http://gli.unl.edu/

Institute for Leadership Research (Texas Tech University)
http://www.ilr.ba.ttu.edu/

Jepson School of Leadership Studies (University of Richmond)
http://www.jepson.richmond.edu

Kravis Leadership Institute (Claremont McKenna College)
http://www.claremontmckenna.edu/kli

Leader to Leader Institute (Drucker Foundation for Nonprofit
    Management)
http://www.leadertoleader.org/

NeuroLeadership Institute
http://www.Neuroleadership.org

New Zealand Leadership Institute (University of Auckland)
http://www.excelerator.co.nz

School of Global Leadership & Entrepreneurship (Regent University)
http://www.regent.edu/acad/global/home

The Lancaster Leadership Centre (Lancaster University)
http://www.lums.lancs.ac.uk/leadership/

The Leadership Trust (Ross-on Wye, UK)
http://www.leadership.co.uk/

Wharton Center for Leadership and Change Management (University of
    Pennsylvania)
http://leadership.wharton.upenn.edu/welcome/index.shtml

twenty-four movies about leadership really worth viewing

Apollo 13 (1995) Director: Ron Howard
Bagdad Cafe (1987) Director: Percy Adlon
Bridge Over the River Kwai (1957) Director: David Lean
Castle Under Fiery Skies (2000). Director: Tanaka Mitsutoshi
Dead Poets' Society (1989) Director: Peter Weir
Downfall (Der Untergang) (2004) Director: Oliver Hirschbiegel
Gandhi (1982) Director: Richard Attenborough
Glory (1989) Director: Edward Zwick
Hoosiers (1986) Director: David Anspaugh
Hotel Rwanda (2004) Director: Terry George
Kagemusha (1980) Director: Akira Kurosawa
Lawrence of Arabia (1962) Director: David Lean
Malcolm X (1992) Director: Spike Lee
Michael Collins (1996) Director: Neil Jordan

Norma Rae (1970) Director: Martin Ritt
Saint Joan (1957) Director: Otto Preminger
Spartacus (1960) Director: Stanley Kubrick
The Election (2005) Director: Johnny To
The Last King of Scotland (2006) Director: Kevin Macdonald
Thirteen Days (2000) Director: Roger Donaldson
Twelve Angry Men (1957) Director: Sidney Lumet
Wall Street (1987) Director: Oliver Stone
Whale Rider (2002) Director: Niki Caro
When We Were Kings (1996) Director: Leon Gast

References

Adams, S. (1996) *The Dilbert Principle*. New York: HarperCollins.

Adler, N.J. (1996) 'Global women political leaders: An invisible history, and increasingly important future', *Leadership Quarterly*, 7 (1): 133–61.

Ailon, G. (2007) *Global Ambitions and Local Identities: An Israeli–American High-tech Merger*. New York: Berghahn Books.

Ailon, G. (2008) 'Mirror, mirror on the wall: Culture's consequences in a value test of its own design', *Academy of Management Review*, 33 (4): 885–904.

Ailon, G. (2009) 'Who is the fairest of them all? Galit Ailon's mirror', *Academy of Management Review*, 34 (3): 571–3.

Ailon-Souday, G. and Kunda, G. (2003) 'The local selves of global workers: The social construction of national identity in the face of organizational globalization', *Organization Studies*, 24 (7): 1073–96.

Alimo-Metcalfe, B. and Alban-Metcalfe, R.J. (2001) 'The development of a new Transformational Leadership Questionnaire', *Journal of Occupational and Organizational Psychology*, 74: 1–28.

Alvarez, J.L. and Svejenova, S. (2005) *Sharing Executive Power*. Cambridge: Cambridge University Press.

Alvesson, M. (1993) *Cultural Perspectives on Organization*. Cambridge: Cambridge University Press.

Alvesson, M. and Spicer, A. (eds) (2010) *Metaphors We Lead By*. London: Routledge.

Alvesson, M. and Sveningsson, S. (2003a) 'Managers doing leadership: The extraordinarization of the mundane', *Human Relations*, 56 (12): 1435–59.

Alvesson, M. and Sveningsson, S. (2003b) 'The great disappearing act: Difficulties in doing "leadership"', *Leadership Quarterly*, 14 (3): 359–81.

Amit, K., Popper, M., Gal, R., Mamane-Levy, T. and Lisak, A. (2009) 'Leadership-shaping experiences: A comparative study of leaders and non-leaders', *Leadership & Organization Development Journal*, 30 (4): 302–18.

Antonakis, J. and Dalgas, O. (2009) 'Predicting elections: Child's play', *Science*, 323: 1183.

Astin, H.S. and Leland, C. (1992) *Women of Influence, Women of Vision: A Cross-Generational Study of Leaders and Social Change*. San Francisco, CA: Jossey-Bass.

Avolio, B.J. (1999) *Full Leadership Development: Building Vital Forces in Organizations*. Newbury Park, CA: Sage.

Avolio, B.J. (2005) *Leadership Development in Balance: MADE/Born*. Mahwah, NJ: LEA.

Avolio, B.J. and Bass, B. (1995) 'Individual consideration viewed at multiple levels of analysis: A multi-level framework for examining the diffusion of transformational leadership', *Leadership Quarterly*, 6 (2): 199–218.

Avolio, B.J. and Gardner, W.L. (2005) 'Authentic leadership development: Getting to the root of positive forms of leadership', *Leadership Quarterly*, 16 (3): 315–38.

Avolio, B.J., Gardner, W.L. and Walumbwa, F.O. (2005) Preface in W.L. Gardner, B.J. Avolio and F.O. Walumbwa (eds), *Authentic Leadership Theory and Practice: Origins, Effects, and Development* (Vol. 3). New York: Elsevier. pp. xxi–xxix.

Avolio, B.J., Gardner, W.L., Walumbwa, F.O., Luthans, F. and May, D.R. (2004) 'Unlocking the mask: A look at the process by which authentic leaders impact follower attitudes and behaviors', *Leadership Quarterly*, 15 (6): 801–23.

Avolio, B.J., Howell, J.M. and Sosik, J.J. (1999b) 'A funny thing happened on the way to the bottom line: Humor as a moderator of leadership style effects', *Academy of Management Journal*, 42 (2): 219–27.

Avolio, B.J., Kahai, S. and Dodge, G.E. (2001) 'E-leadership: Implications for theory, research, and practice', *Leadership Quarterly*, 11 (4): 615–68.

Avolio, B.J. and Luthans, F. (2006) *The High Impact Leader: Moments Matter in Accelerating Authentic Leadership Development*. New York: McGraw-Hill.

Avolio, B.J., Reichard, R.J., Hannah, S.T., Walumbwa, F.O. and Chan, A. (2009a) 'A meta-analytic review of leadership impact research: Experimental and quasi-experimental studies', *The Leadership Quarterly*, 20 (5): 764–84.

Avolio, B.J., Sivasubramaniam, N., Murry, W.D., Jung, D. and Garger, J.W. (2003) 'Assessing shared leadership: Development and preliminary validation of a team multifactor leadership questionnaire', in C.L. Pearce and J.A. Conger (eds), *Shared Leadership: Reframing the Hows and Whys of Leadership*. Thousand Oaks, CA: Sage. pp. 143–72.

Avolio, B.J., Walumbwa, F.O. and Weber, T.J. (2009) 'Leadership: Current theories, research, and future directions', *Annual Review of Psychology*, 60: 421–49.

Awamleh, R. and Gardner, W.L. (1999) 'Perceptions of leaders charisma and effectiveness: The effects of vision content, delivery, and organizational performance', *Leadership Quarterly*, 10 (3): 345–73.

Babiak, P. (1996) 'Psychopathic manipulation in organizations: Pawns, patrons, and patsies', in D.J. Cooke, A.E. Forth, J.P. Newman and R.D. Hare (eds), *Issues in Criminological and Legal Psychology: No. 24, International Perspectives on Psychopathy*. Leicester, UK: British Psychological Society, pp. 12–17.

Badaracco, J.L. (2002) *Leading Quietly: An Unorthodox Guide to Doing the Right Thing*. Boston, MA: Harvard Business Press.

Baker, S.D. (2007) 'Followership: The theoretical foundation of a contemporary construct', *Journal of Leadership and Organizational Studies*, 14 (1): 50–60.

Bandura, A. (1997) *Social Learning Theory*. Englewood Cliffs, NJ: Prentice-Hall.

Banker, R.D., Field, J.M., Schroeder, R.G. and Sinha, K.K. (1996) 'Impact of work teams on manufacturing performance: A longitudinal field study', *Academy of Management Journal*, 39: 867–90.

Barker, J.R. (1993) 'Tightening the iron cage: Concertive control in self-managing teams', *Administrative Science Quarterly*, 38 (3): 408–37.

Barker, R.A. (1997) 'How can we train leaders if we do not know what leadership is?', *Human Relations*, 50 (4): 343–62.

Barnard, C.I. (1938) *The Functions of the Executive*. Cambridge, MA: Harvard University Press.

Bartone, P.T., Eid, J., Johnsen, B.H., Laberg, J.C. and Snook, S.A. (2009) 'Big five personality factors, hardiness, and social judgement as predictors of leader performance', *Leadership and Organization Development Journal*, 30 (6): 498–521.

Bass, B.M. (1985) *Leadership and Performance Beyond Expectations*. New York: The Free Press.

Bass, B.M. (1990) 'Concepts of leadership', in B.M. Bass and R.M. Stodgill (eds), *Handbook of Leadership: Theory, Research and Managerial Applications*. New York: The Free Press.

Bass, B.M. (1997) 'Does the transactional and transformational leadership paradigm transcend organizational and national boundaries?', *American Psychologist*, 52 (2): 130–9.

Bass, B.M. (1998) *Transformational Leadership: Industrial, Military and Educational Impact*. Mahwah, NJ: Lawrence Erlbaum.

Bass, B.M. and Avolio, B.J. (1990) 'The implications of transactional and transformational leadership for individual, team, and organizational development', *Research in Organizational Change and Development*, 4: 231–72.

Bass, B.M. and Avolio, B.J. (1994) 'Shatter the glass ceiling: Women may make better managers', *Human Resource Management*, 33: 549–60.

Bass, B.M. and Steidlmeier, P. (1999) 'Ethics, character, and authentic transformational leadership behaviour', *Leadership Quarterly*, 10 (2): 181–217.

Bathurst, R., Jackson, B. and Statler, M. (2010) 'Leading aesthetically in uncertain times', *Leadership*, 6 (3): 311–30.

Bedell-Avers, K., Hunter, S.T., Angie, A.A., Eubanks, D.L. and Mumford, M.D. (2009) 'Charismatic, ideological, and pragmatic leaders: An examination of leader–leader interactions', *Leadership Quarterly*, 20 (3): 209–315.

Beechler, S. and Javdian, M. (2007) *Leading with a Global Mindset*. London: Emerald.

Benefiel, M. (2005) 'The second half of the journey: Spiritual leadership for organizational transformation', *Leadership Quarterly*, 16: 723–47.

Bennis, W. (2007) 'The challenges of leadership in the modern world', *American Psychologist*, 62 (1): 2–5.

Bennis, W.G. and Nanus, B. (1985) *Leaders: The Strategies for Taking Charge*. New York: Harper & Row.

Berson, Y. and Avolio, B. (2004) 'Transformational leadership and the dissemination of organizational goals: A case study of a telecommunication firm', *Leadership Quarterly*, 15 (5): 625–46.

Bligh, M.C. (2011) 'Followership and follower-centered approaches', in A. Bryman, D. Collinson, K. Grint, B. Jackson and M. Uhl-Bien (eds), *Sage Handbook of Leadership*. London: Sage. pp. 423–34.

Boal, K.B. and Hooijberg, R. (2000) 'Strategic leadership research: Moving on', *Leadership Quarterly*, 11 (4): 515–49.

Boje, D.M. (2001*) Narrative Methods for Organizational and Communication Research*. Thousand Oaks, CA: Sage.

Boje, D.M. and Rhodes, C. (2005) 'The virtual leader construct: The mass mediatization and simulation of transformational leadership', *Leadership*, 1 (4): 407–28.

Bolden, R. (ed.) (2005) *What is Leadership Development?: Purpose and Practice*. Exeter: Centre for Leadership Studies, University of Exeter.

Bolden, R. and Gosling, J. (2006) 'Leadership competencies: Time to change the tune', *Leadership*, 2 (2): 147–63.

Bolman, L.G. and Deal, T.E. (1997) *Reframing Organizations*. San Francisco, CA: Jossey-Bass.

Boyce, L.A., Zaccaro, S.J. and Wisecarver, M.Z. (2010) 'Propensity for self-development of leadership attributes: Understanding, predicting and supporting performance of leader self-development', *The Leadership Quarterly*, 21 (1): 159–78.

Bratton, J., Grint, K. and Nelson, D.L. (2004) *Organizational Leadership*. New York: Thomson.

Brown, M.E. and Gioia, D.A. (2002) 'Making things click: Distributive leadership in an online division of an offline organization', *Leadership Quarterly*, 13 (4): 397–419.

Brown, M.E. and Trevino, L.K. (2006) 'Ethical leadership: A review and future directions', *Leadership Quarterly*, 17: 595–616.

Brown, M.E., Trevino, L.K. and Harrison, D. (2005) 'Ethical leadership: A social learning perspective for construct development and testing', *Organizational Behaviour and Human Decision Processes*, 97: 117–34.

Brungardt, C. (1996) 'The making of leaders: A review of the research in leadership development and education', *The Journal of Leadership Studies*, 3 (3): 81–95.

Bryman, A. (1992) *Charisma and leadership in organizations*. London: Sage.

Bryman, A., Stephens, M. and à Campo, C. (1996) 'The importance of context: Qualitative research and the study of leadership, *Leadership Quarterly*, 7 (3): 353–70.

Burgoyne, J. (2004) 'How certain are we that management and leadership development is effective?' Paper presented at the Management Learning and Leadership Workshop, Lancaster University, July.

Burke, C.S., Sims, D.E., Lazzara, L.H. and Salas, E. (2007) 'Trust in leadership: A multi-level review and integration', *Leadership Quarterly*, 18: 606–32.

Burke, K. (1975) 'The five key terms of Dramatism', in D. Brissett and C. Edgley (eds), *Life as Theater: A Dramaturgical Sourcebook*. Chicago, IL: Aldine. pp. 445–52.

Burke, R.J. and McKeen, C.J. (1996) 'Do women at the top make a difference? Gender Proportions and the experiences of managerial and professional women, *Human Relations*, 49 (8): 1093–104.

Burns, J.M. (1978) *Leadership*. New York: Harper & Row.

Burns, J.M. (2003) *Transforming Leadership: A New Pursuit of Leadership*. New York: Atlantic Monthly Press.

Burns, J.M. (2005) 'Leadership', *Leadership*, 1 (1): 11–12.

Cable, D.M. and Judge, T.A. (2003) 'Managers' upward influence tactic strategies: The role of manager personality and supervisor leadership style', *Journal of Organizational Behaviour*, 24 (2): 197–214.

Cacioppe, R. (1998) 'An integrated model and approach for the design of effective leadership programmes', *Leadership and Organization Development Journal*, 19 (1): 44–53.

Calás, M.B. and Smircich, L. (1997) 'Voicing seduction to silence leadership', in K. Grint (ed.), *Leadership: Classical, Contemporary and Critical Approaches*. Oxford: Oxford University Press.

Calder, B.J. (1977) 'An attribution theory of leadership', in B.M. Staw and G.R. Salancik (eds), *New Directions in Organizational Behaviour*. Chicago, IL: St Clair. pp. 179–204.

Cameron, K.S., Dutton, J.E. and Quinn, R.E. (2003) *Positive Organizational Scholarship: Foundations of a New Discipline*. San Francisco, CA: Berrett-Koehler.

Cammock, P. (2002) *The Dance of Leadership*. Auckland, NZ: Prentice-Hall.

Carroll, B. and Levy, L. (2008) 'Defaulting to management: Leadership defined by what it is not', *Organization*, 15 (1): 75–96.

Carroll, B. and Levy, L. (2010) 'Leadership development as identity construction', *Management Communication Quarterly*, 24: 211–32.

Carroll, B. and Levy, L. and Richmond, D. (2008) 'Leadership as practice: Challenging the competency paradigm', *Leadership*, 4 (4): 363–79.

Caza, A. and Carroll, B. (in press) 'Critical theory and POS', in K.S. Cameron and G.M. Spreitzer (eds), *Handbook on Positive Organizational Scholarship*. Oxford: Oxford University Press.

Caza, A. and Jackson, B. (2011) 'Authentic leadership', in A. Bryman, D. Collinson, K. Grint, B. Jackson and M. Uhl-Bien (eds), *Sage Handbook of Leadership*. London: Sage. pp. 350–62.

Chan, A. (2005) 'Authentic leadership measurement and development: Challenges and suggestions', in W.L. Gardner, B.J. Avolio and F.O. Walumbwa (eds), *Authentic Leadership Theory and Practice: Origins, Effects, and Development* (Vol. 3). New York: Elsevier. pp. 227–50.

Chatman, J.A. and O'Reilly, C.A. (2004) 'Asymmetric reactions to work group sex diversity among men and women', *Academy of Management Journal*, 47 (2): 193–208.

Chen, C.C. and Meindl, J.R. (1991) 'The construction of leadership images in the popular press: The case of Donald Burr and People Express', *Administrative Science Quarterly*, 36: 521–55.

Chhokar, J.S., Brodbeck, F.C. and House, R.J. (eds) (2007) *Culture and Leadership across the World: The Globe Book of In-depth Studies of 25 Societies*. Mahwah, NJ: Lawrence Erlbaum.

Christensen, R.A. (1991) 'A personal perspective on tribal Alaska native gifted and talented education', *Journal of American Indian Education*, 31 (1): 10–14.

Ciulla, J.B. (1995) 'Leadership ethics: Mapping the territory', *Business Ethics Quarterly*, 5 (1): 5–28.

Ciulla, J.B. (1998) *Ethics: The Heart of Leadership*. Boston, MA: Praeger.

Ciulla, J.B. (2005) 'The state of leadership ethics and the work that lies ahead', *Business Ethics: A European Review*, 14 (4): 323–35.

Ciulla, J.B. and Forsyth, D.R. (2011) 'Leadership ethics', in A. Bryman, D. Collinson, K. Grint, B. Jackson and M. Uhl-Bien (eds), *Sage Handbook of Leadership*. London: Sage. pp. 227–39.

Clegg, S.R. (2006) 'Why is organization theory so ignorant? The neglect of total institutions', *Journal of Management Inquiry*, 15 (4): 426–30.

Cluley, R. (2008) 'The psychoanalytic relationship between leaders and followers', *Leadership*, 4 (2): 201–12.

Cohen, S.G. and Ledford, G.E. (1994) 'The effectiveness of self-managing teams: A field experiment', *Human Relations*, 47: 13–43.

Collins, D.B. (2001) 'Organizational performance: The future focus of leadership development programs', *The Journal of Leadership Studies*, 7 (4): 43–54.

Collins, J. (2001a) *Good to Great: Why Some Companies Make the Leap … and Others Don't*. New York: HarperCollins.

Collins, J. (2001b) 'Level 5 leadership: the triumph of humility and fierce resolve', *Harvard Business Review*, 79 (1): 67–76.

Collins, J. and Porras, J.I. (1995) *Built to Last: Successful Habits of Visionary Companies*. New York: HarperCollins.

Collinson, D. (2011) 'Critical leadership studies' in A. Bryman, D. Collinson, K. Grint, B. Jackson and M. Uhl-Bien (eds), *Sage Handbook of Leadership*. London: Sage. pp: 179–92.

Collinson, D.L. (2005a) 'Dialectics of leadership', *Human Relations*, 58 (11): 1419–42.

Collinson, D.L. (2005b) 'Questions of distance', *Leadership*, 1 (2): 235–50.

Collinson, D.L. (2006) 'Rethinking followership: A post-structuralist analysis of follower identities', *Leadership Quarterly*, 17 (2): 179–89.

Conger, J.A. (1989) *The Charismatic Leader: Behind the Mystique of Exceptional Leadership*. San Francisco, CA: Jossey-Bass.

Conger, J.A. (1990) 'The dark side of leadership', *Organizational Dynamics*, 19: 44–55.

Conger, J.A. (1991) 'Inspiring others: The language of leadership', *Academy of Management Executive*, 5 (1): 31–45.

Conger, J.A. (1992) *Learning to Lead: The Art of Transforming Managers into Leaders*. San Francisco, CA: Jossey-Bass.

Conger, J.A. (1996) 'The dark side of leadership', in R.M. Steers, L.W. Porter and G.A. Bigley (eds), *Motivation and Leadership at Work* (6th edn). New York: McGraw-Hill. pp. 658–71.

Craig, S.B. and Gustafson, S.B. (1998) 'Perceived leader integrity scale: An instrument for assessing employee perceptions of leader integrity', *Leadership Quarterly*, 9 (2): 127–45.

Daft, R.L. (1999) *Leadership Theory and Practice*. New York: The Dryden Press.

Dansereau, F. and Yammarino, F.J. (2006) 'Is more discussion about levels of analysis really necessary? When is such discussion sufficient?', *Leadership Quarterly*, 17 (5): 537–52.

Day, D. (2000) 'Leadership development: A review in context', *Leadership Quarterly*, 11 (4): 581–613.

Day, D. (2011) 'Leadership development', in A. Bryman, D. Collinson, K. Grint, B. Jackson and M. Uhl-Bien (eds), *Sage Handbook of Leadership*. London: Sage. pp. 37–50.

Day, D., Gronn, P. and Salas, E. (2004) 'Leadership capacity in teams', *Leadership Quarterly*, 15 (6): 857–80.

Deal, T.E. and Kennedy, A.A. (1982) *Corporate Cultures: The Rites and Rituals of Corporate Life*. New York: Addison-Wesley.

Den Hartog, D.N. and Dickson, M.W. (2004) 'Leadership and culture', in J. Antonakis, A.T. Cianciolo and R.J. Sternberg (eds), *The Nature of Leadership*. London: Sage. pp. 249–78.

Den Hartog, D.N., House, R.J., Hanges, P.J., Ruiz-Quintanilla, S.A., Dorfman, P.W., Field, R.H.G. et al. (1999) 'Culture-specific and cross-culturally generalizable implicit leadership theories: Are attributes of charismatic/transformational leadership universally endorsed?', *Leadership Quarterly*, 10 (2): 219–56.

Den Hartog, D.N., Van Muijen, J.J. and Koopman, P.L. (1997) 'Transactional versus transformational leadership: An analysis of the MLQ', *Journal of Occupational and Organizational Psychology*, 70 (1): 19.

Dent, E.B., Higgins, M.E. and Wharff, D.M. (2005) 'Spirituality and leadership: An empirical review of definitions, distinctions, and embedded assumptions', *The Leadership Quarterly*, 16 (5): 625–53.

Dickson, M.W., Den Hartog, D. and Mitchelson, J. (2003) 'Research on leadership in a cross-cultural context: Making progress, and raising new questions', *Leadership Quarterly*, 14 (6): 729–68.

Dickson, M.W., Resick, C.J. and Hanges, P.L. (2006) 'Systematic variations in organizationally-shared prototypes of effective leadership based on organizational form', *Leadership Quarterly*, 17 (5): 487–505.

Dionne, S.D., Yammarino, F.J., Howell, J.P. and Villa, J. (2005) 'Substitutes for leadership, or not', *Leadership Quarterly*, 16 (1): 169–93.

Dobson, J. (1999) *The Art of Management and the Aesthetic Manager: The Coming Way of Business*. Westport, CT: Quorum Books.

Doh, J.P. (2003) 'Can leadership be taught? Perspectives from management educators', *Academy of Management Learning and Education*, 2 (1): 54–68.

Dorfman, P.W. (2003) 'International and cross-cultural leadership research', in B.J. Punnett and O. Shenkar (eds), *Handbook for International Management Research*. Ann Arbor, MI: University of Michigan Press.

Drath, W. (2001) *The Deep Blue Sea: Rethinking the Source of Leadership*. San Francisco, CA: Jossey-Bass and Center for Creative Leadership.

Drucker, P. (1955) *The Practice of Management*. New York: Harper & Row.

Dvir, T., Eden, D., Avolio, B.J. and Shamir, B. (2002) 'Impact of transformational leadership on follower development and performance: A field experiment', *Academy of Management Journal*, 45 (4): 735–44.

Eagly, A.H. (1987) *Sex Differences in Social Behaviour: A Social-Role Interaction*. Hillsdale, NJ: Erlbaum.

Eagly, A.H., Johannesen-Schmidt, M.C. and van Engen, M. (2003) 'Transformational, transactional and laissez-faire leadership styles: A meta-analysis comparing women and men', *Psychological Bulletin*, 95: 569–91.

Eagly, A.H. and Johnson, B. (1990) 'Gender and leadership: A meta-analysis', *Psychological Bulletin*, 108: 233–56.

Eigel, K.M. and Kuhnert, K.W. (2005) 'Authentic development: Leadership development level and executive effectiveness', in W.L. Gardner, B.J. Avolio and F.O. Walumbwa (eds), *Authentic Leadership Theory and Practice: Origins, Effects, and Development* (Vol. 3). New York: Elsevier. pp. 357–85.

Elkin, G., Jackson, B. and Inkson, K. (2004) *Organizational Behaviour in New Zealand*. Auckland: Prentice-Hall.

Elmes, M. and Barry, M. (1999) 'Deliverance, denial, and the death zone: A study of narcissism and regression in the May 1996 Everest climbing disaster', *Journal of Applied Behavioral Science*, 35: 163–87.

Erakovic, L. and Jackson, B. (2009) 'Promoting leadership in governance and governance in leadership: Establishing a research agenda', *Proceedings of the the 13th Asian and Pacific Region Organisation Studies Conference, Monterrey, Mexico*.

Fairclough, N. (1992) *Discourse and Social Change*. Cambridge, UK: Polity Press.

Fairhurst, G.T. (2009) 'Considering context in discursive leadership research', *Human Relations*, 62: 1607–33.

Fairhurst, G.T. (2011) *The power of framing: Creating the language of leadership*. San Francisco, CA: Jossey-Bass.

Faris, N. and Parry, K.W. (2011, in press) 'Islamic organizational leadership within a western society: The problematic role of external context', *The Leadership Quarterly*, 22: in press.

Fernando, M. (2007) *Spiritual Leadership in the Entrepreneurial Business: A Multifaith Study*. Cheltenham: Edward Elgar.

Fernando, M. (2011) 'Spirituality and leadership', in A. Bryman, D. Collinson, K. Grint, B. Jackson and M. Uhl-Bien (eds), *Sage Handbook of Leadership*. London: Sage. pp. 481–92.

Fernando, M., Beale, F. and Geroy, G. (2009) 'The spiritual dimension in leadership at Dilmah Tea', *Leadership and Organization Development Journal*, 30 (6): 522–39.

Fiedler, F.E. (1967) *A Theory of Leadership Development*. New York: McGraw-Hill.

Fletcher, J.K. and Käufer, K. (2003) 'Shared leadership: Paradox and possibility', in C.L. Pearce and J.A. Conger (eds), *Shared Leadership: Reframing the Hows and Whys of Leadership*. Thousand Oaks, CA: Sage. pp. 21–47.

Follett, M.P. (1924) *Creative Experience*. New York: Longmans Green.

Foucault, M. (1977) *Discipline and Punish: The Birth of the Prison*. London: Allen Lane.

Foucault, M. (1980) *Power/Knowledge: Selected Interviews and Other Writings 1972–1977*. Brighton: Harvester Books.

Freud, S. (1921) 'Group psychology and the analysis of the ego', in J. Strachley (ed.), *The Standard Edition of the Complete Works of Sigmund Freud: Vol 28. Beyond the Pleasure Principle, Group Psychology and Other Works*. London: Hogarth Press. pp. 65–143.

Friedrich, T.L., Vessey, W.B., Schuelke, M.J., Ruark, G.A. and Mumford, M.D. (2009) 'A framework for understanding collective leadership: The selective utilization of leader and team expertise within networks', *The Leadership Quarterly*, 20 (6): 933–58.

Fry, L.W. (2003) 'Toward a theory of spiritual leadership', *Leadership Quarterly*, 14 (6): 693–727.

Fry, L.W. (2006) 'Toward a paradigm of spiritual leadership', *Leadership Quarterly*, 16 (5): 619–22.

Fry, L.W. and Cohen, M. (2009) 'Spiritual leadership as a paradigm for organizational transformation and recovery of extended work hours culture', *Journal of Business Ethics*, 84: 265–78.

Fullan, M. (2001) *Leading in a Culture of Change*. San Francisco, CA: Jossey-Bass.

Gabriel, Y. (1997) 'Meeting God: When organizational members come face to face with the supreme leader', *Human Relations*, 50 (4): 315–42.

Gabriel, Y. (2005) 'MBA and the education of leaders: The new playing fields of Eton?', *Leadership*, 1 (2): 147–63.

Gagliardi, P. (1996) 'Exploring the aesthetic side of organizational life', in S.R. Clegg, C. Hardy and W.R. Nord (eds), *Handbook of Organization Studies*. London: Sage. pp. 565–80.

Gardiner, M. and Tiggemann, M. (1999) 'Gender differences in leadership style, job stress and mental health in male and female-dominated industries', *Journal of Occupational and Organizational Psychology*, 72: 301–15.

Gardner, H. (1995) *Leading Minds*. New York: Basic Books.

Gardner, W.L. and Avolio, B.J. (1998) 'The charismatic relationship: A dramaturgical perspective', *Academy of Management Review*, 23: 32–58.

Gardner, W.L., Avolio, B.J., Luthans, F., May, D.R. and Walumbwa, F.O. (2005) 'Can you see the real me? A self-based model of authentic leader and follower development', *Leadership Quarterly*, 16 (3): 343–72.

Gardner, W.L., Avolio, B.J. and Walumbwa, F.O. (2005) *Authentic Leadership Theory and Practice: Origins, Effects, and Development*. New York: Elsevier.

Gardner, W.L. and Schermerhorn, J.R. (2004) 'Unleashing individual potential: Performance gains through positive organizational behavior and authentic leadership', *Organizational Dynamics*, 33 (3): 270–81.

Gemmill, G. and Oakley, J. (1992) 'Leadership: An alienating social myth?', *Human Relations*, 45 (2): 113–29.

George, B. (2003) *Authentic Leadership: Rediscovering the Secrets of Creating Lasting Value*. San Francisco, CA: Jossey-Bass.

George, B. and Sims, P. (2007) *True North: Discover Your Authentic Leadership*. San Francisco, CA: Jossey-Bass.

Giacalone, R., Jurkiewicz, C. and Fry, L. (2005) 'From advocacy to science: The next steps in workplace spirituality research', in R. Paloutzian and C. Park (eds), *Handbook of the Psychology of Religion and Spirituality*. New York: Guilford Press. pp. 515–28.

Goethals, G.R. (2005) 'The psychodynamics of leadership: Freud's insights and their vicissitudes', in D.M. Messick and R.M. Kramer (eds), *The Psychology of Leadership*. Mahwah, NJ: Lawrence Erlbaum Associates. pp. 97–112.

Goffee, R. and Jones, G. (2005) 'Managing authenticity: The paradox of great leadership', *Harvard Business Review*, December: 83 (12): 86–94.

Goffman, E. (1959) *The Presentation of Self in Everyday Life*. New York: Doubleday Anchor.

Goffman, E. (1961) *Asylums*. Harmondsworth, UK: Penguin.

Goldman, B.M. and Kernis, M.H. (2002) 'The role of authenticity in healthy psychological functioning and subjective well-being', *Annals of the American Psychotherapy Association*, 5 (Nov/Dec): 18–20.

Goleman, D. (1995) *Emotional Intelligence: Why It Can Matter More than IQ*. New York: Bantam.

Goleman, D. (1998) 'What makes a leader?', *Harvard Business Review*, 76: 92–102.

Gooderham, P. and Nordhaug, O. (2001) 'Are cultural differences in Europe on the decline?', *European Business Forum*, Winter.

Gordon, J. (1992) 'Work teams: How far have they come?', *Training*, October: 59–65.

Gordon, R. (2002) 'Viewing the dispersion of leadership through a power lens: Exposing unobtrusive tensions and problematic processes', in K.W. Parry and J. Meindl (eds), *Grounding Leadership Theory and Research: Issues, Perspectives, and Methods*. Greenwich, CT: Information Age Publishing. pp. 39–56.

Graen, G.B. (2006) 'In the eye of the beholder: Cross-cultural lessons in leadership from Project GLOBE. A response viewed from the Third Culture Bonding (TCB) model of cross-cultural leadership', *Academy of Management Perspectives*, 20 (4): 95–101.

Graen, G.B. and Hui, C. (1999) 'Transcultural global leadership in the twenty-first century: Challenges and implications for development', in W.H. Mobley (ed.), *Advances in Global Leadership* (Vol. 7). Stamford, CT: JAI Press. pp. 9–26.

Graen, G.B. and Uhl-Bien, M. (1995) 'Relationship-based approach to leadership: Development of leader-member-exchange (LMX) theory over 25 years: Applying a multi-level, multi-domain perspective', *Leadership Quarterly*, 6: 219–47.

Greenleaf, R.K. (1977) *Servant Leadership: A Journey into the Nature of Legitimate Power and Greatness*. New York: Paulist Press.

Grey, C. (2005) *A Very Short, Fairly Interesting and Reasonably Cheap Book about Studying Organizations*. London: Sage.

Grey, C. (2009) *A Very Short, Fairly Interesting and Reasonably Cheap Book About Studying Organizations* (2nd edn). London: Sage.

Griffey, E. and Jackson, B. (2010) 'The portrait as leader: Commissioned portraits and the power of tradition', *Leadership*, 6 (2): 1–25.

Grint, K. (2001) *The Arts of Leadership*. Oxford: Oxford University Press.

Grint, K. (2005a) *Leadership: Limits and Possibilities*. New York: Palgrave Macmillan.

Grint, K. (2005b) 'Problems, problems, problems: The social construction of leadership', *Human Relations*, 58 (11): 1467–94.

Grint, K. (2007) 'Learning to lead: Can Aristotle help us find the road to wisdom?', *Leadership*, 3 (2): 231–46.

Grint, K. (2011) 'A history of leadership', in A. Bryman, D. Collinson, K. Grint, B. Jackson and M. Uhl-Bien (eds), *Sage Handbook of Leadership*. London: Sage. pp. 3–14.

Gronn, P. (2002) 'Distributed leadership as a unit of analysis', *Leadership Quarterly*, 13 (4): 423–51.

Guillet de Monthoux, P. and Statler, M. (2008) 'Aesthetic play as an organizing principle', in D. Barry, and H. Hansen (eds), *Sage Handbook of New Approaches in Management and Organization*. London: Sage. pp. 423–35.

Gustafson, S.B. and Ritzer, D.R. (1995) 'The dark side of normal: A psychopathy-linked pattern called aberrant self-promotion', *European Journal of Personality*, 9: 147–83.

Guthey, E. (2005) 'Management studies, cultural criticism and American dreams', *Journal of Management Studies*, 42 (2): 451–66.

Guthey, E., Clark, T. and Jackson, B. (2009) *Demystifying Business Celebrity*. London: Routledge.

Guthey, E. and Jackson, B. (2005) 'CEO portraits and the authenticity paradox', *Journal of Management Studies*, 42 (5): 1057–82.

Guthey, E. and Jackson, B. (2011) 'Cross-cultural leadership revisited', in A. Bryman, D. Collinson, K. Grint, B. Jackson and M. Uhl-Bien (eds), *Sage Handbook of Leadership*. London: Sage. pp. 163–76.

Hall, E.T. and Hall, M.R. (1990) *Understanding Cultural Differences*. Yarmouth, ME: Intercultural Press.

Hambrick, D. and Mason, P. (1984) 'Upper echelons: The organization as a reflection of its top managers', *Academy of Management Review*, 9: 193–206.

Hanges, P.J. and Dickson, M.W. (2006) 'Agitation over aggregation: Clarifying the development of and the nature of the GLOE scales', *Leadership Quarterly*, 17 (5): 522–36.

Hannah, S.T., Uhl-Bien, M., Avolio, B.J. and Cavarretta, F.L. (2009) 'A framework for examining leadership in extreme contexts', *The Leadership Quarterly*, 20 (6): 897–919.

Hansen, H. and Bathurst, R. (2011) 'Aesthetics and leadership', in A. Bryman, D. Collinson, K. Grint, B. Jackson and M. Uhl-Bien (eds), *Sage Handbook of Leadership*. London: Sage. pp. 253–64.

Hansen, H., Ropo, A. and Sauer, E. (2007) 'Aesthetic leadership', *The Leadership Quarterly*, 18 (6): 544–60.

Hardy, C. (1994) 'Power and politics in organizations', in C. Hardy (ed.), *Managing Strategic Action: Mobilizing Change*. London: Sage. pp. 220–37.

Harter, S. (2002) 'Authenticity', in C.R. Snyder and S.J. Lopez (eds), *Handbook of Positive Psychology*. New York: Oxford University Press. pp. 382–94.

Harzing, A. (2006) 'Response styles in cross-national survey research: A 26-country study', *International Journal of Cross Cultural Management*, 6 (2): 123–41.

Haslam, S.A. and Ryan, M.K. (2008) 'The road to the glass cliff: Differences in the perceived suitability of men and women for leadership position in succeeding and failing organizations', *The Leadership Quarterly*, 19: 530–46.

Heenan, D.A. and Bennis, W. (1999) *Co-leaders: The Power of Great Partnerships*. New York: John Wiley & Sons.

Heifetz, R. (1994) *Leadership without Easy Answers*. Cambridge, MA: Harvard University Press.

Heifetz, R.A. and Laurie, D.L. (1997) 'The work of leadership', *Harvard Business Review*, January-February, 75 (1): 124–34.

Henry, E. and Pene, H. (2001) 'Kaupapa Maori: Locating indigenous ontology, epistemology and methodology in the academy', *Organization*, 8 (2): 234–42.

Hersey, P. and Blanchard, K. (1977) *The Management of Organizational Behaviour*. Englewood Cliffs, NJ: Prentice-Hall.

Hicks, D.A. (2002) 'Spiritual and religious diversity at the workplace: Implications for leadership', *Leadership Quarterly*, 13: 379–96.

Hickson, D.J. and Pugh, D.S. (2001) *Management Worldwide: Distinctive Styles amid Globalization*. London: Penguin.

Hock, D. (1999) *Birth of the Chaordic Age*. San Francisco, CA: Berrett-Koehler.

Hofstede, G. (1980) *Culture's Consequences: International Differences in Work-related Values*. Beverly Hills, CA: Sage.

Hofstede, G. (1991) *Cultures and Organizations: The Software of the Mind*. New York: McGraw-Hill.

Hofstede, G. (2002) 'Dimensions do not exist: A reply to Brendan McSweeney', *Human Relations*, 55 (11): 1355.

Hofstede, G. (2006) 'What did GLOBE really measure? Researchers' minds versus respondents' minds', *Journal of International Business Studies*, 37 (6): 882–96.

Hofstede, G. (2009) 'Who is the fairest of them all? Galit Ailon's mirror', *Academy of Management Review*, 33 (4): 570–2.

Hofstede, G. and Bond, M.H. (1988) 'The Confucius Connection: From cultural roots to economic growth', *Organizational Dynamics*, 16 (4): 4–21.

Hogg, M.A. (2005) 'Social identity and leadership', in D.M. Messick and R.M. Kramer (eds), *The Psychology of Leadership*. Hillsdale, NJ: Lawrence Erlbaum Associates. pp. 53–80.

Hogg, M.A., Fielding, K.S., Johnston, D., Masser, B., Russell, E. and Svensson, A. (2001) 'On glass ceilings and demographic disadvantage: Social identity and leadership in small groups'. Unpublished manuscript, University of Queensland Centre for Research on Group Processes, Brisbane, QCD Australia.

Hollander, E.P. (1958) 'Conformity, status, and idiosyncratic credit', *Psychology Review*, 65: 117–27.

Hollander, E.P. (1995) 'Ethical challenges in the leader–follower relationship', *Business Ethics Quarterly*, 5 (1): 55–65.

Holmes, J. (2007) 'Humour and the construction of Maori leadership at work', *Leadership*, 3 (1): 5–27.

Holmes, J. and Marra, M. (2004) 'Relational practice in the workplace: Women's talk or gendered discourse?', *Language in Society*, 33: 377–98.

Holmes, J., Marra, M., Vine, B., Pfeifer, D. and Jackson, B. (2008) 'Exploring co-leadership talk through interactional sociolinguistics', *Leadership*, 4 (3): 339–60.

Hooker, J. (2003) *Working across Cultures*. Stanford, CA: Stanford University Press.

Hosking, D.M. (1988) 'Organizing, leadership and skilful process', *Journal of Management Studies*, 25: 147–66.

Hosking, D.M. (1991) 'Chief executives, organising processes, and skill', *European Journal of Applied Psychology*, 41: 95–103.

Hosking, D.M. (2007) 'Not leaders, not followers: A post-modern discourse of leadership processes', in B. Shamir, R. Pillai, M. Bligh and M. Uhl-Bien (eds), *Follower-Centered Perspectives of Leadership: A Tribute to the Memory of James R. Meindl*. Greenwich, CT: Information Age Publishing. pp. 167–86.

House, R.J. (1971) 'A path–goal theory of leader effectiveness', *Administrative Science Quarterly*, 16: 321–39.

House, R.J. (1977) 'A 1976 theory of charismatic leadership', in J.G. Hunt and L.L Larson (eds), *Leadership: The Cutting Edge*. Carbondale, IL: Southern Illinois University Press. pp. 189–207.

House, R.J., Hanges, P., Javidan, M., Dorfman, P. and Gupta, V. (eds) (2004) *Culture, Leadership and Organizations: The GLOBE Study of 62 Societies*. Thousand Oaks, CA: Sage.

House, R.J. and Howell, J.M. (1992) 'Personality and charismatic leadership', *The Leadership Quarterly*, 3: 81–108.

House, R.J., Javidan, M., Dorfman, P.W. and De Luque, M.S. (2006) 'A failure of scholarship: Response to George Graen's critique of GLOBE', *Academy of Management Perspectives*, 20 (4): 102–14.

House, R.J., Javidan, M., Hanges, P. and Dorfman, P. (2002) 'Understanding cultures and implicit leadership theories across the globe: An introduction to project GLOBE', *Journal of World Business*, 37: 3–10.

Howell, J.P. and Mendez, M.J. (2008) 'Three perspectives on followership', in R.E. Riggio, I. Chaleff and J. Lipman-Blumen (eds), *The Art of Followership: How Great Followers Create Great Leaders and Organizations*. San Francisco, CA: Jossey-Bass. pp. 25–40.

Huczynski, A. and Buchanan, D. (2006) *Organizational Behaviour.* New York: Prentice-Hall.

Hughes, L.W. and Avey, J.B. (2009) 'Transforming with levity: Humour, leadership and follower attitudes', *Leadership & Organization Development Journal*, 30 (6): 540–62.

Hummel, R.P. (1975) 'Psychology of charismatic followers', *Psychological Reports*, 37: 759–70.

Huxham, C. and Vangen, S. (2000) 'Leadership in the shaping and implementation of collaboration agendas: How things happen in a (not quite) joined up world', *Academy of Management Journal*, 43 (6): 1159–75.

Iles, P. and Preece, D. (2006) 'Developing leaders or leadership? The Academy of Chief Executives' programmes in the North East of England', *Leadership*, 2 (3): 317–40.

Ilies, R., Morgeson, F.P. and Nahrgang, J.D. (2005) 'Authentic leadership and eudaemonic well-being: Understanding leader–follower outcomes', *Leadership Quarterly*, 16 (3): 373–94.

Jackall, R. (1988) *Moral Mazes.* Oxford: Oxford University Press.

Jackson, B. (2001) *Management Gurus and Management Fashions: A Dramatistic Inquiry.* London: Routledge.

Jackson, B. and Parry, K.W. (2001) *The Hero Manager: Learning from New Zealand's Top Chief Executives.* Auckland: Penguin.

Javidan, M., Teagarden, M. and Bowen, D. (2010) 'Making it overseas', *Harvard Business Review*, 88 (4): 109–13.

Jepson, D. (2009) 'Studying leadership at cross-country level: A critical analysis', *Leadership*, 5 (1): 61–80.

Jones, A.M. (2005) 'The anthropology of leadership: Culture and corporate leadership in the American South', *Leadership*, 9 (1): 259–78.

Jones, A.M. (2006) 'Developing what? An anthropological look at the leadership development process across cultures', *Leadership*, 2 (2): 481–98.

Judge, T.A., Bono, J.E., Ilies, R. and Gerhardt, M.W. (2002) 'Personality and leadership: A qualitative and quantitative review', *Journal of Applied Psychology*, 87 (4): 765–80.

Judge, T.A., Piccolo, R.F. and Kosalka, T. (2009) 'The bright and dark sides of leaders traits: A review and theoretical extension of the leader trait paradigm, *Leadership Quarterly*, 20: 855–75.

Jung, D., Yammarino, F.J. and Lee, J.K. (2009) 'Moderating the role of subordinates' attitudes on transformational leadership and effectiveness: A multi-cultural and multi-level perspective', *Leadership Quarterly*, 20: 586–603.

Kanter, R.M. (1977) *Men and Women of the Corporation.* New York: Basic Books.

Kanter, R.M. and Corn, R.I. (1994) 'Do cultural differences make a business difference? Contextual factors affecting cross-cultural relationship success', *Journal of Management Development*, 13 (2): 5–23.

Keller, T. (2003) 'Parental images as a guide to leadership sensemaking: an attachment perspective on implicit leadership theories', *Leadership Quarterly*, 14 (2): 141–60.

Kellerman, B. (2004) *Bad Leadership*. Boston, MA: Harvard Business Press.

Kellerman, B. and Webster, S.W. (2001) 'The recent literature on public leadership: Reviewed and considered', *Leadership Quarterly*, 12 (4): 485–514.

Kelley, R.E. (1988) 'In praise of followers', *Harvard Business Review*, 66 (6): 141–8.

Kelley, R.E. (1992) *The Power of Followership: How to Create Leaders People Want to Follow and Followers Who Lead Themselves*. New York: Doubleday.

Kelloway, E.K., Barling, J. and Helleur, J. (2000) 'Enhancing transformational leadership: the roles of training and feedback', *The Leadership & Organizational Development Journal*, 21 (3): 145–9.

Kempster, S. (2006) 'Leadership learning through lived experience', *Journal of Management and Organization*, 12 (1): 4–22.

Kempster, S., Jackson, B. and Conroy, M. (in press) 'Leadership as purpose: Exploring the role of purpose in leadership practice', *Leadership*.

Kernis, M.H. (2003) 'Toward a conceptualization of optimal self-esteem', *Psychological Inquiry*, 14 (1): 1–26.

Kerr, S. and Jermier, J. (1978) 'Substitutes for leadership: Their meaning and measurement', *Organizational Behavior and Human Performance*, 22: 374–403.

Kessler, E.H. and Wong-MingJi, D.J. (eds) (2009) *Cultural Mythology and Global Leadership*. Cheltenham, UK: Edward Elgar.

Kets de Vries, M. (2004) 'Putting leaders on the couch', *Harvard Business Review*, January, (82: 1).

Kets de Vries, M. (2006) *The Leader on the Couch*. Chichester, West Sussex: Jossey-Bass.

Kets de Vries, M. and Balazs, K. (2011) 'The shadow side of leadership', in A. Bryman, D. Collinson, K. Grint, B. Jackson and M. Uhl-Bien (eds), *Sage Handbook of Leadership*. London: Sage. pp. 378–90.

Kets de Vries, M.F.R. and Engellau, E. (2004) *Are Leaders Born or Are they Made?* London: Karnac.

Kets de Vries, M.F.R. and Miller, D. (1985) 'Narcissism and leadership: An object relations perspective', *Human Relations*, 38 (6): 583–601.

Khoo, S.W. and Burch, G. (2008) 'The "dark side" of leadership personality and transformational leadership: An exploratory study', *Personality and Individual Differences*, 44 (1): 86–97.

Kluckhohn, F. and Strodtbeck, F.L. (1961) *Variations in Value Orientations*. Westport, CT: Greenwood Press.

Knights, D. and Willmott, H. (1992) 'Conceptualizing leadership processes: A study of senior managers in a financial services company', *Journal of Management Studies*, 29: 761–82.

Kotter, J.P. (1990) *A Force for Change: How Leadership Differs from Management*. New York: The Free Press.

Kouzes, J.M. and Posner, B.Z. (1998) *Encouraging the Heart*. San Francisco, CA: Jossey-Bass.

Kraidy, M. (2005) *Hybridity, or the Cultural Logic of Globalization*, Philadelphia, PA: Temple University Press.

Krakauer, J. (1997) *Into Thin Air: A Personal Account of the Mount Everest Disaster*. New York: Anchor Books.

Krantz, J. (2006) 'Leadership, betrayal and adaptation', *Human Relations*, 59 (2): 221–40.

Kriger, M. and Seng, Y. (2005) 'Leadership with inner meaning: A contingency theory of leadership based on the worldviews of five religions', *The Leadership Quarterly*, 16 (5): 771–806.

Kunda, G. (1992) *Engineering Culture: Control and Commitment in a High-Tech Corporation*. Philadelphia, PA: Temple University Press.

Ladkin, D. (2006) 'The enchantment of the charismatic leader: Charisma reconsidered as aesthetic encounter', *Leadership*, 2 (2): 165–79.

Ladkin, D. (2008) 'Leading beautifully: How mastery, congruence and purpose create the aesthetic of embodied leadership practice', *The Leadership Quarterly*, 19 (1): 31–41.

Ladkin, D. and Taylor, S.V. (2010) 'Enacting the "true self": Towards a theory of embodied authentic leadership', *Leadership Quarterly*, 21: 64–74.

Levy, L. (2004) 'The call for leadership', *University of Auckland Business Review*, 6 (1): 1–8.

Liden, R.C. and Antonakis, J. (2009) 'Considering context in psychological leadership research', *Human Relations*, 62: 1587–605.

Ligon, G.S., Hunter, S.T. and Mumford, M.D. (2008) 'Development of outstanding leadership: A life narrative approach', *The Leadership Quarterly*, 19 (3): 312–34.

Lindholm, C. (2002) *Charisma*. Self-published PDF version.

Link, W., Corral, T. and Gerzon, M. (2006) *Leadership is Global*. San Francisco: Shinnyo-en Foundation.

Linstead, S., Fulop, L. and Lilley, S. (2004) *Management and Organization: A Critical Text*. New York: Palgrave.

Lipman-Blumen, J. (2007) 'Toxic leaders and the fundamental vulnerability of being alive', in B. Shamir, R. Pillai, M.C. Bligh and M. Uhl-Bien (eds), *Follower-Centered Perspectives on Leadership*. Greenwich, CT: Information Age Publishing. pp. 1–17.

Locke, E.A. (2003) 'Leadership: Starting at the top', in C.L. Pearce and J.A. Conger (eds), *Shared Leadership: Reframing the Hows and Whys of Leadership*. Thousand Oaks, CA: Sage. pp. 271–84.

Lord, R.G. (1985) 'An information processing approach to social perceptions, leadership perceptions and behavioural measurement of organizational settings', in B.M. Staw and L. Cummings (eds), *Research in Organizational Behaviour*. Greenwich, CT: JAI Press. pp. 87–108.

Lord, R.G. and Mayer, K.G. (1991) *Leadership and Information Processing: Linking Perceptions and Performances*. Boston, MA: Unwin Hyman.

Luthans, F. (2002) 'The need for and meaning of positive organizational behavior', *Journal of Organizational Behavior*, 23 (6): 695–706.

Luthans, F. and Avolio, B.J. (2003) 'Authentic leadership development', in K.S. Cameron, J.E. Dutton and R.E. Quinn (eds), *Positive Organizational Scholarship: Foundations of a New Discipline*. San Francisco, CA: Berrett-Koehler Publishers. pp. 241–58.

Luthans, F. and Avolio, B.J. (2009) 'The "point" of positive organizational behavior', *Journal of Organizational Behavior*, 30 (2): 291–307.

Luthans, F., Luthans, K.W., Hodgetts, R.M. and Luthans, B.C. (2001) 'Positive approach to leadership (PAL): Implications for today's organizations', *Journal of Leadership Studies*, 8 (2): 3–20.

Lynham, S.A. (2000) 'The development of a theory of responsible leadership for performance'. St. Paul, MN: University of Minnesota, Human Resource Development Research Centre.

Maak, T. (2007) 'Responsible leadership, stakeholder engagement, and the emergence of social capital', *Journal of Business Ethics*, 4: 329–43.

Maccoby, M. (2000) 'Narcissistic leaders: The incredible pros, the inevitable cons', *Harvard Business Review*, 78 (1): 68–77.

Manz, C.C. and Sims, H.P. (1991) 'SuperLeadership: Beyond the myth of heroic leadership', *Organizational Dynamics*, 19: 18–35.

Martin, J. (1993) *Cultures in Organizations: Three Perspectives*. New York: Oxford University Press.

Maslow, A. (1968) *Towards a Psychology of Being*. New York: Van Nostrand.

Mayer, D.M., Kuenzi, M., Greenbaum, R., Bardes, M. and Salvador, R. (2009) 'How low does ethical leadership flow? Test of a trickle-down model', *Organizational Behaviour and Human Decision Process*, 108: 11–13.

Mayo, M., Meindl, J.R. and Pastor J.C. (2003) 'Shared leadership in work teams', in C.L. Pearce and J.A Conger (eds), *Shared Leadership: Reframing the Hows and Whys of Leadership*. Thousand Oaks, CA: Sage. pp. 193–214.

McCall, M. and Lombardo, M.M. (1988) *The Lessons of Experience*. Lexington, MA: Lexington Books.

McCallum, S. and O'Connor, D. (2009) 'Social capital and leadership development: Building stronger leadership through enhanced relational skills', *Leadership and Organization Development Journal*, 30 (2): 152–66.

McDonald, P. (2009) 'The potential contribution of neuroscience to authentic leadership', *NeuroLeadership Journal*, 2: 53–66.

McSweeney, B. (2002a) 'Hofstede's model of national cultural differences and their consequences: A triumph of faith – a failure of analysis', *Human Relations*, 55 (1): 89–118.

McSweeney, B. (2002b) 'The essentials of scholarship: A reply to Geert Hofstede', *Human Relations*, 55 (11): 1363.

Mead, R. (1994) *International Management: Cross-Cultural Dimensions*. Oxford: Blackwell.

Meek, V.L. (1988) 'Organizational culture: Origins and weaknesses', *Organization Studies*, 9: 453–73.

Meindl, J.R. (1993) 'Reinventing leadership: A radical social psychological approach', in J.D. Murningham (ed.), *Social Psychology in Organizations*. Englewood Cliffs, NJ: Prentice-Hall. pp. 89–118.

Meindl, J.R. (1995) 'The romance of leadership as a follower-centric theory: A social constructionist approach', *Leadership Quarterly*, 6 (3): 329–41.

Meindl, J.R. and Ehrlich, S.B. (1987) 'The romance of leadership and the evaluation of organizational   performance', *Academy of Management Journal*, 30 (1): 91–109.

Meindl, J.R. and Ehrlich, S.B. (1988) 'Developing a "romance of leadership" scale', *Proceedings of the Eastern Academy of Management*.

Meindl, J.R., Ehrlich, S.B. and Dukerich, J.M. (1985) 'The romance of leadership', *Administrative Science Quarterly*, 30 (1): 78–102.

Meindl, J.R., Pastor, J.C. and Mayo, M. (2004) 'Romance of leadership', in G.R. Goethals, G.J. Sorenson and J.M. Burns (eds), *Encyclopedia of Leadership* (Vol. 3). Thousand Oaks, CA: Sage. pp. 233–45.

Messick, D.M. (2005) 'On the psychological exchange between leaders and followers', in D.M. Messick and R.M. Kramer (eds), *The Psychology of Leadership*. Hillsdale, NJ: Lawrence Erlbaum Associates. pp. 81–96.

Michalko, M. (2001) *Cracking Creativity: The Secrets of Creative Genius for Business and Beyond*. Berkeley, CA: Ten Speed Press.

Michie, S. and Gooty, J. (2005) 'Values, emotions, and authenticity: Will the real leader please stand up?', *Leadership Quarterly*, 16 (3): 441–57.

Mitroff, I. and Denton, E. (1999) 'A study of spirituality in the workplace', *Sloan Management Review*, 40 (4): 83–92.

Mobley, W.H. and Weldon, E. (2006) *Advances in Global Leadership* (Vol. 4). New York: Elsevier/JAI Press.

Mumby, D.K. and Clair, R.P. (1997) 'Organizational discourse', in T.A. van Dijk (ed.), *Discourse as Social Interaction*. London: Sage. pp. 181–205.

Mumford, M.D., Antes, A.L., Caughron, J.J. and Friedrich, T.L. (2008) 'Charismatic, ideological, and pragmatic leadership: Multi-level influences on emergence and performance', *The Leadership Quarterly*, 19 (2): 144–60.

Mumford, M.D. and Van Doorn, J. (2001) 'The leadership of pragmatism: Reconsidering Franklin in the age of charisma', *Leadership Quarterly*, 12: 279–310.

Nana, E., Burch, G. and Jackson, B. (2010) 'Attributing leadership personality and effectiveness from leaders' faces: An exploratory study', *Leadership and Organizational Development Journal*, 31 (8): 720–42.

Neale, J. (2001) 'Against the odds: Combining family and the leadership role', in K.W. Parry (ed.), *Leadership in the Antipodes: Findings, Implications and a Leader Profile*. Wellington, NZ: Institute of Policy Studies and the Centre for the Study of Leadership. pp. 141–65.

Nielsen, J. (2004) *The Myth of Leadership: Creating Leaderless Organizations*. Palo Alto, CA: Davies-Black.

O'Connell, W. and Bligh, B. (2009) 'Emerging from ethical scandal: Can corruption have a happy ending?', *Leadership*, 5 (2): 213–35.

O'Toole, J., Galbraith, J. and Lawler, E.E. (2003) 'The promise and pitfalls of shared leadership', in C.L. Pearce and J.A. Conger (eds), *Shared Leadership: Reframing the Hows and Whys of Leadership*. Thousand Oaks, CA: Sage. pp. 250–67.

Offerman, L.R. (2004) 'When followers become toxic', *Harvard Business Review*, January: 82 (1): 55–60.

Osborn, R.N., Hunt, J.G. and Jauch, L.R. (2002) 'Toward a contextual theory of leadership', *Leadership Quarterly*, 13 (6): 797–837.

Osland, J. and Bird, A. (2000) 'Beyond sophisticated stereotyping: Cultural sensemaking in context', *Academy of Management Executive*, 14 (1): 65–77.

Osland, J.S., Bird, A., Delano, J. and Jacob, M. (2000) 'Beyond sophisticated stereotyping: Cultural sensemaking in context', *Academy of Management Executive*, 14 (1): 65–79.

Ospina, S. and Foldy, E. (2009) 'A critical review of race and ethnicity in the leadership literature: Surfacing context, power and the collective dimension of leadership', *Leadership Quarterly*, 20: 876–96.

Ospina, S. and Su, C. (2009) 'Weaving color lines: Race, ethnicity, and the work of leadership in social change organizations', *Leadership*, 5 (2): 131–70.

Oswick, C., Keenoy, T. and Grant, D. (2002) 'Metaphors and analogical reasoning in organization theory: Beyond orthodoxy', *Academy of Management Review*, 27 (2): 294–303.

Ottensmeyer, E. (1996) 'Too strong to stop, too sweet to lose: Aesthetics as a way to know organizations', *Organization*, 3 (2): 189–94.

Padilla, A., Hogan, R. and Kaiser, R.B. (2007) 'The toxic triangle: Destructive leaders, susceptible followers, and conducive environments', *The Leadership Quarterly*, 18 (3): 176–94.

Palmer, I. and Hardy, C. (2001) *Thinking about Management*. Thousand Oaks, CA: Sage.

Parry, K.W. (1999) 'Enhancing adaptability: Leadership strategies to accommodate change in local government settings', *Journal of Organizational Change Management*, 12 (2): 134–56.

Parry, K.W. (2004) *Becoming a Transformational Leader*. Brisbane: Management Press.

Parry, K.W. (2008) 'The thing about metaphors and leadership', *International Leadership Journal*, 1 (1): 6–23.

Parry, K.W. (2009) 'Leadership comes from within', *Australian Financial Review*, 19 October, p. 28.

Parry, K.W. and Bryman, A. (2006) 'Leadership in organizations', in S. Clegg, C. Hardy and W. Nord (eds), *Handbook of Organization Studies* (2nd edn). London: Sage. pp. 447–68.

Parry, K.W. and Proctor-Thomson, S.B. (2002) 'Perceived integrity of transformational leaders in organizational settings', *Journal of Business Ethics*, 35 (2): 75–96.

Parry, K.W. and Proctor-Thomson, S.B. (2003) 'Leadership, culture and performance: The case of the New Zealand public sector', *Journal of Change Management*, 3 (4): 376–99.

Parry, K.W. and Sinha, P. (2005) 'Researching the trainability of transformational organizational leadership', *Human Resource Development International*, 8 (2): 165–83.

Parsons, T. and Shils, E.A. (1951) *Towards a General Theory of Action*. Cambridge, MA: Harvard University Press.

Pearce, C.L. and Conger, J.A. (eds) (2003) *Shared Leadership: Reframing the Hows and Whys of Leadership*. Thousand Oaks, CA: Sage.

Pearce, C.L. and Sims, H.P. (2000) 'Shared leadership: Toward a multi-level theory of leadership', *Advances in the Interdisciplinary Studies of Work Teams*, 7: 115–39.

Pearson, C.A.L. (1992) 'Autonomous work-groups: An evaluation at an industrial site', *Human Relations*, 45: 905–36.

Peters, T. and Austin, N. (1985) *A Passion for Excellence: The Leadership Difference*. New York: HarperCollins.

Peterson, M.F. and Castro, S.L. (2006) 'Measurement metrics at aggregate levels of analysis: Implications of organization culture research and the GLOBE Project', *Leadership Quarterly*, 17 (5): 506–21.

Pfeffer, J. (1977) 'The ambiguity of leadership', *Academy of Management Review*, 2: 104–12.

Pfeffer, J. and Salancik, G.R. (1978) *The External Control of Organizations: A Resource Dependency Perspective*. New York: Harper & Row.

Pfeifer, D., Love, M. and Jackson, B. (2006) 'Exploring intra-national cross-cultural leadership: The case of New Zealand Aotearoa'. Paper presented at the Academy of Management Meeting, Atlanta, GA, August 11–16.

Phillips, N., Sewell, G. and Jaynes, S. (2008) 'Applying critical discourse analysis in strategic management research', *Organizational Research Methods*, 11 (4): 770–89.

Podsakoff, P.M., MacKenzie, S.B., Moorman, R.H. and Fetter, R. (1990) 'Transformational leader behaviours and their effects on followers' trust in leader, satisfaction, and organizational citizenship behaviors', *Leadership Quarterly*, 1: 107–42.

Popper, M. (2001) *Hypnotic Leadership: Leaders, Followers, and the Loss of Self*. Westport, CT: Praeger.

Porter, L.W. and McLaughlin, G.B. (2006) 'Leadership and the organizational context: Like the weather?', *Leadership Quarterly*, 17 (6): 559–76.

Post, J.M. (1986) 'Narcissism and the charismatic leader–follower relationship', *Political Psychology*, 7 (4): 675–87.

Prasso, S. and Dawson, C. (2001) 'POW! BAM! ZAP! Meet Nissan's Superhero', *Business Week*, 3730: 12.

Price, T.L. (2000) 'Explaining ethical failures in leadership', *Leadership and Organizational Development Journal*, 21 (4): 177–84.

Price, T.L. (2005) *Understanding Ethical Failures in Leadership*. Cambridge: Cambridge University Press.

Prince, L. (2005) 'Eating the menu rather than the dinner: Tao and leadership', *Leadership*, 1 (1): 105–26.

Pye, A. (2005) 'Leadership and organizing: Sense-making in action', *Leadership*, 1 (1): 31–50.

Raelin, J. (2003) *Creating Leaderful Organizations: How to Bring out Leadership in Everyone*. San Francisco, CA: Berrett-Koehler.

Reave, L. (2005) 'Spiritual values and practices related to leadership effectiveness', *Leadership Quarterly*, 16 (5): 655–87.

Reeves, B., Malone, T.W. and O'Driscoll, T. (2008) 'Leadership's online labs', *Harvard Business Review*, May: 86 (5): 3–14.

Riggio, R.E., Chaleff, I. and Lipman-Blumen, J. (eds) (2008) *The Art of Followership: How Great Followers Create Great Leaders and Organizations*. San Francisco, CA: Jossey-Bass.

Ringleb, A.H. and Rock, D. (2008) 'The emerging field of Neuro-Leadership', *NeuroLeadership Journal*, 1: 3–19.

Rogers, C.R. (1963) 'The actualizing tendency in relation to "motives" and to consciousness', in M.R. Jones (ed.), *Nebraska Symposium on Motivation* (Vol. 11). Lincoln, NB: University of Nebraska Press. pp. 1–24.

Ropo, A. and Eriksson, M. (1997) 'Managing a theatre production: Conflict, communication, and competence', in M. Fitzgibbon and A. Kelly (eds), *From Maestro to Manager: Critical Issues in Arts and Culture Management*. Dublin: Oak Tree Press.

Ropo, A., Parviainen, J. and Koivunen, N. (2002) 'Aesthetics in leadership: From absent bodies to social bodily presence', in K.W. Parry and J.R. Meindl (eds), *Grounding Leadership Theory and Research: Issues, Perspectives and Methods*. Greenwich, CT: Information Age Publishing. pp. 21–38.

Rosener, J.B. (1997) 'Sexual static', in K. Grint (ed.), *Leadership: Classical, Contemporary and Critical Approaches*. Oxford: Oxford University Press. pp. 211–33.

Rosenthal, S.A. and Pittinsky, T.L. (2006) 'Narcisstic leadership', *Leadership Quarterly*, 17: 617–33.

Rost, J.C. (1993) *Leadership for the Twenty-First Century*. Westport, CT: Praeger.

Rost, J.C. (2008) 'Followership: An outmoded concept', in R.E. Riggio, I. Chaleff and J. Lipman-Blumen (eds), *The Art of Followership: How Great Followers Create Great Leaders and Organizations*. San Francisco, CA: Jossey-Bass. pp. 53–64.

Rule, N. and Ambady, N. (2008) 'The face of success: Inferences from chief executive officers' appearance predict company profits', *Psychological Science*, 19: 109–11.

Rule, N.O. and Ambady, N. (2009) 'She's got the look: Inferences from female chief executive officers' faces predict their success', *Sex Roles*, 61: 644–52.

Sally, D. (2002) 'Co-leadership: Lessons from republican Rome', *California Management Review*, 44: 65–83.

Sashkin, M. (1988) 'The visionary leader', in J.A. Conger and R.N. Kanungo (eds), *Charismatic Leadership: The Elusive Factor in Organizational Effectiveness*. San Francisco, CA: Jossey-Bass.

Sass, J.S. (2000) 'Characterizing organizational spirituality: An organizational communication culture approach', *Communication Studies*, 51: 195–207.

Schein, E.H. (2004) *Organizational Culture and Leadership* (3rd edn). San Francisco, CA: Jossey-Bass.

Schneider, A. (2004) *Tony Soprana on Management: Leadership Lessons Inspired by America's Favourite Mobster*, NY: Berkley.

Schneider, B. (1987) 'The people make the place', *Personnel Psychology*, 40: 437–53.

Schwartz, S.H. (1999) 'Cultural value differences: Some implications for work', *Applied Psychology: An International Review*, 48: 23–48.

Schyns, B. and Hansbrough, T. (eds) (2010) *When Leadership Goes Wrong: Destructive Leadership, Mistakes and Ethical Failures*. Charlotte, NC: Information Age Publishing.

Schyns, B. and Meindl, J.R. (2005) *Implicit Leadership Theories*. Greenwich, CT: Information Age Publishing.

Seligman, M.E.P. and Csikszentmihalyi, M. (2000) 'Positive psychology: An introduction', *American Psychologist*, 55: 5–14.

Sendjaya, S. and Sarros, J.C. (2002) 'Servant leadership: Charting its origin, development and application in the organization', *Journal of Leadership & Organizational Studies*, 9 (2): 57–64.

Shackleton, E. (1999) *South: The Endurance Expedition*. New York: Signet.

Shamir, B. (1992) 'Attribution of influence and charisma to the leader: The romance of leadership revisited', *Journal of Applied Social Psychology*, 22: 386–407.

Shamir, B. (2007) 'From passive recipients to active co-producers', in B. Shamir, R. Pillai, M.C. Bligh and M. Uhl-Bien (eds), *Follower-Centered Perspectives on Leadership*. Greenwich, CT: Information Age Publishing. pp. ix–xxxix.

Shamir, B. and Eilam, G. (2005) 'What's your story? A life-stories approach to authentic leadership development', *Leadership Quarterly*, 16 (3): 395–417.

Shamir, B., House, R.J. and Arthur, M.B. (1993) 'The motivational effects of charismatic leadership: A self-concept based theory', *Organisation Science*, 4 (4): 577–94.

Shamir, B. and Howell, J.M. (1999) 'Organizational and contextual influences on the emergence and effectiveness of charismatic leadership', *Leadership Quarterly*, 10 (2): 257–83.

Shamir, B. and Lapidot, Y. (2003) 'Shared leadership in the management of group boundaries', in C.L. Pearce and J.A. Conger (eds), *Shared Leadership: Reframing the Hows and Whys of Leadership*. Thousand Oaks, CA: Sage. pp. 235–49.

Shamir, B., Pillai, R., Bligh, M.C. and Uhl-Bien, M. (eds) (2007) *Follower-Centered Perspectives on Leadership*. Greenwich, CT: Information Age Publishing.

Shane, S., Venkataraman, V. and MacMillan, I. (1995) 'Cultural differences in innovation championing roles', *Journal of Management*, 26: 931–52.

Shaw, J.B. (1990) 'A cognitive categorization model for the study of intercultural management', *Academy of Management Review*, 15: 626–45.

Sims, H.P. and Lorenzi, P. (1992) *The New Leadership Paradigm*. Newbury Park, CA: Sage.

Sinclair, A. (2005) 'Body possibilities in leadership', *Leadership*, 1 (4): 387–406.

Sinclair, A. (2007) *Leadership for the Disillusioned*. Crows Nest, NSW: Allen & Unwin.

Smircich, L. (1993) 'Concepts of culture and organizational analysis', *Administrative Science Quarterly*, 28: 339–58.

Smircich, L. and Morgan, G. (1982) 'Leadership: The management of meaning', *Journal of Applied Behavioural Science*, 18: 257–73.

Smith, J.A. and Rayment, J.J. (2007) 'The Global SMP Fitness Framework: A guide for leaders exploring the relevance of spirituality in the workplace', *Management Decision*, 45 (2): 217–34.

Smith, M.A. and Canger, J.M. (2004) 'Effects of superior "big five" personality on subordinates attitudes', *Journal of Business and Psychology*, 18 (4): 465–81.

Smith, P.B. (2006) 'When elephants fight, the grass gets trampled: The GLOBE and Hofstede projects', *Journal of International Business Studies*, 37 (6): 915–21.

Søderberg, A.-M. and Holden, N. (2002) 'Rethinking cross-cultural management in a globalizing business world', *International Journal of Cross-Cultural Management*, 2 (1): 103–21.

Sonnenfeld, J.A. and Ward, A. (2007) *Firing Back: How Great Leaders Rebound after Career Setbacks*. Cambridge, MA: HBS Press.

Sosik, J., Avolio, B. and Kahai, S. (1997) 'Effects of leadership style and anonymity on group potency and effectiveness in a group decision support system environment', *Journal of Applied Psychology*, 82 (1): 89–103.

Stafsudd, A. (2004) 'People are strange when you're a stranger: Senior executives select similar successors', *European Management Review*, 3: 177–89.

Starratt, R.J. (1993) *The Drama of Leadership*. London: Falmer Press.

Stech, E.L. (2004) 'Psychodynamic approach', in P.G. Northouse (ed.), *Leadership Theory and Practice*. London: Sage. pp. 235–63.

Stewart, C. (2007) *Creolization: History, Ethnography, Theory*. Walnut Creek, CA: Left Coast Press.

Stogdill, R.M. (1974) *Handbook of Leadership*. New York: The Free Press.

Storey, J. (2004) 'Changing theories of leadership and leadership development', in J. Storey (ed.), *Leadership in Organizations: Current Issues and Key Trends*. London: Routledge. pp. 11–37.

Strang, E.E. and Kuhnert, K.W. (2009) 'Personality and leadership developmental levels as predictors of leader performance', *The Leadership Quarterly*, 20 (3): 421–33.

Strati, A. (1992) 'Aesthetic understanding of organizational life', *Academy of Management Review*, 17 (3): 568–81.

Tayeb, M.H. (1996) 'Conducting research across cultures: Overcoming drawbacks and obstacles', *International Journal of Cross-Cultural Management*, 1 (9): 91–108.

Taylor, S. (2002) 'Overcoming aesthetic muteness: Researching organizational members' aesthetic experience', *Human Relations*, 55 (7): 821–40.

Thomas, D. and Inkson, K. (2004) *Cultural Intelligence: People Skills for Global Business*. San Francisco, CA: Berrett-Koehler.

Tichy, N. and Devanna, M.A. (1986) *The Transformational Leader*, NY: Wiley.

Ting-Toomey, S. (1988) 'Intercultural conflict styles', in Y. Kim and W. Gudykunst (eds), *Theories in Intercultural Communication*. Thousand Oaks, CA: Sage. pp. 213–35.

Tourish, D., and Vatcha, N. (2005) 'Charismatic leadership and corporate cultism at Enron: The elimination of dissent, the promotion of conformity and organizational collapse', *Leadership*, 1 (4): 455–80.

Tourish, D.T., Craig, R. and Amernic, J. (2010) 'Transformational leadership education and agency perspectives in business school pedagogy: A marriage on inconvenience', *British Journal of Management*, 21: S40–59.

Tourish, D.T. and Tourish, N. (2010) 'Spirituality at work, and its implications for leadership and followership: A post-structuralist perspective', *Leadership*, 6 (2): 207–24.

Triandis, H. (1980) *Handbook of Cross-Cultural Psychology*. Boston, MA: Allyn & Bacon.

Trompenaars, F. and Hampden-Turner, C. (1997) *Riding the Waves of Culture: Understanding Cultural Diversity in Business*. London: Nicholas Brealey.

Turner, V. (1974) *Dramas, Fields, and Metaphors*. Ithaca, NY, and London: Cornell University Press.

Uhl-Bien, M. (2006) 'Relational leadership theory: Exploring the social processes of leadership and organising', *Leadership Quarterly*, 17: 654–76.

Uhl-Bien, M. and Pillai, R. (2007) 'The romance of leadership and the social construction of followership', in B. Shamir, R. Pillai, M.C. Bligh and M. Uhl-Bien (eds), *Follower-Centred Perspectives on Leadership*. Greenwich, CT: Information Age Publishing. pp. 187–209.

Van Knippenberg, D. and De Cremer, D. (2008) 'Leadership and fairness: Taking stock and looking ahead', *European Journal of Work and Psychology*, 17 (2): 173–9.

Van Knippenberg, D. and Hogg, M.A. (2003) 'A social identity model of leadership effectiveness in organizations', in B.M. Staw and R.M. Kramer (eds), *Research in Organizational Behaviour* (Vol. 25). New York: Elsevier. pp. 243–95.

Van Vugt, M., Hogan, R. and Kaiser, R.B. (2008) 'Leadership, followership and evolution', *American Psychologist*, 63 (3): 182–96.

Vroom, V.H. and Yetton, P.W. (1973) *Leadership and Decision-making*. Pittsburgh, PA: University of Pittsburgh Press.

Waldman, D.A., Bass, B.M. and Yammarino, F.J. (1990) 'Adding to contingent reward behaviour: The augmenting effect of charismatic leadership', *Group and Organization Studies*, 15 (4): 381–94.

Waldman, D.A., Siegel, D.S. and Javidan, M. (2006) 'Components of CEO transformational leadership', *Journal of Management Studies*, 43 (8): 1703–25.

Walker, H., Ilardi, B., McMahon, A. and Fennell, M. (1996) 'Gender, interaction, and leadership', *Social Psychology Quarterly*, 59: 255–72.

Walumbwa, F.O., Avolio, B.J., Gardner, W.L., Wernsing, T.S. and Peterson, S.J. (2008) 'Authentic leadership: Development and validation of a theory-based measure', *Journal of Management*, 34 (1): 89–126.

Warner, L.S. and Grint, K. (2006) 'American Indian ways of leading and knowing', *Leadership*, 2 (2): 225–44.

Watson, T.J. (1994) *In Search of Management*. London: Routledge.

Weick, K.E. (1995) *Sensemaking in Organizations*. Thousand Oaks, CA: Sage.

Weick, K.E. (2007) 'Romancing, following, and sensemaking: James Meindl's legacy', in B. Shamir, R. Pillai, M.C. Bligh and M. Uhl-Bien (eds), *Follower-Centred Perspectives on Leadership*. Greenwich, CT: Information Age Publishing. pp. 279–91.

Westley, F. and Mintzberg, H. (1989) 'Visionary leadership and strategic management', *Strategic Management Journal*, 10: 17–32.

Wong-MingJi, D.J. (2009) 'Cultural mythology and global leadership in China', in E.H. Kessler and D.J. Wong-MingJi (eds), *Cultural Mythology and Global Leadership*. Cheltenham, UK; Edward Elgar. pp. 289–305.

Woolley, L., Caza, A., Levy, L. and Jackson, B. (2007) 'Three steps forward and one step back: Exploring relationships between authentic leadership, psychological capital, and leadership impact', *Proceedings of the Australia and New Zealand Academy of Management*, Sydney, December 4 (7).

Yammarino, F.J., Dionne, S.D., Schriesheim, C.A. and Dansereau, F. (2008) 'Authentic leadership and positive organizational behavior: A meso, multi-level perspective', *Leadership Quarterly*, 19 (6): 693–707.

Yukl, G.A. (1999) 'An evaluation of conceptual weaknesses in transformational and charismatic leadership theories', *Leadership Quarterly*, 10 (2): 285–305.

Yukl, G.A. (2002) *Leadership in Organizations*. Upper Saddle River, NJ: Prentice-Hall.

Zaleznik, A. (1970) 'Power and politics in organizational life', *Harvard Business Review*, 48: 47–60.

Zaleznik, A. (1977) 'Managers and leaders: Are they different?', *Harvard Business Review*, 55: 67–78.

Index

Academy of Management (AOM) 11–12
accountability 42
achievement orientation 18, 79
acquaintance phase 64
acquiescence response style (ARS) 86
action learning 138
Adams, S. 73
adaptability 31
adaptive change 15
Advances in Global Leadership 92
aesthetics 123–6, 133
affective societies 81
affiliation needs 18
agreeableness 38
Ailon, Galit 83–4, 90
Alban-Metcalfe, R. J. 32–3, 34
Alexander the Great 17
Alimo-Metcalfe, B. 32–3, 34
altruism 113
Alvarez, J. L. 61, 99, 102
Alvesson, M. 62, 71, 131
American-Indian leadership 90–1
Amernic, J. 67
Amit, K. 17
analogy 127
anthropology 10, 90, 144
Antonakis, J. 70
Aristotle 145
art 128
aspiration 18
assertiveness 84
Astin, H. S. 27–8
asymmetry, power 97
attraction-similarity-attrition (ASA) 70
attractiveness 16
attribution approach 36
Austin, Nancy 12–13
authentic leadership 34, 43, 113, 116–19, 121, 133
authoritarian style 54
autoethnography 6, 10
autonomous leadership 85

autonomy 78–9
Avery, J. B. 127
Avolio, Bruce J. 8, 31–2, 98, 100, 126, 127, 130, 148
    authentic leadership 116–17, 118, 119
    followers 103
    gender 27
    life stream 7
    nature/nurture 16, 25
    technology 105
    TMLQ 108
Awamleh, R. 52

Babiak, P. 39
bad leadership 39–41, 44
Badaracco, Joseph 42–3
Baker, S. D. 46
Balazs, K. 39
Bandura, A. 115
Barker, J. R. 95, 107–8, 135
Barry, M. 40
Bartone, P. T. 38
Bass, Bernard M. 12, 27, 31–2, 33, 34, 36, 100, 103, 115, 117, 119–20, 126
Bathurst, Ralph 10–11, 125
Beale, F. 121
beautiful leadership 112, 124
Beechler, S. 92, 93
behavioural approach 27, 28, 30, 36
behavioural view of power 96
Bennis, W. 19, 25, 98, 100–1
Berson, Y. 98
Bird, A. 83
Blair, Tony 3, 36, 65
Blanchard, K. 48
Bligh, B. 115
Bligh, Michelle C. 46, 61
Boal, K. B. 102
bodily knowledge 124
Boje, David 35, 109
Bolden, R. 142, 143
Bolman, L. G. 69

Bond, M. H. 81
Bowen, D. 93
Boyce, L. A. 142
Branson, Richard 40, 53, 65
Bratton, J. 65
Brenner, Rick 128
Brent Spar 20
'bright side' 40, 44
Brodbeck, F. C. 85
Brown, M. E. 105, 113, 115
Bryman, Alan 30, 102, 105, 122
Buchanan, D. 21, 73
Buffet, Warren 42
Burch, G. 126
Burke, R. J. 28, 116
Burns, James MacGregor 11, 15, 57, 99–100
Burns Paradox 15
Burr, Donald 52–3

Cacioppe, R. 139
Calás, M. B. 130
Cammock, Peter 127
captaincy 132
Carroll, B. 19, 135, 142–3
Caza, A. 116, 119
celebrity CEO phenomenon 53
Chan, A. 118
charismatic leadership 23, 31, 36–7, 44, 52, 56, 84–7, 122, 130
Chatman, J. A. 28
Chen, C. C. 52–3
Chhokar, J. S. 85
Chinese culture 81
Christensen, R. A. 91
Ciulla, Joanne B. 112, 114, 116
Clair, R. P. 97
Clark, T. 53
Clegg, Stewart 97–8
Clinton, Bill 3
Clinton, Hilary 30, 125
Cluley, R. 57
co-leadership 24, 61, 95, 98–9, 110, 141
Cohen, M. 120
collective leadership 102
collectivism 78–9, 82, 84
Collins, Jim 41–2, 104–5
Collinson, D. L. 66, 143

'colluders' 66
command 20, 21
competency models 142
concertive control 107–8
confidence 18
'conformers' 66
Conger, Jay A. 36, 39–40, 99, 129, 136, 141
connection 18
Conroy, M. 113
conscientiousness 38
context 21, 34, 68–71, 102, 142
contingency theory 21, 48, 49, 69
contingent reward/punishment 32
control 73, 81–2, 107–8
Corn, R. I. 83
corporate social responsibility 74, 116
Corral, T. 92
corrective avoidant leadership 32
counter-dependent followers 54–5
Covey, Stephen 56
Craig, R. 67
Craig, S. B. 38
creolization 89
critical discourse analysis 96
Critical Management Studies 23
critical perspectives 95–111
critical problems 20
cross-cultural leadership 75–6, 78–94
cult leaders 56
cultural intelligence 75–6
cultural theory of leadership 90
culture 23, 68–94
   embedding mechanism 72–3
   followers 46
   paradoxes 83
   shock 75

Daft, R. L. 121
dance 127
'dark side' 39, 40, 44
Darwin, Charles 55
Day, D. 62, 143
De Cremer, D. 115
Deal, T. E. 69, 72
deep power structures 104
delegating style of leadership 49

Den Hartog, Deanne 33, 68, 77, 78, 85, 86
Dent, E. B. 120
dependent followers 54–5
destructive leadership 39, 41, 66
development assessment centres 137
development of leaders 8, 24, 134–45
developmental assignments 137–8
developmental exchange 32
Dickson, M. W. 68, 77, 78, 86
discourse 96, 98–9
dispersed leadership 24, 102, 104, 110
distributed leadership 61–2, 95–111
Dodge, G. E. 105
Doh, J. P. 136
Dorfman, Peter 87–8, 89
dot.com bubble 43
drama 130
Drucker, Peter 19
Dukerich, J. M. 47, 52
Dvir, T. 141
dyadic processes 35

e-commerce 105–6
Eagly, A. H. 27, 28
Eastern perspective 76, 81, 91–2
ecological fallacy 86
effective leaders 16, 17–18
Ehrlich, S. B. 47, 51–2
Eigel, K. M. 118
Eilam, G. 117
Elkin, G. 100
Elmes, M. 40
embeddedness 78–9
'emic' approach 89–93
emotional dimension 80–1
emotional intelligence 18, 140
emotional stability 18, 38
Enron 24, 36–7
Erakovic, L. 20–1
Eriksson, M. 124
essentialist view 89
ethical leadership 43–4, 113–16, 133
ethnicity 59, 88
ethnography 10, 11
'etic' approach 89

European Journal of Work and Organizational Psychology 115
European Management Journal 116
executive coaching 138
experience 136–7, 145
Exploring Leadership and Learning Theories in Asia (ELLTA) 92
external culture 81
extraversion 38
extreme contexts 70–1
extreme response style (ERS) 86

Fairclough, N. 96
Fairhurst, Gail 70, 128
feedback 64, 137
femininity 80, 82
feminization 28
Fernando, M. 120, 121
financial crisis 20, 24, 43, 144
Fiorina, Carly 29
Fletcher, J. K. 99
Foldy, E. 88
Follett, Mary Parker 64
follower-centred perspectives 36, 45–67, 103
followers 15, 23, 103, 143–4
    as co-producers of leadership 63–7, 68, 103
    as constructors of leadership 47, 51–60, 67
    as leaders 47, 61–3
    as moderators of leadership 47, 48–9, 67
    narcissism 40
    as recipients of leadership 47, 48, 103
    self-concept 36
    as substitutes for leadership 47, 49–51, 67
Forsyth, D. R. 114
Foucault, M. 96
frames 69, 128
Franklin, Benjamin 122–3
Freud, Sigmund 54, 55
Friedrich, Tamara 102
Fry, L. W. 120–1
Fulop, L. 96
fundamental attribution error 83
future orientation 84

Gabriel, Y. 55, 57, 144
Gardiner, M. 28
Gardner, Howard 1, 4, 14
Gardner, W. L. 43, 52, 117, 118, 119, 130
gender 27–30, 59
  egalitarianism 84
  Hofstede's dimensions 80, 82
  stereotypes 130
George, B. 118
Geroy, G. 121
Gerzon, M. 92
Ghosn, Carlos 88–9
Gioia, D. A. 105
glass ceiling 59
glass cliff 29
global leadership 92–3
Global Leadership Network 92
Global Mindset Inventory 93
globalization 75–6, 88–9
GLOBE study 84–7, 89, 93
goal-setting 141
goals of leadership 41
Goethals, George 55, 56–7
Goffman, E. 97–8
Goldman, B. M. 118
Goleman, Daniel 18, 140
Gooderham, P. 82
Gooty, J. 117
Gordon, J. 106
Gordon, R. 104, 142
Gosling, J. 142
governance 20–1
Graen, George B. 64, 76, 86–7
Greenleaf, Robert 63
Grey, Chris 21, 22
Griffey, Erin 128
Grint, Keith 13–14, 19–20, 64, 65, 90, 110, 114, 127, 130, 140–1, 145
Gronn, P. 62
grounded theory 104
Group Support Systems (GSP) 105
guardian leaders 63
Gustafson, S. B. 38, 39
Guthey, Eric 43, 53, 83, 86, 88, 89

haiku 128
Hall, E. T. 80

Hall, M. R. 80
Hambrick, D. 101
Hammer, Michael 56
Hampden-Turner, C. 81, 82
Hannah, S. T. 70
Hardy, Cynthia 74, 96
harmony cultures 82
Harnsbrough, T. 39
Harrison, D. 115
Harter, S. 117
Harzing, Anne-Will 86
Haslam, S. A. 29
Heenan, D. A. 98, 100–1
Heifetz, Ron 15
Henry, E. 91
hero leaders 80, 103, 144
hero manager backlash 43
Hersey, P. 48
Hesse, Herman 63
Hicks, D. A. 120
hierarchy 79
Hitler, Adolf 112–13
Hock, Dee 61
Hofstede, Geert 71–2, 77, 78–9, 80, 81, 82–4, 85, 87
Hogan, R. 66
Hogg, M. A. 57, 58–9
Holden, N. 89
Hollander, Edwin 46, 63
Hooijberg, R. 102
Hosking, D. M. 103–4, 144
House, Robert J. 36, 41, 84, 85, 86–7
Howell, Jane M. 32, 36, 41, 127
Hubbard, Dick 74
Huczynski, A. 21, 73
Hughes, L. W. 127
Hui, C. 76
human nature assumptions 81
Human Relations 69–70
humane orientation 84
humanities-based perspective 89–93, 95
Hummel, R. P. 36
humour 127, 128
Hunt, J. G. 68–9
Huxham, C. 102
hyper-reflexivity 10

identity 19, 25–7, 44, 127
Iles, P. 143
Ilies, R. 118, 119
Immelt, Jeff 43
implicit leadership theory 7, 84, 112
in-group collectivism 84
inauthentic transformational
    leadership 34
independent followers 54–5
indigenous leadership 77,
    88, 90–1
individualism 78–9, 82
individualistically oriented
    cultures 46
informal leadership 33
information technology 105–6, 143
Ingarden, Roman 125
Inkson, Kerr 75–6, 100
institutional collectivism 84
integrity 18, 38–9, 42, 86, 113
interdisciplinary research 9–12
internal culture 81
internal locus of control 18
International Conference on
    Studying Leadership 12
International Leadership Association
    (ILA) 11
International Worldly Leadership
    Summit 92
internationalization 11–12
interpersonal leadership 28–9
Islamic leadership 63, 95
'Isrocom' 90

Jackall, Robert 149
Jauch, L. R. 68–9
Javidan, M. 92, 93, 116
Jaynes, S. 96
Jepson, Doris 86
Jermier, John 50
job rotation 138
Johnson, B. 27, 28
Jones, A. M. 90, 143, 144
Jones, Jim 56
Journal of Management
    Studies 116
Judge, T. A. 37, 38, 40
Jung, Carl 54
Jung, D. 77

Kahai, S. 105
Kaiser, R. B. 66
Kant, Immanuel 37, 114
Kanter, R. M. 83, 149
Käufer, K. 99
Kaupapa Maori 91
Keller, T. 54
Kellerman, Barbara 39, 100
Kelley, R. E. 49
Kempster, Steve 112, 113, 135, 138
Kennedy, A. A. 72
Kennedy, John F. 4
Kernis, M. H. 117, 118
Kerr, Steven 50
Kessler, E. H. 76
Kets de Vries, Manfred 17, 34, 39,
    41, 56
Khrushchev, Nikita 79
King, Martin Luther 129
Kluckhohn, F. 81
Knights, D. 104
Koivunen, N. 124
Koresh, David 56
Kosalka, T. 40
Kotter, J. P. 19, 33
Kouzes, J. M. 103
Kraidy, Marwan 89
Krantz, J. 58
Kuhnert, K. W. 38, 118
Kunda, Gideon 73, 149

Ladkin, D. 37, 112, 116, 124, 125
laissez-faire leadership 32, 49, 54
language 80–1, 96
Lapidot, Y. 109
Laurie, Donald 15
Lay, Kenneth 37
LEAD programme 135, 138
leader behaviour/identity 25–7, 44
leader categories/schemas 57–8
leader-centred perspectives
    22–3, 25–44, 103
Leader-Member Exchange
    (LMX) 63–4
leaderful models 23–4
leaderless workgroups 95, 106–8
Leadership 11
leadership-as-practice approach
    142–3

The Leadership Quarterly 10, 50, 70, 86, 95, 116
Leadership Trust 92, 138
Lee, J. K. 77
Leland, C. 27–8
'level 4' leadership 42, 43
'level 5' leadership 41–2, 43, 104–5
Levy, Lester 19, 135, 142–3
Liden, R. C. 70
life stream 7
Lilley, S. 96
Lindholm, C. 36, 56
Link, W. 92
Linstead, S. 96
Lipman-Blumen, Jean 56
listening 27–8, 98
Locke, E. A. 100
long-term orientation 81
Lord, Robert G. 57, 84
Lorenzi, P. 102
Luthans, F. 116–17, 118, 119

Maak, T. 116
McCallum, S. 143
Maccoby, Michael 34, 40, 41
McDonald, P. 140
McFerrin, Bobby 124
McKeen, C. J. 28
McLaughlin, Grace 69
MacMillan, I. 80
McSweeney, Brendan 82
management 33, 103
    fads and fashions 110
    gurus 19, 42, 56, 73, 110, 147
    leadership difference 19–21
management-by-exception 32
manager-in-charge 26
managers of meaning 31, 69
Mandela, Nelson 3, 80
Manson, Charles 56
Manz, C. C. 102
Maori 77, 88, 91
Martin, J. 73
masculinity 80, 82
Mason, P. 101
mastery cultures 81–2
mature phase 64
Mayer, D. M. 115
Mayer, K. G. 84

Mayo, M. 45, 108–9
Mead, R. 82
media 2, 3, 52–3
Meek, V. L. 73
Meindl, James R. 7, 45, 47, 51–3, 84, 108–9
mentoring 138
Messick, D. M. 63
metaphors 127, 130–2, 142
method acting 125
methodology 147–8, 149
Michalko, Michael 130
Michie, S. 117
middle response style (MRS) 86
Mill, John Stuart 114
Miller, D. 34, 41
mindfulness 76
mirroring strategy 83
Mitchelson, J. 68
Mobley, W. H. 92
Morgan, G. 31, 126
movies 2–3, 65, 129
multi-source feedback 137
Multifactor Leadership Questionnaire (MLQ) 32, 77
Mumby, D. K. 97
Mumford, Mike 41, 122–3
mythology 76

Nana, E. 126
Nanus, B. 19
narcissism 34, 40–1, 44, 55
narrative analysis 109
natural leaders 16–17
nature-nurture debate 16–17, 25–6
Neale, Jenny 30
Nelson, D. L. 65
NeuroLeadership 140
neutral countries 81
'new leadership' 22, 30–1, 33–5, 44
newspapers 2
Nielsen, Jeffrey 62
Nixon, Richard 79
non-contingent reward/ punishment 32
non-violent/ideological leaders 41
non-violent/non-ideological leaders 41
Nordhaug, O. 82

Obama, Barack 13–14
O'Connell, D. 143
O'Connell, W. 115
Offerman, Lynn 56
O'Reilly, C. A. 28
organizational culture 72–5
Orthwein, Peter 42
Osborn, R. N. 68–9
Osland, J. S. 82–3
Ospina, Sonia 88
outdoor challenge programmes 138

Padilla, A. 66
Palmer, Ian 74
parenting 16–17, 54, 64–5, 131
Parsons, T. 79
participatory style of leadership 49
Parviainen, J. 124
Pastor, J. C. 45, 108–9
Pearce, C. L. 99, 108
peer-based organization 62
Pene, H. 91
Perceived Leader Integrity Scale
    (PLIS) 38
permanence orientation 84
personality traits 16–17, 18, 21,
    25–6, 27, 37–41, 44, 85
personalized leadership 41
Peters, Tom 12–13
Pfeifer, Dale 98
Phillips, N. 96
Piccolo, R. F. 40
Pillai, Rajnandini 60
Pittinsky, T. L. 40
Podsakoff, Phil 32, 33
poetry 128
political leadership 36, 58, 96
political psychology 10
political view of power 96
Popper, Micha 56
Porter, Lyman 69
Posner, B. Z. 103
Post, J. M. 41
power 96
    asymmetry 97
    behavioural view 96
    concentration 84
    critical perspectives 95, 96–8
    decentralization 84

power cont.
    deep structures 104
    gender 30
    political view 96
power distance 79
power motivation 18
practices of leadership 104
pragmatic leadership 122–3, 133
Preece, D. 143
Price, T. 114, 116
primal horde 55
Prince, Lesley 91
privacy 148–9
Proctor-Thomson, Sarah 38–9,
    103, 142
projection 55–6
prototypes 57–9, 84–7
pseudo transformational leaders 117
psychoanalytic theories 36, 54–7,
    59–60
psychodynamic approach 54–7
psychology of leadership 69–70
purpose of leadership 113, 114
Pye, Annie 31, 121, 126

qualitative methods 34–5
quantitative methods 35
The Queen 65

race 88
Raelin, Joseph 61
RAMPP 103
reflection 6–7, 145
relational power 96
relational view 144
relationship behaviour 49
relationship-orientation 21, 28, 50
research bias 76–8
research and development 134–45
resilience 18
responsibility 42
responsible leadership 116
Rhodes, Carl 35
rhythm 129
Richmond, D. 135, 142–3
righteous leaders 63
Ringleb, A. H. 140
Ritzer, D. R. 39
Roc, D. 140

Roddick, Anita 29, 53
role modelling 72, 113, 115, 131
romance of leadership 51–4, 59–60
Ropo, A. 124
Rosener, J. B. 130
Rosenthal, S. A. 40
Rost, Joseph 12, 14–15, 45
rule-breaking 16–17
Russo, Patricia 29
Ryan, M. K. 29

Salas, E. 62
sampling, GLOBE study 86
Schein, Edgar 72–3, 74
Schermerhorn, J. R. 118
Schneider, B. 70
schooling 132
Schwartz, S. H. 78, 81–2
Schyns, B. 7, 39, 84
self-awareness 102–3
self-concept 16, 36
self-consciousness 102–3
Self Leadership 102–3
self-managing teams 107–8
self-protective leadership 85
selling style of leadership 49
semi-autonomous workgroups 106
Senge, Peter 56
sensemaking 31, 126–30
servant leadership 63, 121
Sewell, G. 96
Shackleton, Ernest 63, 69
Shamir, Boas 36, 47–8, 50, 55, 58,
    59–60, 66, 103, 109, 117, 121
Shane, S. 80
shared leadership 15, 24, 61–2,
    99–102, 108, 110, 141–2
Shaw, J. B. 84
Shils, E. A. 79
short-term orientation 81
Siegal, D. S. 116
Sims, H. P. 102, 108
Sims, P. 118
Sinclair, A. 134, 144–5
Sinha, Paresha 103, 141
situational analysis 34
situational leadership 48–9, 69
Skilling, Jeffrey 37
skills 103–4

Smircich, L. 31, 121, 126, 130
Smith, Peter 87
social capital 143
social constructionism 19–20, 52,
    69, 70, 130
social contagion 52
social identity theory 57–60
social network approach 108–9
social role theory 28
socialized leadership 41
Søderberg, A.-M. 89
song 129
The Sopranos 66
Sosik, John J. 32, 105, 127
Spicer, A. 131
spiritual leadership 43, 113, 119–22,
    133, 147
Statler, M. 125
status 79
Stech, E. L. 54
Steidlmeier, P. 34, 115, 117
stereotypes 57–8, 82–3, 130
Stewart, Martha 53
Stogdill, R. M. 12
Storey, John 8, 10, 102, 122
Strang, E. E. 38
stranger phase 64
Strati, Antonio 124
Strodtbeck, F. L. 81
style counselling theories 21
Super Leadership 102
surface-level empowerment 104
Svejenova, S. 61, 99, 102
Sveningsson, S. 62
Swan, Kate 29
symbolic resources 90

tame problems 20
Taoism 91
task-orientation 21, 28, 50
Tayeb, M. H. 82
Taylor, S. 116, 124, 125
Teagarden, M. 93
team leadership 95, 108–10
Team Multifactor Leadership
    Questionnaire (TMLQ) 108
team orientation 85
telling style of leadership 49
Thatcher, Margaret 29, 80

Thomas, David 75–6
Thompson, Wade 42
Thor Industries 42
Tiggemann, M. 28
Ting-Toomey, S. 81
total institution 97–8
Tourish, Dennis 37, 66–7, 121–2
Tourish, N. 121–2
toxic leaders 56
toxic triangle 66
training programmes 138–40
traits *see* personality traits
transactional leadership 22, 23,
    31–3
transcultural creative leaders 76
transference 55–6
transformational leadership 22, 23,
    30–5, 43, 98, 117, 119–20,
    122, 141
  gender 27
  humour 127
  shared 99–102
Transformational Leadership
    Questionnaire (TLQ)
    32–3, 34
translation 86
transmission model 98
Trevino, L. K. 113, 115
Triandis, H. 89
Trompenaars, F. 81, 82
Trump, Donald 40
trust 116

Uhl-Bien, Mary 60, 64
uncertainty avoidance 79–80, 82, 84
unmet needs 60
Upper Echelons Theory 101

Van Doorn, J. 122–3
Van Knippenberg, D. 57, 115
Vangen, S. 102
Vatcha, Naheed 37
Venkataraman, V. 80
Vine, Bernadette 98
violent/ideological leaders 41
violent/non-ideological leaders 41
Virtual Leader Construct
    (VLC) 35
virtuous betrayal 58
visionary leadership 31

Waldman, D. A. 33, 116
Walker, H. 28
Walumbwa, F. O. 117, 118, 148
Warner, Linda Sue 90
Washington, George 55
Watson, Tony 149
Weber, Max 37
Weber, T. J. 148
Webster, S. W. 100
Weick, Karl 31, 46, 126
Welch, Jack 40
Weldon, E. 92
Western perspective 76–7, 90–1
wicked problems 20
Willmott, H. 104
Wisecarver, M. Z. 142
Wong-MingJi, D. J. 76
Woolley, L. 118

Yammarino, F. J. 77, 117
Yukl, Gary A. 18, 34–5, 137, 139

Zaccaro, S. J. 142
Zaleznik, A. 19, 36